AF897415

Protecting Cultural Property in Armed Conflict

International Humanitarian Law Series

VOLUME 29

Editors-in-Chief

H.E. Judge Sir Christopher Greenwood
Professor Timothy L.H. McCormack

Editorial Advisory Board
Professor Georges Abi-Saab
H.E. Judge George H. Aldrich
Madame Justice Louise Arbour
Professor Ove Bring
Professor Antonio Cassese
Professor John Dugard
Professor Dr. Horst Fischer
Dr. Hans-Peter Gasser
Professor Leslie C. Green
H.E. Judge Geza Herczegh
Professor Frits Kalshoven
Professor Ruth Lapidoth
Professor Gabrielle Kirk McDonald
H.E. Judge Theodor Meron
Captain J. Ashley Roach
Professor Michael Schmitt
Professor Jiří Toman

The International Humanitarian Law Series is a series of monographs and edited volumes which aims to promote scholarly analysis and discussion of both the theory and practice of the international legal regulation of armed conflict.
The series explores substantive issues of International Humanitarian Law including,

- protection for victims of armed conflict and regulation of the means and methods of warfare
- questions of application of the various legal regimes for the conduct of armed conflict
- issues relating to the implementation of International Humanitarian Law obligations
- national and international approaches to the enforcement of the law and
- the interactions between International Humanitarian Law and other related areas of international law such as Human Rights, Refugee Law, Arms Control and Disarmament Law, and International Criminal Law.

The titles in this series are listed at the end of this volume.

Damaged mural representing St. Peter, Matejce Monastery, Former Yugoslav Republic of Macedonia. Photo: Joris D. Kila, 2002.

Protecting Cultural Property in Armed Conflict

An Insight into the 1999 Second Protocol to the Hague Convention of 1954 for the Protection of Cultural Property in the Event of Armed Conflict

Edited by
Nout van Woudenberg and Liesbeth Lijnzaad

MARTINUS
NIJHOFF
PUBLISHERS

LEIDEN • BOSTON
2010

Printed on acid-free paper.

Library of Congress Cataloging-in-Publication Data

Protecting cultural property in armed conflict : an insight into the 1999 second protocol to the Hague Convention of 1954 for the Protection of Cultural Property in the Event of Armed Conflict / edited by Nout van Woudenberg and Liesbeth Lijnzaad.

p. cm. -- (International humanitarian law series ; v. 29)

Includes bibliographical references and index.

ISBN 978-90-04-18377-3 (hardback : alk. paper) 1. Cultural property--Protection (International law) 2. Convention for the Protection of Cultural Property in the Event of Armed Conflict (1954) 3. Cultural property--Protection--Law and legislation. I. Woudenberg, Nout van. II. Lijnzaad, Liesbeth.

K3791.P722 2010

344'.094--dc22

2010019167

ISBN: 978 9004 18377 3

Copyright 2010 by Koninklijke Brill NV, Leiden, The Netherlands.

Koninklijke Brill NV incorporates the imprints Brill, Hotei Publishing, IDC Publishers, Martinus Nijhoff Publishers and VSP.

http://www.brill.nl

All rights reserved. No part of this publication may be reproduced, stored in a retrieval system, or transmitted in any form or by any means, electronic, mechanical, photocopying, microfilming, recording or otherwise, without written permission from the Publisher.

Authorization to photocopy items for internal or personal use is granted by Koninklijke Brill NV provided that the appropriate fees are paid directly to The Copyright Clearance Center, 222 Rosewood Drive, Suite 910, Danvers MA 01923, USA. Fees are subject to change.

PRINTED AND BOUND IN THE NETHERLANDS.

Table of Contents

Documents

Introduction

Nout van Woudenberg and Liesbeth Lijnzaad

Historical buildings, sites, archaeological discoveries, archives, and collections of musea all form part of our collective cultural memory. They tell us who we are, and how we have become what we are today. The loss of cultural heritage deprives people of tangible remnants of their past, which have great significance for them. Moreover, the loss of a people's cultural heritage is a loss for all humanity.

The Netherlands has long been strongly committed to the protection of cultural property from armed conflict. As early as 1899, the Hague Regulations concerning the Laws and Customs of War on Land additional to Hague Convention respecting the Laws and Customs of War on Land referred to the protection of cultural property. In collaboration with UNESCO and its Member States, the Netherlands played a key role in drafting the 1954 Hague Convention for the Protection of Cultural Property in the Event of an Armed Conflict (the 1954 Hague Convention). The 1954 Hague Convention is probably best known for its distinctive emblem: a shield, pointed below, with a royal blue square and a royal blue triangle above the square on a white background. Cultural property bears this emblem to facilitate its recognition and protection. In the Netherlands alone, there are about 4000 cultural goods protected under the 1954 Hague Convention.

In the last decade of the 20th century, it however became evident that the 1954 Hague Convention needed updating. Archaeological sites proved particularly vulnerable in the two Gulf Wars. The armed conflict in former Yugoslavia led to major damage to historic cities like Sarajevo, Dubrovnik and Mostar. This update got the form of the 1999 Second Protocol, which was a major step forward in protecting cultural property under international humanitarian law. It strengthened and supplemented the Convention by introducing more effective international rules. In particular, a tribute must be paid to the Dutch chairman of the 1999 Diplomatic Conference, dr Adriaan Bos, who ably guided the conference towards the Protocol's conclusion, at a time the conflict in Kosovo unfolded.

On Thursday 26 March 2009, it was exactly ten years ago that the 1999 Second Protocol was adopted. To celebrate this anniversary, the Dutch Ministry of Foreign Affairs, joined by the Ministry of Defence and the Ministry of Education, Culture and Science, organised a symposium in the Peace Palace in The Hague. The book before you is largely a reflection of the symposium.

The aim of the symposium has been to assess the Second Protocol's significance for international law. The symposium focused on the innovative aspects of the Protocol, as "enhanced protection", "criminal responsibility and jurisdiction", and "the protection of cultural property in armed conflicts not of an international character". It was hoped that the symposium would inspire States that had not yet acceded to the 1999 Second Protocol to do so. In fact, four new States have since joined the 51 States Parties at the time of the symposium.

Given the value of the contributions at the symposium, and the importance of enhancing participation in the 1999 Second Protocol we have decided to compile and publish the symposium's highlights, supplemented by a few other relevant texts. We are happy to present a variety of contributions focussing on the legal as much as the cultural aspects of the Second Protocol. Scholars as well as military officers have contributed, and some country specific studies are included. We are grateful to all the authors who have spoken at the seminar, or have contributed texts. The content of the contributions obviously remains the responsibility of the authors.

We are indebted to the Dutch Ministry of Foreign Affairs for facilitating the publication of this book. We very much hope that the book will contribute to further improving the protection of cultural property in times of armed conflict, and that it will serve as a tool to facilitate increased participation in the Second Protocol.

For ease of reference, the 1954 Hague Convention, the Regulations and both Protocols have been included in the back of the book.

Nout van Woudenberg
Liesbeth Lijnzaad

Message from Mr Koïchiro Matsuura, Director-General of UNESCO,* on the occasion of the symposium of the 10th Anniversary of the Second Protocol to the Hague Convention of 1954 for the Protection of Cultural Property in the Event of Armed Conflict

I am very sorry that I cannot be with you personally for today's celebration of the tenth anniversary of a milestone in international humanitarian law: the adoption of the Second Protocol to the Convention for the Protection of Cultural Property in the Event of Armed Conflict. It is particularly fitting that this commemoration should take place in The Hague, where the Second Protocol was adopted on 26 March 1999.

Allow me first to reiterate UNESCO's gratitude to the Netherlands authorities for their constant support and promotion of the Hague Convention and its two Protocols. Indeed, the Netherlands played a key role in their elaboration and adoption, and The Hague is the cradle of international law and the seat of a number of international tribunals and courts, which have often shaped the course of key events in recent decades. Since 1899, when it played host to its first Peace Conference, The Hague has rightfully earned its reputation as "the international city of justice and peace".

However, peace cannot be achieved by any individual State alone. It requires the concerted efforts of all nations. For this reason, UNESCO works closely with its 193 Member States to build "peace in the minds of men" through education, the sciences, culture and communication. Our success in mobilizing the international community has been clearly demonstrated by the wide ratification of many of UNESCO's standard-setting instruments, not least the Hague Convention and its two Protocols – one of our principal tools for protecting cultural heritage in the name of peace. To date the Hague Convention boasts 122 High Contracting Parties, and 51 States have become party to the Second Protocol. I am very pleased to announce that the United States of America recently deposited its instrument of ratification. This will contribute towards the universality of the Convention in the long term.

The establishment of the Committee for the Protection of Cultural Property in the Event of Armed Conflict on 26 October 2005 was a landmark event in the life of the Second Protocol. Among its principal tasks in this first phase of its life, is the development of the Draft Guidelines for the Implementation of the Second Protocol to the Hague Convention. Thus far, six chapters of this document have been drafted, and an upcoming meeting will continue this process to ensure that the institutional mechanism of the Second Protocol will be operational in the near future.

In addition to celebrating this tenth anniversary of the adoption of the Second Protocol, you will also discuss the Protocol's innovative features and underlying prin-

* 1999-2009.

ciples as well as the most effective means to promote wider implementation at the national level and ratification of this instrument.

I hope that today's encounter may serve as an occasion to reflect on our past and current accomplishments, and to intensify our future efforts to promote the implementation and universality of the Second Protocol.

I wish you much success in your deliberations and thank you very much for your attention.

Koïchiro Matsuura

Words of Welcome

*Adriaan Bos**

As Chairman of the 1999 Diplomatic Conference, which drafted the Second Protocol to the Hague Convention of 1954, it gives me great pleasure to say a few words to welcome you all to this symposium. Today we commemorate the adoption ten years ago of the Second Protocol. This is a time for reflection, for looking back and looking forward.

Let me first note, not without a certain pride, that the Netherlands has long played an important role in the protection of cultural property in the event of armed conflict. The first measures to offer this protection resulted from the First Hague Peace Conference in 1899. This Conference, together with the Second Conference in 1907, played a pioneering role in developing the protection of cultural property in times of armed conflict. For example, Article 27 of the Regulations respecting the Laws and Customs of War on Land provided that in sieges and bombardments, attacking forces must take all necessary steps to spare, as far as possible, certain specified, culturally valuable buildings as long as they are not being used at the time for military purposes. It was the duty of the besieged State to indicate the presence of such buildings or places with distinctive signs, which the enemy was to be notified of beforehand. These signs should however not be confused with the distinctive white-and-blue emblem that has since been developed under the 1954 Hague Convention. The rules embodied in the Hague Convention and Regulations of 1899/1907, including Article 27, are today recognised as part of international customary law and as such are binding on all States.

After the Hague Peace Conferences, the codification of rules for the protection of cultural property mainly took place in two distinct forums: on the one hand the ICRC, active in the codification and development of international humanitarian law, and on the other hand UNESCO, active in the codification of rules relating to culture. Through the years these two organisations have cooperated closely in these fields.

In 1954, after the experiences of the Second World War and in the light of new methods of warfare, the Hague Convention was drafted. Its preamble declared: '*Damage to cultural property belonging to any people whatsoever means damage to the cultural heritage of all mankind, since each people makes its own contribution to the culture of the world.*' These words underscore the importance of cultural property for humanity as a whole. Destroying cultural heritage affects the identity of a people and conse-

* Dr Adriaan Bos is a former Legal Adviser, Ministry of Foreign Affairs of the Netherlands, and was Chairman of the 1999 Hague Diplomatic Conference.

quently has a destabilising and disintegrating effect on their society. In his famous book *The Law of Nations*, Emmerich de Vattel wrote:

"For whatever reason a belligerent plunders a country, he should spare buildings that are the pride of mankind and do not strengthen the enemy. Temples, tombstones, public buildings, and all other works of art distinguished for their beauty; what can be the advantage of destroying them? Only an enemy of mankind can thoughtlessly deprive humanity of those monuments of art, the exemplars of artistry."

The innovative step taken in 1954 was to require States to take measures in peacetime so that they would be prepared for an armed conflict. The Convention thus became a landmark. It can be seen as 'a true code for cultural property', as the distinguished Professor Jirí Toman has stated. In spite of many efforts by UNESCO to promote the Convention's implementation, however, the number of States Parties fell short of expectations for many years. Moreover, probably due in part to the Convention's not always very concrete wording, States Parties often failed to take the national measures necessary for its implementation.

In the light of a continuing succession of armed conflicts (such as the Gulf Wars, the conflict in the former Yugoslavia and the war in Afghanistan) and the consequent serious harm to cultural heritage in many historic places around the world, the question arose whether the 1954 Hague Convention was still an adequate instrument to cope with these problems. The Netherlands decided to include a review of the 1954 Convention in its contribution to the United Nations Decade of International Law. The Netherlands and UNESCO agreed to jointly commission and fund a review of the objectives and operation of the Convention and Protocol, with a view to proposing measures to improve its application and effectiveness and to considering the necessity of revising the Convention itself. Patrick J. Boylan was appointed to undertake this review, to be completed in time for the May 1993 meeting of the UNESCO Executive Board. He presented his very valuable report in 1993.

Following up on these developments, representatives of governments began preparatory work for a review of the 1954 Convention. A Diplomatic Conference was held, open to all members of the United Nations. The Parties to the Hague Convention participated on the same footing as non-Parties, and all these participants were ultimately able to adopt the Second Protocol by consensus. Moreover, the Protocol was ready in time for the celebration of the centenary of the First Hague Convention, which coincided with the end of the UN Decade on International Law.

The Second Protocol is founded on the rules stemming from the First Hague Peace Conference, developed and modified in the light of present-day developments in international law. Its rules are applicable to both international and internal conflicts. The 1954 Hague Convention has not been amended, but rather supplemented with such new features as the definition of military necessity, the introduction of the new category of 'enhanced protection' and the creation of an intergovernmental Committee for the Protection of Cultural Property in the Event of Armed Conflict, a new monitoring body for the implementation of the Protocol. These new tools reflect developments in international humanitarian and international criminal law, which have undeniably been undergoing rapid change. These rapid developments are evident notably in the area of individual criminal responsibility, where they are manifest in particular in the Statutes of international criminal tribunals. The Protocol applies to cultural property the approach taken in those Statutes to individual criminal responsibility for serious international crimes. States are obliged to try or extradite offenders. This obligation is an important contribution to the effective implementation of the rules.

A joint effort by military leaders and international lawyers led to the inclusion in the Protocol of a balanced definition of the concept of military necessity. This concept was so controversial in 1954 that it was not defined at all. Reaching agreement on this issue was a major achievement of the 1999 Conference.

Nevertheless, after ten years, one must admit that the number of Parties to the Protocol definitely needs to grow, and that not all regions of the world are equally represented. Nor has the preparatory work necessary for its implementation been completed. Armed conflicts, on the other hand, continue to occur. There is even evidence that the destruction of cultural property has sometimes become a goal in itself in these conflicts.

First and foremost, it is necessary to increase the number of Parties to the Second Protocol, so that it can be seen as an instrument with truly universal support. It is also of great importance for States Parties to incorporate, in peacetime, the provisions of the Protocol into their national legislation. These current States Parties will then have the task of helping future States Parties implement the Protocol. The intergovernmental Committee set up under the Protocol can also play a crucial role in this respect. If we can attain these goals, we may expect respect for the cultural property during international and non-international armed conflicts to increase.

Adriaan Bos

Chapter 1

The road to the 1999 Second Protocol

*Jiří Toman**

1. Introduction

This contribution will address the question 'Why a Second Protocol to 1954 Hague Convention?'

But before I begin let me however mention an important recent event. On 13 March 2009, the Director-General of UNESCO received from the United States of America the instrument of ratification of the 1954 Hague Convention for the Protection of Cultural Property in the Event of Armed Conflict (the 1954 Hague Convention for short), entering into force immediately and, with some exceptions related to penal aspects, being self-executing. This is a very important step. During the negotiations at the 1954 Hague Conference, the delegates made several concessions requested by the UK and US delegations, in the hope that they would become Parties to the Convention.[1] The international community had to wait 55 years to see at least one of them become a Party. We are still waiting for the UK to take the same step.

The US representative[2] was right to indicate that US military personnel were trained in and familiar with the provisions of the 1954 Hague Convention and with numerous customary rules on the protection of cultural property. Nonetheless, we have recently seen a number of violations. This occurred in particular during the Iraqi campaign, as described in several books[3] and reported at the seminar on mili-

---

* Jiří Toman is – among other things – Professor of Law at Santa Clara University (USA). He has written an extensive Article by Article Commentary on the 1954 Hague Convention and First Protocol. Recently he published a very detailed Article by Article Commentary on the 1999 Second Protocol: Cultural Property in War: Improvement in Protection, Unesco, 2009.

1 See for example Jiří Toman, *The Protection of Cultural Property in the Event of Armed Conflict* (Aldershot/Paris, Dartmouth/UNESCO, 1996), p. 60.

2 Mr. Steve Engelken, Chargé d'Affaires a.i. of the United States of America to UNESCO. See also UNESCO Flash Info No. 040-2009, dated 16 March 2009.

3 Philippe Flandrin, *Le Pillage de l'Irak* (Paris: Editions du Rocher, 2004); Lawrence Rothfield, ed., *Antiquities under Siege: Cultural Heritage Protection after the Iraq War* (Lanham, MD: AltaMira Press, 2008); Peter G. Stone and Joanne Farchakh Bajjaly, eds., *The Destruction of Cultural Heritage in Iraq* (Woodbridge: Boydell Press, 2008).

Nout van Woudenberg and Liesbeth Lijnzaad (eds.) Protecting Cultural Property in Armed Conflict
© *2010 Koninklijke Brill NV. Printed in The Netherlands.* *ISBN 978 9004 18377 3 pp. 1–19.*

tary operations on 25 March 2009 in The Hague.[4] We have high expectations of US participation as a High Contracting Party to the Convention. With its help we can perhaps breathe new life into the 1954 Hague Convention. We are looking forward to the US considering becoming a Party to the 1999 Second Protocol as well.[5]

2. Towards the 1954 Convention

The 1954 Hague Convention satisfied a desire that many philosophers had expressed over the course of centuries. It was also the result of prolonged efforts, which started with the 1863 Lieber Code, the 1874 Brussels Draft Declaration and the 1899 and 1907 Hague Conventions – not to forget the famous 1935 Roerich Pact, which is still in force. It would also be unjust not to mention the 1938 draft convention prepared by a Committee of Experts of the International Museums Office, chaired by Charles de Visscher and composed of some of the most famous lawyers of the time, which undoubtedly left its mark on the final text of the 1954 Hague Convention.[6]

Also in 1938 and 1939 it had been the Dutch government which was in charge of preparing a Diplomatic Conference on the basis of a draft Convention. The Netherlands sent the draft to sixty-two States, and received responses from forty States. In the meantime, however, the Second World War had begun. The International Museums Office tried to cope with this new situation by suggesting that the States adopt a declaration of principle. A draft Declaration consisting of ten articles was therefore prepared. After making a few changes to the text of the Declaration, the governments of Belgium and the Netherlands had decided to adopt the draft when the military events of May 1940 brought the two countries into the war.[7]

It was only after the Second World War – in the context of post-war enthusiasm for human rights and humanitarian law – that the first universal convention for the protection of cultural property in armed conflict was adopted. The 1954 Hague Convention inspired high hopes in its drafters, who considered it an instrument "of great importance for all peoples of the world".[8] However, they were also conscious of the concessions that had been made to military exigencies. The Dutch Minister of

---

4 Seminar on 'Cultural property protection in the event of armed conflict', organised by the Dutch Ministry of Defence in the Peace Palace on 25 March 2009.

5 At the signing ceremony of the Second Protocol on 16 May 1999, the then Secretary of State Colin Powers mentioned that 'it is appropriate to all States to consider thoroughly this Second Protocol and to joint their voices to those of other civilised peoples for the survival of human behaviour, preserving of human lives and the maintenance of a rich heritage to be handed o n to future generations.' (Text distributed at the ceremony, p. 6).

6 Jiří Toman, op.cit., pp. 18-9.

7 'Project of a Declaration concerning the Protection of Monuments and Works of Art in case of Armed Conflict', in Marcel Deltenre and Firmin van den Bosch eds., *General Collection of the Laws and Customs of War on Land, on Sea, under Sea and in the Air* (Brussels: Éditions Fred. Wellens-Pay, 1943), pp. 754-9.

8 Preamble to the 1954 Hague Convention.

Public Instruction, Art and Science[9] considered that the law, supported by the views of various High Commands and military experts, had been more conservative than "prudent moderation" demanded.[10]

3. Implementation and application of the 1954 Hague Convention

Nevertheless, the Convention's first years were not disappointing. It seemed to satisfy Charles de Visscher's characterisation of the rules of international law: "Every rule of positive international law thus presents two essential aspects for critical examination on different levels: the degree in which its content corresponds to social needs, and the accuracy of its formal expression compared with the practice of States. The rule of international law retains its full force in application only in so far as it satisfies this double requirement."[11] This was not surprising, as the world had just emerged from the Second World War and was fully aware of the dangers that continued to threaten it. The 1954 Hague Convention thus fitted into the context of other very progressive developments in the field of human rights[12] and humanitarian law.[13]

3.1 Parties to the 1954 Hague Convention

By the end of 1954, the Convention had been signed by 21 Third World States, 22 Western States and 7 Eastern European States. It entered into force on 7 August 1956, three months after the deposit of the fifth instrument of ratification.

During the Convention's first decade (1954-1964), a further 52 States became Parties: 26 Third World countries, 16 Western countries and all the Eastern European countries (10), undoubtedly still under the influence of the post-war period. Then a period of slower progress followed: between 1964 and 1974 only 12 States acceded and between 1974 and 1984 only 6 more, making a total of 70 States Parties. Between 1984 and 1994, the number of States Parties grew again: 15 States acceded, perhaps under the influence of the end of the Cold War, changes in the Soviet Union / Russian Federation and the conflict in the former Yugoslavia. Between 1994 and 2004 28 States acceded to the Convention, because of the start of the new codification process. In the last five years, however, only 10 States have acceded. As a result 123 States are now Parties to the Convention, including – as mentioned before – the US.

3.2 Implementation of the 1954 Hague Convention

The practical implementation of the 1954 Hague Convention followed at the very beginning the same rhythms as the ratification and accession. The post-war situation influenced not only the drafting of the text and the number of the States that

9 Mr. J.M.L.Th. Cals.

10 Jiří Toman, op.cit., p. 23, n. 46.

11 Charles de Visscher, *Theory and Reality in Public International Law*, translated from French by P. E. Corbett (Princeton: Princeton University Press, 1957), p. 133.

12 Such as the 1948 Universal Declaration of Human Rights.

13 Such as the 1949 Geneva Conventions.

became Parties to it, but also the practical steps in its implementation. In this respect too the Convention's first years were ones of great activity.

The Middle East

The Middle East seemed predestined to face problems related to the protection of cultural property in armed conflict. It is in this part of the world that the practical application of the Convention started. In 1956 and 1957 Professor Gerard Garitte of the University of Louvain, at the request of the Member States of UNESCO, carried out a mission to Egypt and Israel. On this occasion, he prepared a detailed report on the state of the Saint Catherine Monastery (in the Sinai) and made several suggestions for its protection.

The procedures prescribed by the Convention were brought into practice. Following the 1967 Middle East conflict, the States concerned designated representatives for cultural property, as required by the Convention.[14] Moreover, they appointed commissioners-General in accordance with the procedure stipulated in the Regulations,[15] by using the good offices of Switzerland. Karl Brunner of Switzerland was chosen by Jordan, Lebanon, Egypt and Syria; J. Reinink of the Netherlands by Israel. After Karl Brunner's death, De Angelis d'Ossat of Italy was appointed. The two commissioners-General resigned in 1977. The procedure for their replacement unfortunately did not lead to the appointment of new commissioners-General.

When the civil war began in Lebanon in 1975, the officials responsible for cultural property, in particular the director of the Beirut National Museum, took many precautionary measures, including the transfer of invaluable objects to the French Institute of Archaeology in Damascus. In 1982, at Lebanon's request a mission was sent to the archaeological site of the Lebanese city of Tyre. In his call for the site to be safeguarded and his decision to send a mission, the Director-General of UNESCO based himself on the provisions of the 1954 Hague Convention, in particular Article 23, and on a special mandate conferred by Resolution 4/13 adopted by the UNESCO General Conference at its 21st session.[16] As the site was occupied by the Israeli army, the Director-General asked the Israeli authorities to cooperate and transmitted to them the Lebanese request.

This mission is an example of cooperation between governments, various UN authorities and the local population, despite the insoluble character of the problems of Tyre, caught between the needs of the archaeological sites and of protecting the past, and the needs of its present-day inhabitants, who are trying to survive in spite of many difficulties. The mission was constrained only by the absence of Lebanese archaeologists, despite the steps taken by the Lebanese and Israeli authori-

14 Regulations for the Execution of the Convention for the Protection of Cultural Property in the Event of Armed Conflict, Article 2(a).

15 Regulations for the Execution of the Convention for the Protection of Cultural Property in the Event of Armed Conflict, Article 2 (c).

16 Belgrade, 23 September – 28 October 1980.

ties. The mission report,[17] which was impartial and objective, made a number of recommendations, several of which could not be carried out without UNESCO's help. One hundred and fifty distinctive signs were placed at the disposal of the Lebanese authorities to mark Tyre's archaeological sites and monuments.

Obstacles to the implementation of special protection

Special protection was a weak point in the 1954 Hague Convention however. Only five States[18] requested registration. Following these requests, eight refuges and monumental centres were registered. These were the Vatican City (18 January 1960), a refuge located at Alt-Aussee in Austria (17 November 1967), six refuges in the municipalities of Zandvoort, Heemskerk, Steenwijkerwold and Maastricht in the Netherlands (12 May 1969) and the central refuge Oberrieder Stollen in the Federal Republic of Germany (22 April 1978). At the request of the States, three refuges in the Netherlands and one in Austria have been removed from the list in 2000.

Another reason for the failure of special protection were the practical difficulties encountered when applying Article 8, in particular with regard to cultural property in the middle of large cities or close to major urban, political, and industrial centres. Many countries announced that a request for registration was being studied but never actually submitted it.[19] Libya took another approach: in response to a request for registration, an abridged list of cultural property was drawn up, but the government would not commit to diverting transport routes or to not using the nearby ports in the event of conflict. It never came to registration. Yet other reasons can be given for the failure of special protection. The increasing politicisation resulting from the Cold War and the tensions that pervaded relations between States, including any cultural measures. The example of Cambodia is revealing.

Cambodia

On 31 March 1972 Cambodia submitted a request to the Director-General of UNESCO for the registration of the centres containing the monuments of Angkor and Roluos, the sanctuaries located at Phnom Bok and Phnom Krom, and a refuge at Angkor. The Director-General informed the High Contracting Parties of Cambodian request on 25 April 1972, while referring to Article 14 of the Regulations for the Execution of the Convention, which states that any High Contracting Party

17 Doc. 22 C/ Inf., dated 12 September 1983. See: http://unesdoc.unesco.org/images/0005/000572/057227e0.pdf.

18 Austria, the Federal Republic of Germany, Cambodia, the Netherlands and Vatican City.

19 According to the country reports, applications were examined by the following States but never submitted: Czechoslovakia (1979), Egypt (1970), France (1983), the Federal Republic of Germany (in addition to Oberried), Hungary (1970), Italy (1967), Liechtenstein (1983), Romania (1962), San Marino (1967), Spain (1962) and Yugoslavia (1979). Some countries – such as Bulgaria, Poland and the USSR (1970) – seem to have made reservations concerning the provisions of Article 8 that constituted an obstacle to any application for special protection. See J. Toman, op.cit., p. 109.

may lodge an objection to the registration of cultural property by letter addressed to the Director-General.

Within the period stipulated for the receipt of communications,[20] the Director-General received letters from four High Contracting Parties – Cuba, Egypt, Romania and Yugoslavia – stating that the application for registration had not been presented by the authority that they considered the government entitled to represent Cambodia. The Director-General therefore did not proceed to register these cultural properties. In the troubled atmosphere of the Cold War, the value of property that undeniably formed part of the cultural heritage of humanity was sacrificed to transitory political considerations. This example demonstrates the failure of the concept of special protection due to the increased politicisation that resulted from the Cold War and the tensions that poisoned relations between States.

Actions undertaken by UNESCO and the initiatives of the Director-General

The character of wars and armed conflicts changed in the decades that followed the adoption of the Hague Convention in 1954. It was thus necessary to resort to other, more flexible methods to ensure the protection of cultural property.

UNESCO explored the possibility of using Article 23 (Assistance of UNESCO), as well as its 'general mandate of cultural initiative' under the UNESCO Constitution. Article 1 of its Constitution states that the Organisation can pursue its aims to "[M]aintain, increase and diffuse knowledge: by assuring the conservation and protection of the world's inheritance of books, works of art and other monuments of history and science, and recommending to the nations concerned the necessary international conventions."[21] The World Conference on Cultural Policies in Mexico City in 1982[22] noted that in a world torn by disturbances that imperil the cultural values of the different civilisations, UNESCO's Member States and Secretariat should increase their efforts to preserve these values and take more intensive action to further the development of humanity.

An excellent example of a UNESCO initiative goes back to 1969, when hostilities started in the 'Football War' between Honduras and El Salvador.[23] The Director-

20 Four months. See Article 14 of the mentioned Regulations.

21 Constitution of the United Nations Educational, Scientific and Cultural Organisation, adopted in London on 16 November 1945. Article 1, paragraph 2(c), 4 UNTS 275.

22 http://portal.unesco.org/culture/en/files/12762/11295421661mexico_en.pdf/mexico_en.pdf.

23 The 'Football War' (*La guerra del fútbol*) was a four-day war caused by political conflicts between Honduras and El Salvador, namely issues concerning immigration from El Salvador to Honduras. The tensions coincided with rioting during the second North American qualifying round for the 1970 FIFA World Cup, when the two nations were pitted against each other. Disturbances broke out during the first game in Tegucigalpa, and escalated during the second match in San Salvador. Early in the morning of 14 July 1969, the Salvadorian army launched an attack against Honduras. The Organisation of American States negotiated a ceasefire which took effect on 20 July, and the Salvadorian troops withdrew in early August. Eleven years later the two nations signed

General launched an appeal to the two governments, suggesting that they become Parties to the Convention to ensure the protection of the cultural property on their territory. Although neither of them was then a Party at the time,[24] both heeded the call and acceded.

The Director-General adopted the practice of reminding States of their duties at the beginning of hostilities, particularly when they were Contracting Parties to the 1954 Hague Convention. At the time of the internal conflict in Nigeria (1967-1970), the Director-General, referring to Article 19 of the 1954 Hague Convention, offered UNESCO's services to the Nigerian authorities. The offer was not accepted, but the authorities sent documentation showing that they would respect the Convention.

Similar messages were sent in 1971 to India and Pakistan, in 1974 to Cyprus and Turkey at the time of the conflict in Cyprus, and in 1980 to Iraq and Iran, both Parties to the Convention. The authorities on both sides responded and declared that they would respect their obligations.

Fact-finding missions were also undertaken in Cyprus, both before and after the *de facto* partition of the island in 1974. Also measures were taken to safeguard the historic Mediterranean city of Tyre after the Israeli occupation of southern Lebanon in 1982 and more recently in the former Yugoslavia, notably Dubrovnik.

The Director-General has intervened many times, through either diplomatic channels or public appeals and declarations at conferences, particularly at UNESCO's General Conference. One public appeal was launched jointly with the Secretary-General of the United Nations.[25] UNESCO regularly sends observers, representatives and experts to conflict situations, and the General Conference adopts resolutions reminding States of their obligations.

4. The 1983 Meeting of Legal Experts on the 1954 Hague Convention

In 1983, UNESCO invited high-level legal experts from eleven countries to meet in Vienna, where they reaffirmed the importance of the Convention and made many suggestions to renew and improve its application. The main difficulties facing States Parties mentioned were the very complex technical work required, the shortage of experts to do the work, the small number of countries that had marked their monuments with the emblem of the 1954 Hague Convention, the limited use of special protection, difficulties with and lengthy negotiations over the appointment of Commissioners-General, and finally the fact that not all States were willing to apply the system of international control. The experts were also aware of the problems of implementation in situations of international and non-international armed conflicts,

---

a peace treaty on 30 October 1980, agreeing to bring their border dispute before the International Court of Justice.

24 El Salvador ratified the Convention on 19 July 2001; Honduras acceded on 25 October 2002.

25 Joint Declaration by the Secretary-General of the United Nations and the Director-General of UNESCO on the Situation in Yugoslavia, 24 October 1991.

of inadequate implementation, and lack of interest in providing reports on peacetime implementation.

The Meeting extensively discussed the question of UNESCO's right of initiative under Articles 19 and 23 of the 1954 Hague Convention. It was suggested that UNESCO should assist States draw up inventories of cultural property that would warrant inclusion in the International Register of Cultural Property under Special Protection. The connection with the World Heritage Convention was underlined. At that time, the experts considered it unnecessary to amend the Convention, and preferred to concentrate on efforts to improve its application.[26] They noted the lack of reports on how States were complying with their obligation to impose sanctions under their criminal legislation. They also stated that UNESCO should provide assistance in accelerating the appointment of Commissioners-General.

Several remedies for the reported difficulties with the 1954 Hague Convention were proposed: an appeal by the Director-General, the adoption of a resolution by the General Conference, the establishment of high-level contacts in States, the preparation of an information campaign and the organisation of training programmes. At the same time it was considered essential that countries take action to promote awareness of the need to protect cultural heritage in armed conflict. One of the ways to achieve this was the establishment of national associations.[27] The possibility of a conference on heritage protection of all UNESCO Member States was also mentioned.[28]

This 1983 meeting was my first encounter with the issue. I recommended several measures, mostly institutional: the creation of national coordinating bodies and non-governmental associations to support the governmental bodies, the appointment of a technical advisory committee to UNESCO, the establishment of intervention teams, the setting up of a fund for the protection of cultural property, the development of teaching and research on the Convention, and wider dissemination of the Convention. The experts adopted the recommendation for a permanent technical advisory committee, which had been made earlier at the meeting of the High Contracting Parties in 1962.[29]

Following the post-World War II enthusiasm, the lack of interest at the 1983 expert meeting was due to the tense international political situation of the Cold War, rapid advances in military technology, and doubts as to whether in these cir-

---

26 1983 Meeting of Legal Experts on the Convention for the Protection of Cultural Property in the Event of Armed Conflict (The Hague, 1954), Vienna 17 – 19 October 1983, CLT-83/CONF.641/1, p. 10.

27 Idem, p. 4.

28 Idem, p. 14.

29 "Such a committee could be established within UNESCO, which would not require a revision of the Convention. It would fall within the framework of the technical assistance foreseen in Article 23 of the Convention. The Committee could take the form of a committee of experts appointed by the Director-General in their personal capacity or of a subsidiary body of the Executive Board [...]. It was furthermore recalled that a proposal to establish a permanent council of representatives of High Contracting Parties had been made at The Hague Conference in 1954." Idem, p. 12.

cumstances the Convention could still be effective.[30] The experts considered that the review process clearly reflected the evolution of international relations since the Second World War. The ineffectiveness that had been observed was essentially due to the lack of political will to apply all the protective measures that had been provided for.[31]

5. New conflicts in the 1980s and 1990s

5.1 Iran – Iraq[32]

Another example of action by UNESCO took place during the war between Iran and Iraq in the 1980s. In this conflict, the Executive Board and Director-General expressed their concern, and stressed UNESCO's willingness to help protect human lives, educational, scientific and cultural institutions, and cultural and natural heritage threatened by the conflict. In conjunction with the President of the General Conference, the Director-General sent a telegram to the foreign ministers of the two Member States. Towards the end of the war, when troop numbers and resources were declining on both sides, military operations focused on the cities: Iran attempted to capture Basra and attacked Baghdad while Iraq attacked 65 Iranian cities.

As 'the war of the cities' gradually led to a ceasefire, it was finally possible to have more frequent contacts with the permanent delegates of the two countries. Stressing the importance of the 1954 Hague Convention, the Director-General proposed specific measures. The resolutions of the 23rd[33] and 24th[34] sessions of the General Conference as well as the decisions of the Executive Board called upon both States to end the war, seek a peaceful solution and observe international humanitarian principles, in particular those on the protection of cultural and natural heritage, the environment, and educational, scientific and cultural institutions. The Director-General sent a team of two personal representatives – Dr Abdulgani and Professor Lemaire – to Iran (from 31 October to 7 November 1985) and Iraq (from 11 to 15 January 1986).[35] They visited the sites and monuments that had suffered from the war and the places

30 Idem, p. 3. At the signing ceremony of the Second Protocol to the Hague Convention for the Protection of Cultural Property in the Event of Armed Conflict at The Hague on 16 May 1999, Colin Power said, "However, there was a period when the mechanisms of the Hague Convention of 1954 were thoughts to have been superseded by technology: how could painting a sign on the roof of a museum to indicate a protected site be an adequate warning when the menace was an intercontinental ballistic missile? Thus little attention was paid to the Convention in the 1970s and 1980s." (Text distributed at the signing ceremony, p. 3).

31 Idem, p. 12.

32 1980-1988.

33 http://unesdoc.unesco.org/images/0006/000684/068427e.pdf.

34 http://unesdoc.unesco.org/images/0007/000769/076995e.pdf.

35 UNESCO Executive Board, 126th Session, 126 ex./ìnf. 3, Paris 18 may 1987: "I also informed you that I had sent a mission consisting of two of my personal representatives, Dr Abdulgani and Professor Lemaire, to Iran in October 1985 and, subsequently, to Iraq in January 1986."

that the authorities of the two countries were willing to show them. They had discussions with the authorities of the two States who affirmed their willingness to respect the Convention's provisions. The two governments committed themselves to examining the possibility of appointing a Commissioner-General for Cultural Property, but the war ended before such an appointment could occur.

5.2 Yugoslavia[36]

The war in former Yugoslavia was a watershed in the systematic destruction of cultural heritage. It undoubtedly constituted a major persuasive element leading to the adoption of the Second Protocol. The destruction of the bridge at Mostar and the bombing of Dubrovnik, a historic city registered on the World Heritage List, became symbols of the total failure of protection.

Worst of all was the confirmation that the destruction had been intentional, that cultural destruction was a military objective in itself. The aim had not simply been the destruction of cultural property, but the disruption of the ordinary life and the peaceful coexistence of different peoples that it symbolised, and their communities' urban and religious life.

The Yugoslav armed forces were familiar with the Convention's provisions, as Yugoslavia had been actively engaged in the dissemination, reaffirmation and development of humanitarian law. This shows that knowledge of the Convention's provisions is not enough; there is a clear need for political goodwill as well.

From the outset of the conflict, following the Slovene and Croatian declarations of independence, the Director-General repeatedly called for cultural property to be respected, based on the 1954 Hague Convention and the 1972 World Heritage Convention. UN Security Council resolution 780 (1992) established a UN Commission of Experts.[37] UNESCO sent missions, and the Director-General made a joint appeal with the UN Secretary-General.[38]

Later, UNESCO established contacts with the International Criminal Tribunal for the former Yugoslavia as the ICTY dealt with several well-known cases concerning the destruction of cultural property.[39]

---

36 1992-1995.

37 On 6 October 1992, at its 3119th meeting, the Security Council authorised the "Secretary-General to establish, as a matter of urgency, an impartial Commission of Experts to examine and analyse the information submitted pursuant to resolution 771 (1992) and the present resolution, [...] with a view to providing the Secretary-General with its conclusions on the evidence of grave breaches of the Geneva Convention and other violations of international humanitarian law committed in the territory of the former Yugoslavia." The conclusions of the Commission of Experts were delivered to the President of the UN Security Council on 24 May 1994 and included a chapter on the destruction of cultural property (Final report of the Commission of Experts established pursuant to Security Council Resolution 780 (1992), S/1994/674, paragraphs 285 – 301).

38 See footnote 25.

39 Theodor Meron, 'The Protection of Cultural Property in the Event of an Armed Conflict within the Case-law of the International Criminal Tribunal for the Former Yugoslavia', *Museum International* 228 (December 2005), pp. 41-60.

5.3 *The first Gulf War*[40]

Immediately after the occupation of Kuwait began, Iraq's Director of Antiquities came to Kuwait to remove the al-Sabah collection and transport it to Baghdad. The collection remained in the cellars of the Iraq National Museum and was thus protected from the bombing. So although plundering did not take place at the beginning of the war, the Iraqis themselves seized antiquities. After the war, between 14 September and 20 October 1991, 25,082 objects from the Kuwaiti National Museum and the al-Sabah collection of Islamic art were returned by Iraq to Kuwaiti representatives in Baghdad, under the supervision of the UN Return of Property group (UNROP), which carried out an inventory, inspection and evaluation of the damage. Once the property was restored, UNDP and UNESCO ensured that experts were appointed to repair the damaged objects.

The war itself caused damage. Operation Desert Storm was called a 'masterpiece of planning and execution at the strategic and tactical level'. However, the American soldiers reserved their attention to military objectives, and collateral damage could not be avoided. Plundering of archaeological sites and museums thus became a principal concern. The Iraqis presented a list of some 4,000 disappeared objects. With the assistance of UNESCO and many other agencies, information on the stolen objects was transmitted to customs and police officers and antique dealers internationally. Although the trade in cultural objects was prohibited by the Security Council[41], Iraqi antiquities started to appear on the European and American markets. Already in 1997, it was said that enough antiquities had been confiscated at the border with Jordan to mount an exhibition at the National Museum in Baghdad.[42]

Certain objects were saved by placing them in safe repositories to protect them from bombing. The sanctions that followed the war prevented a serious evaluation of the losses and delayed or blocked international assistance. Nonetheless, thanks to aid from UNESCO, the National Museum in Baghdad was restored from 1998 and opened to the public in April 2000.

5.4 *Afghanistan*[43]

During the fighting that followed the Soviet withdrawal from Kabul in 1988, the Afghan National Museum was emptied of its contents. Seventy per cent of the museum's collections disappeared. What remained was finally destroyed by order of the Taliban. The many years of conflicts of all kinds, the civil war, the occupation and extremist fundamentalism of the Taliban led to massive destruction, symbolised by the destruction of the Bamiyan Buddhas, and the plundering of the country's treasures, in particular those in the National Museum in Kabul and the museums of Ghazni and Herat.

---

40 1991.

41 UN Security Council Resolution 1483 (2003), adopted 22 May 2003.

42 Jeremy Lott, *Found Objects: What archaeologists can gain from markets, or lose by ignoring them*, Reason, January 2004.

43 Since 1988.

The destruction was followed by neglect. The end of the Taliban regime did not prevent the plundering and trafficking that stripped Afghanistan of its historical treasures. UNESCO established relationships with Afghan and foreign institutions to preserve the country's heritage. An International Coordination Committee for the Safeguarding of Afghanistan's Cultural Heritage was formed, taking preventive measures against the illicit excavations and illegal export of cultural property and helping with the restoration of a series of monuments.

5.5 The most recent catastrophe: The invasion of Iraq by US and Coalition forces[44]

All the methods mentioned above for the dissemination of humanitarian law and protection of cultural property were recently put to a new test: the invasion of Iraq by the troops of the coalition led by the US army. US Army Field Manual 27-10 contains clear provisions referring to the Hague Regulations, the Roerich Pact and customary international law. At the time of the invasion in 2003, however, the US was not bound by the 1954 Hague Convention.

There are no words to describe the negligence of those who allowed the plundering to take place and proved incapable of preventing the destruction. Several articles and books describe this extensively.[45]

The armed forces were well informed and had been warned. Professor McGuire Gibson of the Oriental Institute of the University of Chicago took part in preparing lists containing several thousand names of archaeological sites. National and international organisations placed necessary information at the army's disposal and issued warnings stressing that Iraq is universally known to have a particularly rich cultural inheritance; the country is often described as the 'cradle of civilisation'. The Director-General of UNESCO approached the US observer, and made him aware of his worries with regard to the danger of plundering and destruction of cultural property. The American authorities responded that they had taken note of international concerns. However, the army was totally negligent, taking no action against the plunderers and those who occupied the National Museum in Baghdad, the National Library and Archive,[46] and the Ministry of Endowments and Religious Affairs Central Library.[47] The newspapers and other media have provided extensive information on what actually occurred.

Plundering started immediately after the troops' entry into Baghdad on 9 April 2003, apparently by two distinct groups: professional robbers (taking objects from the Uruk and Akkadian periods, those most in demand from collectors) and ordinary robbers. Only on 16 April did American tanks arrive at the site of the National Museum. According to Mounir Bouchenaki, the then UNESCO Assistant Director-

44 2003 – present.

45 Flandrin, op.cit, *Antiquities under Siege*, op.cit., and *The Destruction of Cultural Heritage in Iraq*, op.cit., all cited in footnote 3.

46 National Library and Archive (Dar Al-Kutub Wa Al-Watha'Iq).

47 Ministry of Endowments & Religious Affairs Central Library (Maktabat al-Awqaf al-Markaziyya) .

General for Culture, the Americans were not concerned at all with cultural property in Baghdad or elsewhere, but only with their military concerns: to secure a foothold in certain strategic places. Their role in safeguarding the Ministries of Oil and the Interior, situated two or three kilometres from the National Museum, is today generally acknowledged. By contrast, the US army's failure to protect Iraq's cultural heritage is notorious, and it must be held responsible for what happened.

UNESCO sent investigative experts and missions and organised meetings and rescue projects. Many international organisations were mobilised to provide assistance. Interpol, the FBI, American military investigators and the Italian Carabinieri dispatched agents to the spot. Three White House cultural advisers resigned in protest at the armed forces' failure to prepare this aspect of the invasion.[48]

The UN Security Council adopted the following resolutions on the subject: resolution 1483 of 22 May 2003, paragraph 7 of which concerns the protection of Iraqi cultural objects and prohibits international trade in the Iraqi cultural property that had been illegally removed from the National Museum, the National Library and other places;[49] and resolution 1546 of 8 June 2004, "*Stressing* the need for all parties to respect and protect Iraq's archaeological, historical, cultural, and religious heritage."

The International Council of Museums (ICOM) published an urgent red list to help customs officers, police officers and antique dealers identify objects coming from Iraq, stressing that all antiquities coming from Iraq must be viewed with caution. Following their tragic failures, the American authorities took measures – too late – intended to save face. They proceeded to appoint a consultant to the Provisional Authority, to send missions, experts and advisers, and to provide the Iraqi authorities with equipment needed by the National Museum. One of those involved concluded: "Antiquities trafficking will never merit the same attention or resources as terrorism, drugs, human trafficking, or violent street crime. But, at the very least, it deserves to be on the same list. [...] We must expose those who engage in the illegal trade for what they are: criminals."[50]

---

48 See: http://news.bbc.co.uk/2/hi/entertainment/2958009.stm
http://www.wsws.org/articles/2003/apr2003/cult-a19.shtml
Chicago Sun-Times, 18April 2003, Carl Hartman: "White House cultural advisers quiet over looting"

49 Op. 7 of SC Res 1483 (2003) reads: "7. *Decides* that all Member States shall take appropriate steps to facilitate the safe return to Iraqi institutions, of Iraqi cultural property and other items of archaeological, historical, cultural, rare scientific, and religious importance illegally removed from the Iraq National Museum, the National Library, and other locations in Iraq since the adoption of resolution 661 (1990) of 2 August 1990, including by establishing a prohibition on trade in or transfer of such items and items with respect to which reasonable suspicion exists that they have been illegally removed, and calls upon the United Nations Educational, Scientific, and Cultural Organisation, Interpol, and other international organisations, as appropriate, to assist in the implementation of this paragraph."

50 Matthew Bogdanos, 'Thieves of Bagdad', in: *The Destruction of Cultural Heritage in Iraq*. Edited by Peter G. Stone and Joanne Farchakh Bajjaly. Woodbridge, The Boydell Press, 2008, p. 130.

The recent events in Iraq, like those in former Yugoslavia and other parts of the world, show how vital it is to disseminate the legal rules concerning cultural heritage and to train soldiers and civilian personnel.

6. Development of the legal protection of cultural property since the adoption of the 1954 Hague Convention

The 1954 Hague Convention is not the only legal instrument for the protection of cultural property. The process of reaffirming and developing international humanitarian law has addressed the protection of cultural property in other ways as well. The legal approach to protection has developed in two ways: on the one hand, mainly at the initiative of UNESCO, it has followed the path of codifying the rules concerning culture. On the other hand, mainly at the initiative of the International Committee of the Red Cross and to some extent the United Nations, it has addressed cultural property through humanitarian law more broadly.

6.1 Documents adopted within the framework of UNESCO

The Constitution of UNESCO gives the organisation a mandate to assure "the conservation and protection of the world's inheritance of books, works of art and monuments of history and science, and recommend [...] to the nations concerned the necessary international conventions."[51] UNESCO has adopted many recommendations to carry out this mandate. In particular, it has adopted several Conventions with major significance for the protection of cultural property in time of war such as the Convention on the Means of Prohibiting and Preventing the Illicit Import, Export and Transfer of Ownership of Cultural Property,[52] and the Convention concerning the Protection of the World Cultural and Natural Heritage.[53] Also worthy of mention is the UNESCO Declaration concerning the Intentional Destruction of Cultural Heritage.[54]

6.2 Development of international humanitarian law applicable in armed conflicts

The Diplomatic Conference on the Reaffirmation and Development of International Humanitarian Law applicable in Armed Conflicts (Geneva, 1974-1977) adopted two Additional Protocols,[55] each of which contains an article relating to the protection of

51 Article 1 (2) (c) UNESCO Constitution.

52 Adopted by the General Conference at its 16th session in Paris on 14 November 1970, 823 UNTS 231.

53 Adopted by the UNESCO General Conference at its 17th session in Paris on 16 November 1972, 1037 UNTS 151.

54 Adopted by the UNESCO General Conference on 17 October 2003.

55 Protocol I and II Additional to the Geneva Conventions of 12 August 1949, and relating to the Protection of Victims of International Armed Conflicts and of Non-International Armed Conflict, respectively. Both Protocols were adopted 8 June 1977.

cultural property: Article 53 of Protocol I (international armed conflict) and Article 16 of Protocol II (non-international armed conflicts). Initiated by the Diplomatic Conference of 1974-1977 but adopted under the aegis of the United Nations in 1979-1980, the Convention on the Prohibition or Restriction on the Use of Certain Conventional Weapons which may be Deemed to Be Excessively Injurious or Have Indiscriminate Effects (opened for signature on 10 April 1981) also contains several provisions in its Protocols relating to the protection of cultural property.

Spectacular progress in the field of international criminal law was made in the 1990s, notably through the establishment of the International Criminal Tribunal for the former Yugoslavia,[56] whose Statute and case law represent a great step forward in the criminalisation of acts against cultural property. The Statute of the International Criminal Court is another significant step towards criminalising future violations and crimes against cultural property.[57]

The Extraordinary Chambers in the Courts of Cambodia (ECCC)[58] were created in 2001 by the 'Law on the Establishment of the Extraordinary Chambers in the Courts of Cambodia for the Prosecution of Crimes Committed during the Period of Democratic Kampuchea'.[59] Article 7 of this Law provides that the "Extraordinary Chambers shall have the power to bring to trial all Suspects most responsible for the destruction of cultural property during armed conflict pursuant to the 1954 Hague Convention for the Protection of Cultural Property in the Event of Armed Conflict, and which were committed during the period from 17 April 1975 to 6 January 1979."

6.3 *A new approach in the 1990s*

By the 1990's UNESCO was aware of the difficulties and shortcomings in protecting cultural property during armed conflict. After several *ad hoc* measures were taken, the decision was made to improve the text of the 1954 Hague Convention and reinforce the measures for its implementation. The following were the main shortcomings addressed: there was a lack of adequate preparation in time of peace; very few States had recourse to special protection and the registration of cultural property on the list established and administered by UNESCO, due to the clause allowing exceptions on grounds of military necessity, to political obstacles to registration on the list, and to unrealistic conditions for registration; the reference to non-international conflicts needed more precision and clarification; the monitoring system, though based on an original concept, proved to be completely inadequate in practice, and needed to be adapted to the new conditions prevailing in the international community and in particular to the activities of international organisations dealing with the protection of and respect for human rights; the reporting system needed to be strengthened; there was the lack of appropriate sanctions for violations of its provisions.

There was thus a substantial gap between the provisions of the 1954 Hague Convention and the new provisions concerning sanctions introduced by the 1977

56 UN Security Council Resolution S/Res/827 (1993), adopted 25 May 1993.
57 Adopted on 17 July 1998 in Rome, 2187 UNTS 90.
58 Also called Khmer Rouge Tribunal.
59 Nr. NS.RKM/0801/12, dated 10 August 2001.

Additional Protocols, the Statute of the International Criminal Tribunal for the former Yugoslavia, and Statute of the International Criminal Court, which had to be addressed. In institutional terms, the lack of a connection between the Secretariat of the World Heritage Convention and the other agreements, including the 1954 Hague Convention, had – in my view – a negative impact, and contributed to a virtual abandonment of the protection of cultural property in time of war.

It was undoubtedly due to these shortcomings that the 1954 Hague Convention did not receive sufficient support from States. However, the growing number of ratifications of and accessions to the 1954 Hague Convention as the process of revision began (in 1994-1999), made it possible to hope for a renaissance of the protection of cultural property in the event of armed conflict.

Since the adoption of the 1954 Hague Convention the international community and the international legal system has been evolved and changed.

The changes were particularly significant in the field of the law of armed conflicts, but they were also notable in the field of cultural property, where many new Conventions were being adopted. The 1977 Additional Protocols also included articles for the protection of cultural property. The protection of cultural property in the event of armed conflict required a new approach and an adaptation to the new world situation. This is why a new Protocol was proposed.

7. Contribution of the 1999 Second Protocol to the Protection of Cultural Property in the Event of Armed Conflict

The Netherlands and its government deserve congratulations and gratitude for their contribution to the world community in so many fields of international law. The protection of cultural property is only one such field.

The symposium to mark the tenth anniversary of the Second Protocol dealt with a number of issues that the Protocol addressed. It would be presumptuous of me to try to enumerate all the Second Protocol's contributions to improving the protection of cultural property in the event of armed conflict. I will therefore mention just a few of them that relate to better implementation of the 1954 Hague Convention.

The Second Protocol is helpful not only in improving protection, but also in providing aid in interpreting the Convention. Many examples could be mentioned, but let me underline one of them: the safeguarding measures. At the 1954 Diplomatic Conference, UNESCO proposed a fairly substantial provision which was reduced in the end to something minimal. The Second Protocol now provides many examples of the meaning of the safeguarding measures, thus giving an interpretation, which is also useful for States that are not Parties to the Protocol. The same applies to the concept of military necessity, which is the central and most important issue in interpreting the Convention.

7.1 Committee for the Protection of Cultural Property in the Event of Armed Conflict

The idea of a committee on the implementation of the Convention is not new. At the 1954 Conference itself, Italy and Belgium suggested the creation of a permanent or consultative body responsible for monitoring the Convention's execution. Italy proposed an intergovernmental committee; Belgium by contrast had in mind a committee composed of individual delegates, appointed *ad personam*.

At the preparatory meetings for the 1999 Hague Conference most of the contributions supported a committee with an intergovernmental character. I must admit that I took a somewhat heretical view; there are many treaty bodies, some of them useful and efficient (like the Human Rights Committee), others less so. For this reason, at the 1993 meeting I mentioned one such Committee that is extremely efficient, although not a real committee: the International Committee of the Red Cross. It is in fact a huge and efficient administrative body, providing crucial support to the implementation of the 1949 Geneva Conventions and 1977 Additional Protocols. An efficient administrative body to insure the effective protection of cultural property is necessary.[60]

There is another relevant example: the World Heritage Centre which serves as the secretariat to the World Heritage Committee. It is an efficient administrative body with a staff of about 80, established to mark the 20th anniversary of the 1972 World Heritage Convention. The main reason that the World Heritage Convention is implemented efficiently is not only the existence of this Committee, but also the major administrative support behind it. By contrast, the 1954 Hague Convention and the 1999 Second Protocol have an implementing Committee of twelve States, with only one permanent staff member. This is in my view not the most adequate method to improve the protection of cultural property in armed conflict.

In relation to the Committee and the indispensable character of administrative and staff support, we should underline the words of former UNESCO Director-General Frederico Mayor in his address on 15 March 1999 opening the Diplomatic Conference on the draft Second Protocol:

> "In seeking better support for the Convention, the instinct of many experts was to recommend an intergovernmental committee. Many such committees play an important role in furthering UNESCO's work. But this is a time when all international organisations have been trying to streamline their administrations. We therefore thought it appropriate to propose an alternative, lighter structure such as a Bureau, which could perform most of the same functions with less expense and fewer staff resources. But the decision, as with all the issues, rests with you. *If you determine at this meeting that the instrument on which you are deciding must have an intergovernmental committee to support it, then I will, of course, try to see that adequate resources are established for it.*"[61]

We had no reason not to expect his successor to do the same. Nevertheless, no progress has been made in this respect. It is important to note that the Meeting of the Parties to the Second Protocol in 2005, and every meeting of the Committee for the Protection of Cultural Property in the Event of Armed Conflict, have drawn

60 Due to my heretical views, I was not invited to any other preparatory meeting for the 1999 Second Protocol.

61 UNESCO document DG/99/9, p. 5 (emphasis added).

the Director-General's attention to the need "to provide the necessary human and financial resources to the Secretariat to undertake these responsibilities properly."[62] Some time ago, the professional dealing with the 1954 Hague Convention and its two (1954 and 1999) Protocols was for administrative reasons given an office in the World Heritage Centre, only to be transferred elsewhere later. In my view, this staff position should return to the World Heritage Centre, where it belongs.

7.2 Dissemination

Article 25 of the 1954 Hague Convention and Article 30 of the 1999 Second Protocol deal with the important issue of dissemination. It depends very much on the countries how this commitment is met. Reports on the implementation of these two instruments include information on the way the States Parties incorporate the study of the Convention "in their programmes of military and, if possible, civilian training, so that its principles are made known to the whole population, especially the armed forces and personnel engaged in the protection of cultural property."[63]

The dissemination work of the ICRC is a good example to learn from. Dissemination is important to both the military and civilians; and among civilians, particularly important to those who are involved in the field of cultural property.

I would like to refer to a recent experience with dissemination that was probably even more instructive for me than for those for whom it was intended. I have had an opportunity to speak about the 1954 Hague Convention and its Protocols with the staff of the Ministries of Culture and Museums and with archaeologists in Lebanon and Cambodia. In Lebanon I gave my usual presentation, but the request from Cambodia was much more unusual: I was asked to talk to about 100 people from the Ministry and associated sectors for four days, which included a field mission to the temples devoted to the placement of the emblem of the Convention. The training course, which closed with the distribution of certificates, was a tremendous experience. The participants were interested, asked questions, and often wanted information going far beyond the Convention and Protocols, and beyond issues of international law and treaties and international relations. Courses like this one in Cambodia should be organised more often, and in many other countries.

8. Conclusion

The efficient protection of cultural property requires the participation of all. However, efforts have not been successful thus far. Someone who has participated in many military missions, including Iraq, came to a rather pessimistic conclusion: "Most gov-

62 First Meeting of the Parties to the Second Protocol to the Hague Convention for the Protection of Cultural Property in the Event of Armed Conflict, Paris, 26 October 2005, CLT-05/CONF.208/3, par. 4. See also First Meeting of the Committee for the Protection of Cultural Property in the Event of Armed Conflict, Paris 11 June 2007, CLT-07/CONF/210/3, par. 16; Second Meeting of the Committee , 17-19 December 2007, CLT-07/CONF/212/4, Annex I, par. 6; Third Meeting of the Committee, 4-6 June 2008, CLT-07/CONF/204/4, Annex, par. 8.

63 Article 25 1954 Hague Convention.

ernments have their hands full combating terrorism, with few resources left to spare tracking down stolen artefacts. Most international organisations are content to issue proclamations, preferring to hit conference centres rather than the streets. Many cultural organisations and foundations are equally content to issue a call for papers rather than a call for action. As for the art community, some members wash their hands of unpleasant realities and argue that, while technically illegal, the market in purloined antiquities is benign – victimless – as long as it brings the art to those who can properly protect it and appreciate it (namely, themselves)."[64]

Cultural heritage is exposed to many dangers: armed conflicts, natural disasters, earthquakes, terrorism and other different forms of destruction, and even love – not love of art, but desire for money and profit. The economic crisis we are living through today is clear evidence of the ethical crisis of our society. In relation to cultural property it is always useful to remember the words that Stanislaw Nahlik pronounced in the Peace Palace in 1967:

> "The individual human being is mortal, and one human generation succeeds the next. But it is praiseworthy for each of us, however ephemeral our existence, to leave on earth some immortal trace of our talent, embodied in a work of art, a historic monument, or some other cultural object. Let us never forget the link between that which is ephemeral and that which is solely capable of endowing humanity and its works with enduring life. Life is short; art is long."[65]

---

64 Matthew Bogdanos, 'Thieves of Bagdad', in: *The Destruction of Cultural Heritage in Iraq*. Edited by Peter G. Stone and Joanne Farchakh Bajjaly. Woodbridge, The Boydell Press, 2008, p. 121.

65 Author's translation; see: Stanislaw E. Nahlik, 'La protection internationale des biens culturels en cas de conflit armé', *Recueil des cours de l'Académie de droit international de La Haye* 120: II (1967), p. 159.

Chapter 2

New rules for the protection of cultural property in armed conflict: The significance of the Second Protocol to the 1954 Hague Convention for the Protection of Cultural Property in the Event of Armed Conflict

*Jean-Marie Henckaerts**

Alles van waarde is weerloos.[1]

1. Introduction

The 1954 Hague Convention for the Protection of Cultural Property in the Event of Armed Conflict (hereafter: the 1954 Convention) is the paramount international instrument for the protection of cultural property during armed conflicts.[2] Cultural property includes museums, libraries, archives, archaeological sites and monuments of architecture, art or history, whether religious or secular. The 1954 Convention has to date been ratified by 95 States, but the basic principles concerning respect for cultural property enshrined in it have become part of customary international law. A Protocol dealing mainly with the protection of cultural property in occupied territory was adopted at the same time as the Convention, and 79 States are party thereto.[3] The specific content of the Convention will be explained in brief under each of the substantive sections of this chapter.

The effectiveness of the 1954 Convention became a subject of general concern in the early nineties, during the second Gulf War and the war in the former Yugoslavia.

---

* Jean-Marie Henckaerts is a legal adviser in the Legal Division of the ICRC and head of the ICRC's project on customary international humanitarian law. He followed, on behalf of the ICRC (which had observer status at the Diplomatic Conference in the Hague), the negotiation and adoption of the Second Protocol. This article reflects the views of the author and not necessarily those of the ICRC. This article was first published in the International Review of the Red Cross, No. 835, 1999, pp. 593–620. It is reprinted with permission.

1 "All things of value are defenceless." A famous line by the Dutch poet Lucebert (author's translation).

2 Convention for the Protection of Cultural Property in the Event of Armed Conflict, signed at The Hague, 14 May 1954, reprinted in Dietrich Schindler and Jiří Toman (Eds.), *The laws of armed conflicts: A collection of conventions, resolutions and other documents*, 3rd ed., Martinus Nijhoff/Henry Dunant Institute, Dordrecht/ Geneva, 1988, pp. 745-759.

3 Protocol for the Protection of Cultural Property in the Event of Armed Conflict, signed at The Hague, 14 May 1954, *ibid.*, pp. 777-782.

Nout van Woudenberg and Liesbeth Lijnzaad (eds.) Protecting Cultural Property in Armed Conflict
© 2010 Koninklijke Brill NV. Printed in The Netherlands. ISBN 978 9004 18377 3 pp. 21 – 41.

As this article goes to press, that effectiveness is sadly still being tested in the continued war in the Balkans.

In 1991, the Government of the Netherlands decided to include a review of the 1954 Convention as part of its contribution to the United Nations Decade of International Law. As a result, The Netherlands and the United Nations Educational, Scientific and Cultural Organization (UNESCO) jointly commissioned and funded "a review of the objectives and operation of the Convention and Protocol with a view to identifying measures for improving its application and effectiveness and to see whether some revision of the Convention itself might be needed, perhaps by means of an Additional Protocol."[4] That review was published in 1993 by Professor Patrick Boylan.

In the following years, the Government of the Netherlands continued to be the driving force behind the review process, and three expert meetings were organized which resulted in the "Lauswolt document", named after the Dutch town where it was drafted. The Lauswolt document was a new draft treaty based on the findings of the Boylan review.

In March 1997, twenty government experts met at UNESCO headquarters in Paris to review the Lauswolt document. On the basis of their discussions, the UNESCO Secretariat drew up a revised Lauswolt document which it submitted to all States party to the 1954 Convention at a meeting in Paris on 13 November 1997. It was decided that a final preparatory meeting would be convened to discuss certain legal questions further, and the proposal by the Netherlands to convene a diplomatic conference in 1999 to transform the Lauswolt document into an international treaty was welcomed.

The final preparatory meeting was hosted in Vienna in May 1998 by the Austrian Government. The meeting identified five main areas that needed to be addressed in the Second Protocol:

- the exception of military;
- precautionary measures;
- the system of special protection;
- individual criminal responsibility;
- institutional aspects.

After the meeting, a Preliminary Draft Second Protocol to the 1954 Convention was drawn up.[5] States and relevant organizations were invited to submit comments on the draft, in particular with respect to the five areas mentioned above.[6] On the

4 Patrick J. Boylan, *Review of the Convention for the Protection of Cultural Property in the Event of Armed Conflict (The Hague Convention of 1954)*, UNESCO, Paris, 1993, p. 19.

5 UNESCO Doc. HC/1999/1, 9 October 1998.

6 See Synoptic report with its Addendum and Corrigendum of comments on the Preliminary Draft Second Protocol to the 1954 Hague Convention received from High Contracting Parties to the Hague Convention for the Protection of Cultural Property in the Event of Armed Conflict 1954, other UNESCO Member States and international organizations, UNESCO Docs. HC/1999/4, 15 January 1999, HC/1999/4/Add.1, March 1999, and HC/1999/4/Add.1/Corr.1, 18 March 1999. Military and legal aspects of the preliminary draft were further discussed in the light of modern humanitarian

basis of those comments, the UNESCO Secretariat and the Government of the Netherlands together drew up the final draft Second Protocol.[7]

The Diplomatic Conference on the Second Protocol to the Hague Convention of 1954 for the Protection of Cultural Property in the Event of Armed Conflict took place in The Hague from 15 to 26 March 1999. On 26 March 1999, the Conference adopted the Second Protocol to the Hague Convention of 1954 for the Protection of Cultural Property in the Event of Armed Conflict (hereafter : the Second Protocol) without a vote.[8] It was opened for signature in The Hague on 17 May 1999 in the framework of the Centennial celebrations of the First International Peace Conference and signed by 27 States on that date. It remains open for signature at the Hague until 31 December 1999.

The Second Protocol is additional to the 1954 Convention, which remains the basic text. A State can only become a party to the Second Protocol if it has ratified the 1954 Convention. During the entire review process, four options were kept open regarding the treaty technique to be used for improving the 1954 Convention. The first consisted in amending the 1954 Hague Convention; however, any amendments would have required unanimous adoption by all States party to the Convention.[9] Since this was virtually impossible, this option was discarded even though some States had supported it. The second option consisted in the adoption of a new, separate convention. This would have required substantial negotiations and would have had the disadvantage of creating two separate systems. As a result, this option was never really considered.

The third option consisted in the adoption of a Protocol aimed at revising the 1954 Convention. Several delegations strongly advocated this option, but because unanimity would again have been required, it was rejected by the majority of delegations. In the end, the fourth option prevailed, namely that the new treaty would be an additional protocol which would in no way amend the 1954 Convention but would supplement it and would only apply to the States who ratified it. The 1977 Protocols additional to the 1949 Geneva Conventions served as a useful precedent. As a result, every effort was made to make sure that each provision of the Second Protocol was indeed additional to the 1954 Convention.

The purpose of this article is to highlight the major developments embodied in the Second Protocol and to mention certain points of common understanding that were acknowledged at the Diplomatic Conference but not reflected as such in the text of the Protocol itself nor in the Conference's Final Act.

---

law at an Expert Meeting on the Improvement of the 1954 Hague Convention, Leiden (Netherlands), 17-18 December 1998.

7 Draft Second Protocol to the 1954 Hague Convention for the Protection of Cultural Property in the Event of Armed Conflict, UNESCO Doc. HC/1999/1/rev.1, February 1999.

8 Second Protocol to the Hague Convention of 1954 for the Protection of Cultural Property in the Event of Armed Conflict, signed at The Hague, 17 May 1999, UNESCO Doc. HC/1999/7, 26 March 1999.

9 1954 Convention, Article 39(5).

2. Peacetime measures

Pursuant to Article 3 of the 1954 Convention, States undertake to prepare in time of peace for the safeguarding of cultural property against the foreseeable effects of an armed conflict "by taking such measures as they consider appropriate". But the Convention does not provide any further details on measures States should take.

The Second Protocol aims to provide more guidance in this respect, as it provides specific examples of concrete measures to be taken in time of peace:[10]

- the preparation of inventories;
- the planning of emergency measures for protection against fire or structural collapse;
- the preparation for the removal of movable cultural property or the provision of adequate in situ protection of such property;
- the designation of competent authorities responsible for the safeguarding of cultural property.

These measures are of great practical importance for the protection of cultural property in the event of armed conflict.

Clearly, they also require financial resources and know-how. With these requirements in mind, the Second Protocol provides for the setting up of a Fund for the protection of cultural property in the event of armed conflict.[11] The Fund was specifically established to provide financial or other assistance in support of preparatory or other measures to be taken in peacetime. It will be managed by the Committee for the Protection of Cultural Property in the Event of Armed Conflict, which is to be set up pursuant to the Second Protocol.[12] The resources of the Fund shall consist inter alia of voluntary contributions made by States party to the Second Protocol.[13] Some States had sought the inclusion of compulsory contributions, but in the end that proposal was rejected.

In addition, the Second Protocol expands on the rather general provision concerning dissemination contained in the 1954 Convention.[14] Again, specific examples of concrete dissemination measures are listed, especially for the military and civilian authorities who assume responsibilities with respect to the application of the Second Protocol. They are to be fully acquainted with the Protocol, and to that end States party shall, as appropriate:[15]

- incorporate guidelines and instructions on the protection of cultural property in their military regulations;
- develop and implement, in cooperation with UNESCO and relevant governmental and non-governmental organizations, peacetime training and educational programmes;

10 Second Protocol, Article 5.
11 *Ibid.*, Article 29.
12 *Ibid.*, Article 24.
13 *Ibid.*, Article 29(4).
14 1954 Convention, Article 25.
15 Second Protocol, Article 30.

- communicate to one another, through the Director-General of UNESCO, information on laws, administrative provisions and measures taken under the preceding paragraphs;
- communicate to one another, as soon as possible, through the Director-General, the laws and administrative provisions which they may adopt to ensure the application of the Protocol.

The experience of the International Committee of the Red Cross provides ample evidence of the essential role of dissemination when it comes to ensuring respect for international humanitarian law.

3. Respect for cultural property

3.1 All cultural property

Article 4 of the 1954 Convention provides that cultural property shall not be subject to any act of hostility nor used for purposes which are likely to expose it to destruction or damage in the event of armed conflict. It immediately adds, however, that both obligations may be waived in case of "imperative military necessity". Professor Boylan's review identified the lack of a clear definition of this exception as a serious weakness with respect to the basic principle of protection contained in the 1954 Convention.[16]

Although the origins of the principle of military necessity can be traced back to the Lieber Code,[17] the restriction of imperative military necessity was first codified in international law in the 1907 Hague Regulations limiting the destruction or seizure of the enemy's property to that which was imperatively demanded by the necessities of war.[18] The 1954 Convention borrowed this notion as there were few other established limits applicable to the conduct of hostilities.[19]

As history shows, however, the concept of military necessity has not limited warfare in any significant way. The Second World War, for example, was fought under the restriction that no property could be destroyed unless there was an imperative military necessity to do so. Yet entire cities were destroyed.

16 Boylan, *supra* note 4, pp. 54-57.

17 See Burrus M. Carnahan, "Lincoln. Lieber and the laws of war: The origins and limits of the principle of military necessity", *American Journal of International Law*, Vol. 92, 1998, 213, and Horace B. Robertson, Jr., "The principle of military objective in the law of armed conflict", in Michael N. Schmitt (Ed.), *The Law of Military Operations – Liber Amicorum Professor Jack Grunawalt,* International Law Studies, Vol. 72, Naval War College Press, Newport, Rhode Island, 1998, p. 197.

18 Regulations Respecting the Laws and Customs of War on Land, signed at The Hague, 18 October 1907, Article 23(g), reprinted in Schindler and Toman, *supra* note 2, p. 83.

19 This was in part because some documents which had identified such limits had failed to become binding treaty law. See, e.g., Article 24(1) of the Hague Rules of Air Warfare, drafted by a Commission of Jurists at The Hague, Dec. 1922 - Feb. 1923, reprinted in Schindler and Toman, *supra* note 2, p. 210: "Aerial bombardment is legitimate only when directed at a military objective, that is to say, an object of which the destruction or injury would constitute a distinct military advantage to the belligerent."

It appears that the notion of imperative military necessity is too vague to constitute an effective limitation on warfare. Even military lawyers at the Diplomatic Conference admitted that it was difficult to teach their troops how to interpret and work with the concept. In general, matters left to discretionary clauses based on military necessity are those which could not be regulated; and matters which are not regulated provide a field for the law to develop. In order to do so, the military philosophy behind the maxim "Have confidence in the wisdom of the generals"[20] had to be replaced with objective criteria that were binding on the military. The goal of the Diplomatic Conference was to give a content to the notion of imperative military necessity with a view to enhancing its meaning and effect.

Imperative military necessity to commit acts of hostility

Limiting attacks to military objectives would in large part achieve that goal. One should not forget that the 1954 Convention was adopted well before the 1977 Protocols additional to the 1949 Geneva Conventions. It was drafted against the background of the Second World War, at a time when it was still considered acceptable that entire cities would be attacked. In the midst of such a war, the 1954 Convention sought to protect valuable cultural property.

In 1977, the Protocol additional to the Geneva Conventions of 12 August 1949, and relating to the Protection of Victims of International Armed Conflicts (Protocol I) did away with this approach.[21] Henceforth, only military objectives – more clearly defined and more carefully selected – were to be made the object of attack. Civilians and civilian objects were not to be made the object of a direct attack. This approach is a clear example of how international humanitarian law balances military necessity and humanitarian needs: it allows attacks that are necessary but establishes strict humanitarian limits.

It was therefore obvious that any improvement of the 1954 Convention should reflect this modern approach: cultural property is generally civilian property and as such should not be attacked; it may be attacked only if and when it becomes a military objective. This approach also has the advantage of providing a clearer answer to the question of when cultural property may be attacked.

The definition of military objective in Article 52(2) of Additional Protocol I was one of the major achievements of the Diplomatic Conference on the Reaffirmation and Development of International Humanitarian Law Applicable in Armed Conflicts (CDDH), which was convened by the Swiss Government in 1974 and adopted Additional Protocol I on 8 June 1977. States not party to Additional Protocol I, such as the United States, Turkey and India, confirmed the customary law nature of this provision during the 1999 Diplomatic Conference that adopted the Second

20 Yves Sandoz, Christophe Swinarski and Bruno Zimmerman (eds.), *Commentary on the Additional Protocols of 8 June 1977 to the Geneva Conventions of 12 August 1949*, ICRC/Martinus Nijhoff, Dordrecht/Geneva, 1987, p. 395, quoting Éric David, *La protection des populations civiles pendant les conflits armés*, International Institute for Human Rights, VIIIth Teaching Session, July 1977, Strasbourg, p. 52.

21 Protocol Additional to the Geneva Conventions of 12 August 1949, and relating to the Protection of Victims of International Armed Conflicts (Protocol I), reprinted in Schindler and Toman, *supra* note 2, pp. 621-688.

Protocol. This illustrates how the Diplomatic Conference also sought to reaffirm certain rules of humanitarian law while developing others.

The definition of military objective contains two criteria which have to be fulfilled cumulatively before objects can be destroyed, captured or neutralized. They deal with the nature, location, purpose or use of objects and with the military advantage to be gained by destroying, capturing or neutralizing them. The nature, location, purpose or use of the object has to be such that it makes an "effective contribution to military action". The military advantage has to be "definite, in the circumstances ruling at the time". These criteria were as clear as it was possible to negotiate during the CDDH and they are fairly strict.

As such, the notion of military objective incorporates the idea of military necessity. Once an object has become a military objective it can be destroyed, captured or neutralized, subject to certain exceptions. This simple rule recognizes the military necessity of attacking certain objects during war. By limiting those objects to those which are military objectives it incorporates the notion that war has limits. As a result, the concept of military objective embodies the balance that humanitarian law establishes between military interests and humanitarian concerns.

The requirement of the 1954 Convention that the military necessity has to be "imperative" is made sufficiently clear in Article 4 of the Second Protocol by the second condition, namely that no other alternative is available. Military necessity could therefore virtually never be invoked to justify an attack on cultural property standing in the way of an advancing army, as there are almost always alternatives to circumvent the property. This means that when there is a choice between several military objectives and one of them is a cultural property, the latter shall not be attacked. In fact, this provision adds cultural property to the military objectives which, under Article 57(3) of Protocol I, should not be attacked.[22]

The protection of cultural property is enhanced in that the concept of military objective – so widely recognized and used that it has become part of customary international law – is used to define the exception of military necessity. The rule that only military objectives can be targeted is now part and parcel of military manuals and military training worldwide. As many delegates stated at the Diplomatic Conference, it is important to have a simple text which is easy to use and to teach. The concept of military objective fulfils these requirements far better than the vague notion of military necessity.

The final text of Article 4 of the Second Protocol is based on proposals submitted by Austria and the ICRC. The Austrian proposal read: "Imperative military necessity under Article 4, paragraph 2 of the Convention may only be invoked when there is no other feasible alternative for fulfilling the mission and for as long as the reasons for its invocation prevail." The ICRC proposal read: "Objects constituting cultural property lose their general protection from the moment they become mili-

22 *Ibid.*, Article 57(3) which provides that "when a choice is possible between several military objectives for obtaining a similar military advantage, the objective to be selected shall be that the attack of which may be expected to cause the least danger to civilian lives and to civilian objects [and which is not cultural property]." The text in brackets shows how Article 57(3) would read for States having adopted both Additional Protocol I and the Second Protocol.

tary objectives, i.e. when they are used to make an effective contribution to military action and when their total or partial destruction, capture or neutralization offers a definite military advantage in the circumstances ruling at the time."

A Working Group on Chapter 2 was set up under the chairmanship of Austria. Its task was to combine both proposals as the delegates felt both had merit and were in fact complementary. The Austrian proposal sought to define the "imperative" character of military necessity whereas the ICRC proposal sought to use the concept of military objective to give content to the principle of military necessity. A criticism of the ICRC proposal was that it singled out the use of cultural property that could make an effective contribution to military action, whereas Article 52(2) of Additional Protocol I specifies that the nature, location, purpose or use of objects can make an effective contribution to military action. Many delegates, mostly from NATO countries, observed that any definition of military objective had to correspond exactly to the definition given in Article 52(2) of Protocol I.

As a result, the Working Group decided to provide a definition of military objective at the beginning of the Protocol, while Article 4 would limit acts of hostility against cultural property to property "which, by its use, has become a military objective." But even in the Working Group several delegations expressed concern about the restriction "by its use", whereby cultural property could become a military objective by its use only and not by its location, for example. When the draft prepared by the Working Group on Chapter 2 came back to the plenary, the issue of use and location was clearly too controversial and the text was not acceptable to a significant number of delegations.

The Egyptian and Greek delegations were the most active in supporting the restriction whereby cultural property could become a military objective by its use only. The argument was that cultural property which was not used in any way for military action should never be the object of attack. If mere location could turn a cultural property into a military objective, the protection of cultural property would be greatly diminished. Some positive action should be required from the holder of the property before it could become a military objective. The ICRC supported this approach.

Since it was agreed that the nature and purpose of cultural property could never turn it into a military objective, the entire debate centered around the issue of location. The ICRC Commentary to 1977 Protocol I notes that the Working Group of Committee III introduced the location criterion without giving reasons.[23] The same thing could be said of the Second Protocol. No real reasons were given why location had to be included.

One example commonly cited at the Diplomatic Conference was that of historic bridges. This example is misleading, however, because it is really the use of such bridges that can make an effective contribution to military action.

The Canadian delegation offered another specific example: the retreat of troops could be blocked by a historic wall and there might be no way around the wall if it was located in a valley or a mountain pass. To go around the wall would take too much time, and the commander would therefore either have to take casualties or

23 ICRC Commentary, *supra* note 20, p. 636, para. 2021.

break through the wall. In such case, the historic wall would not be used for military action and would become a military objective merely because of its location. This example does not seem realistic as such walls are not usually built in valleys or mountain passes. The need for the criterion of location was not well explained, yet several delegations, mostly from NATO countries, strongly insisted on it.

The ICRC Commentary on Additional Protocol I gives the following examples of objects which by virtue of their location make an effective contribution to military action : a bridge or other construction or a site which is of special importance for military operations in view of its location, either because it is a site that must be seized or because it is important to prevent the enemy from seizing it, or otherwise because it is a matter of forcing the enemy to retreat from it.[24]

As mentioned above with respect to historic bridges, it is really the use of a construction or site that turns it into a military objective. With regard to sites that must be seized because of their location, the question arose at the CDDH what the situation would be if a belligerent in a combat area wished to prevent the enemy army from establishing itself in a particular area or from passing through that area, for example, by means of barrage fire.[25] There can be little doubt, according to the Commentary, that in such a case the area must be considered as a military objective and treated as such.[26] Of course, such a situation could only concern limited areas and not vast stretches of territory. It applies primarily to narrow passages, bridgeheads or strategic points such as hills or mountain passes.[27]

None of these examples constitute convincing evidence of the need to target cultural property because of its location. There is convincing legal evidence, on the other hand, to say that what turns cultural property into a military objective is ultimately its use. In 1907, Article 27 of the Regulations Respecting the Laws and Customs of War on Land already stipulated that "in sieges and bombardments all necessary steps must be taken to spare, as far as possible, buildings dedicated to religion, art, science, or charitable purposes, historic monuments, hospitals, and places where the sick and wounded are collected, provided they are not being used at the time for military purposes" (emphasis added). This text confirms that it is their use which makes these objects lose their protection.

The ICRC Commentary on Article 53 of Additional Protocol I confirms this view. Article 53 prohibits the use of cultural property in support of the military effort.[28] The Commentary notes that "if protected objects were used in support of the military effort, this would obviously constitute a violation of Article 53 of the Protocol, though it would not necessarily justify attacking them. To the extent that it is admit-

24 *Ibid.*, p. 636, para. 2021.

25 *Ibid.*, p. 621, para. 1955.

26 *Ibid.*

27 *Ibid.*

28 Even though Article 53 deals with the use of very special cultural property only, for example cultural property on the International Register of Cultural Property under Special Protection or the new List of Cultural Property under Enhanced Protection, the author will argue below that there is no need to differentiate between the ways in which special or enhanced protection, on the one hand, and general protection, on the other, is lost.

ted that the right to do so does exist with regard to objects of exceptional value, such a right would depend on their being a military objective, or not, as defined in Article 52, paragraph 2."[29] For example, "it is not permitted to destroy a cultural object whose use does not make any contribution to military action, nor a cultural object which has temporarily served as a refuge for combatants, but is no longer used as such."[30]

As a compromise, the sentence "which, by their use, have become military objects" was changed to "which, by their function, have been made into military objects" in the Second Protocol. This represents a twofold change. First, the word "use" was replaced by "function", which does not appear in the definition of a military objective. Secondly, "become" was replaced by the words "been made into".

With regard to the new text, there was a clear understanding that the word "function" referred at the same time to something that was in fact functioning. For example, an old fortification which was not functioning as a fortification could not be considered a military objective. In addition, the new text sought to convey the requirement of an active role on the part of the holder of the cultural property in that the holder made the property into a military objective. This could only happen through use.

It is only by a stretch of imagination that function could cover location: the example of the historic wall blocking retreating soldiers could fall under the new text in that the circumstances make the wall, which functions to block a retreat, into a military objective. But in real life this is not the problem faced by cultural property on the battlefield. In real life the problem is that cultural property is attacked even when it is not used for any military action or is attacked indiscriminately. In real life the rule should be simple: cultural property which is not used to make an effective contribution to military action and whose destruction, seizure or neutralization does not offer a definite military advantage cannot be attacked. It is difficult to imagine how military commanders could teach their soldiers anything else.

It is remarkable that military lawyers who call for texts that are simple to teach and apply argue at such length about a minor difference that will be difficult to apply and teach. The reason why some delegates strongly argued for use only was clear. The mere location of pyramids in Egypt or temples on Greek islands should never serve as a pretext to attack those objects. The insistence on changing use to function is difficult to understand if the only example that could be given was that of an ancient wall blocking a pass. This example could easily have been dealt with under the exception of the prohibition on use of cultural property, thus leaving the overall system consistent, clear and simple. It is to be hoped that it will be taught and applied in that way.

---

29 ICRC Commentary, *supra* note 20, p. 648, para. 2079.

30 *Ibid.* (emphasis added). See also Michael Bothe, Karl Josef Partsch, Waldemar A. Solf, *New Rules for Victims of Armed Conflicts, Commentary on the Two 1977 Protocols Additional to the Geneva Conventions of 1949*, Martinus Nijhoff, The Hague/Boston/London, 1982, p. 334, para. 2.6.

Imperative military necessity to use cultural property

The 1954 Convention also allows the use of cultural property for military action if such use is required for reasons of imperative military necessity. The same problem as explained above applies to the exception with respect to use of cultural property: the content of the exception is not very clear and the protection of cultural property would be enhanced by greater precision.

An absolute prohibition of the use of cultural property for military action is difficult to imagine, as there may indeed be situations in which the military need to avail themselves of cultural property for good reason. A classic example is the case of retreating troops who need to take shelter in a cultural property for defence purposes. Because the exception is limited to cases of "imperative" military necessity, such use can only be made when there is no alternative available. Hence, the Second Protocol provides that a waiver on the basis of imperative military necessity may only be invoked to use cultural property for military action "when and for as long as no choice is possible between such use of the cultural property and another feasible method for obtaining a similar military advantage."[31]

Finally, it should be noted that the decision to attack or use cultural property on the basis of the exceptions explained above shall only be taken by an officer commanding a force equivalent to a battalion or a smaller force where circumstances do not permit otherwise.[32]

3.2 Cultural property under enhanced protection

The 1954 Convention establishes a system of special protection. This system was designed for a limited number of refuges intended to shelter movable cultural property, centres containing monuments and other immovable cultural property of very great importance.[33] Special protection is granted by entry in the International Register of Cultural Property under Special Protection.[34] The system is intended to safeguard cultural property like the Versailles Palace in France or the Taj Mahal in India.

Unfortunately, the system of special protection has had very limited success. Only one centre containing monuments and eight refuges have been listed in the Register.[35] As three refuges were withdrawn from the list in 1994, only one centre containing monuments and five refuges remain. There are a number of reasons why

31 Second Protocol, Article 6(b). It is noteworthy that the Protocol speaks of "a waiver on the basis of imperative military necessity", because that is the language used in Article 4(2) of the 1954 Convention. The Second Protocol is additional to the 1954 Convention.

32 *Ibid.*, Article 6(c).

33 1954 Convention, Article 8(1).

34 *Ibid.*, Article 8(6).

35 These are: Vatican City (18 January 1960), a refuge at Alt-Aussee in Austria (17 November 1967), six refuges in the Netherlands (Zandvoort (2), Heemskerk (2, cancelled on 22 September 1994), Steenwijkerwold (cancelled on 22 September 1994), Maastricht (12 May 1969)) and the central Oberrieder Stollen refuge in Germany (22 April 1978). See International Register of Cultural Property under Special Protection, UNESCO Doc. CLT-97/WS/12, August 1997.

so few objects have been listed. The first is that entry in the list is conditional on the property being situated at an adequate distance from any large industrial centre or from any important military objective.[36] In many cases it is almost impossible to fulfil this condition as so much valuable cultural property is located in the heart of cities surrounded by potential military objectives. In addition, there is no agreement on what constitutes an adequate distance and, as a result, it is difficult to prepare an application for entry or to judge a request. This is yet another indication that the 1954 Convention was adopted well before the developments in humanitarian law reflected in the 1977 Additional Protocols and well before the technological evolution that has lead to means and methods of warfare that allow for more accurate targeting.

Political motivations have also stood in the way of registration. States can object to the entry in the Register and have done so on grounds such as the fact that the requesting authority was not the legitimate representative of the country in question.[37]

As a result, the Second Protocol has done away with the distance criterion and has strictly limited the possibility of lodging objections. Under the new system, three criteria have to be met in order for an object to be listed in the newly established List of Cultural Property under Enhanced Protection (the List):[38]

- the object must be a cultural heritage of the greatest importance for humanity;
- it must be protected by adequate domestic legal and administrative measures recognising its exceptional cultural and historic value and ensuring the highest level of protection;
- it must not be used for military purposes or to shield military sites and a declaration must have been made by the Party which has control over the cultural property, confirming that it will not be so used.

A decision to grant or deny enhanced protection may only be made on the basis of those criteria. In addition, objections against such grant shall be specific and related to facts.[39] This is a clear response to the shortcomings of the previous system.

The fact that the World Heritage List established under the 1972 Paris Convention concerning the protection of the world cultural and natural heritage is widely used – 582 sites are listed – constituted an incentive to try and make the International Register of Cultural Property under Special Protection work. But past efforts showed that this could only happen if the conditions and procedures were adjusted to redress previous shortcomings.[40] The usefulness of such a list lies in its world-wide renown: its mere existence should constitute an effective tool of prevention and protection. UNESCO would remind warring parties of the list and point

36 1954 Convention, Article 8(1)(a).

37 Jiří Toman, *The Protection of Cultural Property in the Event of Armed Conflict*, Dartmouth/Unesco, Aldershot/Paris, 1996, pp. 108-109.

38 Second Protocol, Article 10.

39 *Ibid.*, Articles 11(5) and 11(7).

40 See Toman, *supra* note 37, pp. 108-111, for examples of important cultural property that, for one reason or another, has not been included in the International Register of Cultural Property under Special Protection.

out that any military use of or attack against any property on the list would constitute a serious war crime (see below). The commission of such acts would also have severe negative political implications. When no wartime list was available, as in the case of the attacks on Dubrovnik, UNESCO availed itself of the World Heritage List, which had not necessarily been established for wartime purposes. As a result, Dubrovnik was more or less spared. This example has strengthened the conviction that it would be useful to have a list of exceptionally valuable cultural property to be protected in time of armed conflict. This conviction was clearly articulated by the States represented at the Preparatory Meeting in Vienna in May 1998.

As the Second Protocol is additional to the 1954 Convention, and does not amend it, the existing system of special protection could not be touched and an entirely new system had to be established. As the existing system has had only very limited success, the intention is clearly to start using the new system. States wanting to register any property should start using the new List of Cultural Property under Enhanced Protection established by the Second Protocol, and States that have registered property in the previous list should request a transfer to the new list.

The fact that a new system had to be set up also explains why a new name had to be used. Continued use of the designation "special protection" would have implied an amendment of the existing special protection system. As the Protocol was clearly supplementary, a new name had to be used and a separate and new system had to be set up.

Under the 1954 Convention special protection consists of the fact that the immunity of such property can only be withdrawn "in exceptional cases of unavoidable military necessity."[41] The wording implied a stricter standard than for other cultural property, where a waiver on the basis of "imperative military necessity" was in place. In practice, however, it was not clear what "exceptional cases of unavoidable military necessity" were.

The Second Protocol has clarified the law by establishing more clearly when cultural property under enhanced protection loses its protection, namely "if, and for as long as, the property has, *by its use*, become a military objective", and an "attack is the only feasible means of terminating the use of the property" that made it a military objective.[42]

Loss of enhanced protection is conditional on use of the cultural property so that it becomes a military objective. "Use" was not replaced by "function" as was the case for the general protection system for all cultural property, on the strength of the argument that the *quid pro quo* of enhanced protection was non-use in exchange for enhanced protection. As indicated above, one of the conditions for registration of cultural property for enhanced protection is abstention from its use for military purposes and a declaration confirming that it will not be so used. The argument was that since there is a promise not to use, enhanced protection can only be lost through use. It was further argued that limiting loss of protection for cultural property under enhanced protection to instances of use only was an essential part of the "enhanced" level of protection offered by enhanced protection system. This argument is, however, mistaken.

41 1954 Convention, Article 11(2).

42 Second Protocol, Article 13 (emphasis added).

A common misunderstanding is that there is a difference in the levels of protection afforded cultural property under general and enhanced protection – and the names indeed do suggest that such a difference exists. But there is, in fact, no lower or higher level of protection. The basic protection is the same: the object cannot be destroyed, captured or neutralized. Once protection is lost, it is lost for good: "you use, you lose." There are minor differences in the level of command at which an attack has to be ordered, the warning to be given and the requirement that a reasonable time be given to the opposing forces to redress the situation (see below), but these differences do not change the basic loss of protection.

There is no difference in the level of protection and there is no need to differentiate between two different ways in which cultural property can become a military objective. What is the difference then between enhanced protection and general protection? The main difference lies not in the obligations of the attacker but in the obligations of the holder of the cultural property. In the case of general protection, the holder of the property has the right, if need be, to convert the property into a military objective, by using it for military action. In the case of enhanced protection, the holder of the property has absolutely no right ever to convert the property into a military objective by using it for military action. Registration on the List therefore requires the State party seriously to study whether it would ever be in need of that property for military purposes and to answer in the negative.

Using property on the List for military purposes would amount to a serious violation of the Second Protocol, and the offender would be liable to criminal sanction as a war criminal (see below). The term "enhanced protection" is therefore misleading. The essence of the system is that it concerns some form of "registered" or "certified protection". The holder of the property registers or certifies his promise that the property will never be used for military purposes. As a result, the property can never become the object of an attack. The advantage of putting property on the List is that an adversary will be particularly aware of it and any attack on the property will have serious consequences for the perpetrator (see below).

The registration of an object on the List of Cultural Property under Enhanced Protection can be compared to an internationally recognized declaration establishing a non-defended locality.[43] It is best to make such declaration in peacetime as it guarantees that everything is in place if and when an armed conflict breaks out.

4. Conditions for attack

4.1 All cultural property

Once cultural property has, by its function, become a military objective and there is no feasible alternative, it has lost its protection against attack. Yet the Second Protocol adds a further condition for attack, providing for an extra level of protection for cultural property which has thus become a military objective, beyond the protection enjoyed by all civilian objects. In case of attack, an effective advance warn-

43 See Additional Protocol I, Article 59.

ing shall be given whenever circumstances permit.[44] This duty did not exist under the 1954 Convention. The duty to issue an effective advance warning also exists for attacks which may affect the civilian population.[45] This demonstrates how the protection of cultural property in some respects approximates the protection of the civilian population as such and goes beyond the protection of other civilian objects.

In addition, an attack can only be ordered by an officer commanding a force equivalent to a battalion or a smaller force where circumstances do not permit otherwise.[46]

4.2 Cultural property under enhanced protection

Under the 1954 Convention, an attack on cultural property under special protection can only be ordered by "an officer commanding a force the equivalent of a division in size or larger and whenever circumstances permit, the opposing Party shall be notified, a reasonable time in advance, of the decision to attack."[47]

The Second Protocol seeks to tighten these conditions, but an effort to change the relative duty of notice into an absolute duty and a concomitant effort, supported by the ICRC, to have the decision to attack taken at the highest level of government failed. It would indeed make sense to have the decision taken at the highest level of government because of the political implications thereof. Several delegates, however, argued against this proposal. While they recognized that in some countries such a decision would probably be taken at the highest level of government, for example if the Head of State is the Commander-in-Chief of the armed forces, they felt that the political structures of countries around the world were too diverse to impose such an obligation. Hence, the Second Protocol requires that an attack be ordered at the highest operational level of command.

In addition, a proposal to make it an absolute obligation to order the attack at such level, to give effective advance warning and to give reasonable time to the opposing forces to redress the situation, was rejected. Several delegates argued that if their troops came under fire from cultural property under enhanced protection they would deem it excessive to have to comply with those conditions without being able to return fire immediately. Hence, the three obligations are waived if circumstances do not permit "due to requirements of immediate self-defence".[48] This still represents progress over the 1954 Convention, as the level at which the attack has to be ordered is much higher and as the vague "whenever circumstances permit" has been narrowed considerably. In addition, the requirement that a reasonable time be given to the opposing forces to redress the situation is new and adds an extra layer of protection.

An earlier ICRC proposal to approximate the protection of cultural property under enhanced protection to that given to medical units was not considered. Under

44 Second Protocol, Article 6(d).

45 Additional Protocol I, Article 57(2)(c).

46 *Supra* note 32.

47 1954 Convention, Article 11(2).

48 Second Protocol, Article 13(2)(c).

Article 21 of the 1949 Geneva Convention for the Amelioration of the Condition of the Wounded and Sick in Armed Forces in the Field, the protection to which medical units are entitled shall not cease "unless they are used to commit, outside their humanitarian duties, acts harmful to the enemy. Protection may, however, cease only after a due warning has been given, naming, in all appropriate cases, a reasonable time limit and after such warning has remained unheeded." It was felt that hospitals deserved an exceptional level of protection, beyond that enjoyed by other civilian objects.

5. Precautions in attack

By introducing the notion of military objective, other rules on the conduct of hostilities contained in Additional Protocol I of 1977 could also be included. The Second Protocol therefore incorporates the rules contained in Article 57 of Protocol I and applies them specifically to cultural property. In fact, Article 57 already covers cultural property, as it applies to civilian objects and all cultural property is, in principle, civilian in nature. Nevertheless, it was deemed useful to reaffirm those rules and to spell them out more clearly with respect to cultural property in particular.

6. Precautions against the effect of hostilities

The same can be said of Article 58 of Additional Protocol I dealing with precautions against the effects of attacks, the so-called passive precautions to be taken by the defender (in parallel with the active precautions to be taken by the attacker). Article 8 of the Second Protocol applies the rules contained in Article 58 of Protocol I in a way appropriate for cultural property.

7. Individual criminal responsibility

Article 28 of the 1954 Convention requires States "to take, within the framework of their ordinary jurisdiction, all necessary steps to prosecute and impose penal or disciplinary sanctions upon those persons, of whatever nationality, who commit or order to be committed a breach of the [...] Convention."[49]

This provision has largely remained a dead letter, mainly because it does not list the violations which require a criminal sanction. The experience of the ICRC Advisory Service on International Humanitarian Law proves that such a list is essential if a coherent and complete system of criminal repression of war crimes is to be instituted worldwide.

This is one of the main areas in which the Second Protocol clarifies and develops humanitarian law with respect to cultural property. Building on Additional Protocol I and the Rome Statute of the International Criminal Court, Article 15 defines five acts which constitute serious violations requiring a criminal sanction if committed intentionally and in violation of the 1954 Convention or the Second Protocol:

- making cultural property under enhanced protection the object of attack;

49 1954 Convention, Article 28.

- using cultural property under enhanced protection or its immediate surroundings in support of military action;
- extensive destruction or appropriation of cultural property protected under the Convention and [the Second] Protocol;
- making cultural property protected under the Convention and [the Second] Protocol the object of attack;
- theft, pillage or misappropriation of, or acts of vandalism directed against, cultural property protected under the Convention.

But the definition of serious violations is not in itself sufficient to ensure that persons committing such violations are actually punished. To achieve this would still require effective enforcement at the national level. In order to arrive at effective national enforcement, implementing legislation has to be adopted covering two aspects: (a) criminalizing violations, and (b) establishing jurisdiction to try or extradite.

7.1 Criminalizing violations

As far as the need to criminalize violations under domestic law is concerned, States have the specific duty, under the Second Protocol, to adopt whatever measures are necessary to establish the abovementioned five serious violations as criminal offences under their domestic law and to make the offences punishable by appropriate penalties. Such legislation would ensure that the prohibition to commit any of the serious violations of the Second Protocol is, in practice, enforced.

With regard to the issues of auxiliary crimes (e.g. aiding and abetting), command responsibility and defences, the original proposal to set out these rules was discarded in favor of an obligation to comply with general principles of law and international law in this respect.[50] These rules have been authoritatively restated in the Rome Statute of the International Criminal Court, and many delegates felt there was no need to repeat them in a "mini criminal code".

7.2 Jurisdiction

The list of serious violations is based on proposals submitted by Austria and the ICRC to the Working Group on Chapter 4. This explains why it contains two types of violations.

a) The first three violations correspond to what are called "grave breaches" under the Geneva Conventions and Additional Protocol I, and are based on a proposal by Austria. States have a duty to try or extradite anyone charged with having committed any of these violations on the basis of universal jurisdiction. Specific and detailed provisions regulate the prosecution and extradition of offenders.[51] According to the Chairman of the Working Group, from the point of view of international criminal

50 Second Protocol, Article 18(2).

51 *Ibid.*, Articles 17, 20.

law, these provisions are a major achievement as all elements to form a coherent system of prosecution and extradition are included.[52]

With respect to the specific violations included in this category, it is interesting to note that the first two violations concern cultural property under enhanced protection, and that both an attack on and the use of such property are established as serious violations. Under Protocol I of 1977, only an attack on such property is defined as a grave breach and only in so far as it causes extensive destruction.[53] The Second Protocol establishes a balance between the criminal responsibility of both the attacker and the defender.

A proposal by the delegate from China to prohibit collateral damage to cultural property under enhanced protection was not acted upon. This would have been a significant improvement of the existing system. Since the Second Protocol requires parties to a conflict to refrain from any use of such property or its immediate surroundings in support of military action, such a rule could have fitted into the Second Protocol.

The third serious violation concerns the destruction or appropriation of all cultural property, but the extensive nature of such acts make them serious violations on a par with grave breaches.

States have to establish universal jurisdiction over such violations. This means they have to establish jurisdiction not only when the offence is committed in the territory of the State or when the alleged offender is a national of the State, but also when the offence is committed abroad by a non-national.[54] This reflects the principle of mandatory universal jurisdiction for grave breaches, which implies that all States have to establish jurisdiction to try or extradite non-nationals for war crimes committed abroad who are present in their territory.

At the request of the United States, a provision was included that excludes nationals of States not party to the Second Protocol from the regime of mandatory universal jurisdiction.[55] This would mean that States have no obligation to try or extradite such persons. The extent of this exception is greatly diminished, however, by the acknowledgement that States may establish jurisdiction over such persons under applicable national or international law, including customary international law[56], by the statement of the Chairman of the Working Group on Chapter 4 that nothing in the Second Protocol in any way limits the ability of States to legislate, criminalize or otherwise deal with any offence under the Protocol[57], and by the fact that the entire jurisdictional regime is without prejudice to Article 28 of the 1954 Convention.[58]

Article 28 of the 1954 Convention was in fact already intended to provide for mandatory universal jurisdiction. According to Toman, "[t]he representative of one

52 Horst Fischer, *Presentation of the Results of the Working Group on Chapter 4*, UNESCO Doc. HC/1999/INF.5, 25 March 1999, p. 2.

53 Additional Protocol I, Article 85(4)(d).

54 Second Protocol, Article 16(1).

55 *Ibid.*, Article 16(2)(b).

56 *Ibid.*, Article 16(2)(a).

57 Fischer, *supra* note 52, p. 3.

58 Second Protocol, Article 16(2)(chapeau).

government raised the question of whether a Party to the Convention was obliged to prosecute and impose penal sanctions upon persons having committed breaches outside the territory subject to the criminal jurisdiction of the State in question. The answer is yes, because that is the aim of this provision. It may reasonably be assumed that the country has at its disposal general legislation concerning the protection of its own cultural property and that the criminal act directed against that property would, in any event, be covered by those provisions. What remains to be done – according to Article 28 of the Convention – *is to prosecute those who have committed criminal acts outside the territorial jurisdiction of the State.*"[59]

b) The last two serious violations were added to the list at the suggestion of the ICRC. The reason for this was that these acts had been recognized as war crimes subject to criminal sanction in the Rome Statute of the International Criminal Court. As such, they could not be included in a general provision on "other violations" which would only require States to suppress such acts without specifying the means of doing so. As indicated above, the experience of the ICRC has shown that the vagueness of the category of "other violations" makes it very difficult to convince States that certain of those other violations are indeed war crimes which have to be penalized with a criminal sanction under domestic law.

These two serious violations amount to war crimes, but States only have the obligation to repress them by criminal sanctions using the most common grounds for jurisdiction, namely when the offence is committed in the territory of the State or when the alleged offender is a national of the State. There is no obligation to establish jurisdiction over cases where the alleged offence was committed abroad by a non-national, although States may exercise such jurisdiction.[60] This reflects the principle of permissive universal jurisdiction for war crimes, according to which all States have jurisdiction to try non-nationals for war crimes committed abroad but are under no obligation to do so if the crimes do not amount to grave breaches. This also follows clearly from the acknowledgement that States may establish jurisdiction over such persons under applicable national or international law, including customary international law[61], and from the statement by the Chairman of the Working Group on Chapter 4, referred to above, that nothing in the Protocol limits in any way the ability of the State to legislate, criminalize or otherwise deal with any of the serious violations of the Protocol.[62]

8. The scope of application

The Second Protocol applies equally to international and non-international armed conflicts.[63] The extension of the application of the Second Protocol to non-international armed conflicts is essential. Most modern armed conflicts are non-inter-

59 Toman, *supra* note 37, p. 294 (emphasis in original).
60 Second Protocol, Article 16(2)(a).
61 *Ibid.*, Article 16(2)(a).
62 Fischer, *supra* note 52, p. 3.
63 Second Protocol, Articles 3 and 22.

national, and history has shown that the protection of cultural property in such conflicts can be problematic.

Furthermore, developments since the adoption of the Hague Convention in 1954 should not be forgotten. Additional Protocol I establishes a coherent system of criminal repression but only as far as international armed conflicts are concerned. It is of particular importance, as a result, that the entire Second Protocol, including the section on criminal repression, applies to non-international armed conflicts. This reflects the modern tendency of legislation, for example, no longer to distinguish between international and non-international armed conflict when it comes to repression of violations of international humanitarian law. In addition, under its Statute, the International Criminal Court has jurisdiction over war crimes committed against cultural property in both international and non-international armed conflict.

At the request of China and India, a phrase was added to the effect that nothing in the Protocol shall prejudice "the primary jurisdiction" of a State in whose territory a non-international armed conflict occurs over the serious violations of the Protocol. This means, in reality, that the territorial State has the primary responsibility to exercise jurisdiction over such violations: to investigate, prosecute and punish the offenders. It clearly implies, however, that if such jurisdiction is not exercised, jurisdiction may be exercised by other States or by international criminal tribunals with the competence to do so.

Although Article 22 of the Second Protocol does not spell it out as clearly as it could have, the Protocol applies to all parties to a non-international armed conflict, whether governmental or insurgent forces. This was clearly acknowledged at the final plenary session. A certain confusion arose because Article 1 of the Protocol defines the word "Party" as a State Party to the Second Protocol. However, the understanding was that throughout the text the word "Party" in the phrase "Party to the conflict" includes rebel groups of States party to the Second Protocol but not third States which have not ratified the Second Protocol.[64] The reasoning was that non-governmental forces involved in a non-international armed conflict within a State party to the Protocol are bound by the Protocol through the ratification of the State concerned.[65]

9. Conclusion

The adoption of the Second Protocol is an important step forward in the legal protection of cultural property in armed conflict. The Protocol addresses the weaknesses

64 Third States which have not ratified the Second Protocol are generally referred to as "party" (in lower case).

65 It is unfortunate that recognition of the potential confusion of the definition of "Party" and the use of the term "Party to the conflict" came only in the last hours of the Diplomatic Conference. As a result, there was no discussion on whether the general understanding that the Second Protocol applies to governmental forces and rebel groups in a non-international armed conflict is also valid for Article 11(9). It is difficult to say whether this was indeed the intention of States, as the Working Group on Chapter 3 (Enhanced Protection) did not discuss the issue.

of the 1954 Convention and offers adequate solutions. Its main achievements are that it:

- clarifies the obligations to take precautionary measures and disseminate the Convention and the Second Protocol;
- updates the 1954 Convention by introducing concepts contained in Additional Protocol I of 1977;
- offers the opportunity to make the regime of "special protection" effective by replacing it with a new and improved system of "enhanced protection";
- improves the enforcement mechanism by defining serious violations which have to be punished with a criminal sanction and by imposing a duty upon States to establish jurisdiction over those violations; and
- develops humanitarian law by defining those serious violations and by extending the scope of application to non-international armed conflicts.

Another beneficial effect of the Second Protocol is that more attention has been given to the 1954 Convention itself. As a result, a considerable number of States have ratified the 1954 Convention since the review process started and more are in the process of ratification. As a result, at 1 September 2009, there were 123 States party to the 1954 Convention and 55 States party to the Second Protocol. However, much still remains to be done, especially as far as marking of cultural property and dissemination are concerned, but at least awareness of the problems has been heightened.

While human life is still more important than objects, it is nevertheless essential to have rules protecting cultural property, as such objects constitute the collective memory of humanity, examples of its greatest achievements, and symbolize human life itself. If cultural property is destroyed, civilian life suffers greatly as well.

Chapter 3

Military necessity under the 1999 Second Protocol

*Kevin Chamberlain**

1. Introduction

Let me first state that we owe debt of gratitude to the Government of the Netherlands for the initiative they took, as part of the Decade of International Law, to institute a review of the workings of the 1954 Hague Convention, culminating in the successful diplomatic conference ten years ago when the Second Protocol was adopted and opened for signature. Ten years on, the Protocol has entered into force and there are now over fifty States parties. The Protocol has made a significant contribution to the development of international law in this area.

The Second Protocol introduced a number of significant improvements to the regime for the protection of cultural property in times of armed conflict and I would like to highlight one of those changes, namely, the more stringent rules for invoking the 'military necessity' exception in the 1954 Hague Convention.

2. Military necessity under the 1954 Convention

A common thread that ran through all international instruments designed to protect cultural property in time of armed conflict was that such protection had to take second place to the notion of military necessity. Article 27 of the Hague Regulations 1907 required States to take all necessary measures to spare historic monuments and buildings dedicated to religion and art but was qualified by the phrase 'as far as possible'. Article 53 of the Fourth Geneva Convention prohibited the destruction of property belonging to the State, public authorities and private persons but the prohibition did not apply when destruction was rendered 'absolutely necessary by military operations'. It was hardly surprising that the question of providing for an exception for military necessity was a matter of some controversy in the negotiations leading to the adoption of the 1954 Hague Convention. The exception to the general

* Barrister, former Deputy Legal Adviser Foreign and Commonwealth Office, former legal adviser to the Ministerial Advisory Panel on Illicit Trade in Cultural Objects, independent consultant to the Department for Culture, Media and Sport on applications for immunity from seizure of works of art imported for temporary exhibitions, Member NATO Appeals Board, author *War and Cultural Heritage* (2004) Institute of Art and Law.

Nout van Woudenberg and Liesbeth Lijnzaad (eds.) Protecting Cultural Property in Armed Conflict
© *2010 Koninklijke Brill NV. Printed in The Netherlands.* *ISBN 978 9004 18377 3 pp. 43–49.*

obligation to protect cultural property on grounds of '*imperative* military necessity' was intended to represent a compromise between those delegations that believed there should be no exceptions to this obligation and those who believed it essential for there to be a military necessity exception. The protection accorded to cultural property under the regime of special protection was in practice no stronger since it could still be waived 'in exceptional cases of unavoidable military necessity'. The biggest practical problem with the notions of 'imperative military necessity' and 'exceptional cases of unavoidable military necessity' was that they were not defined. It was therefore up to each State party, or more likely the officer in command of an attacking or defending force, to interpret the exceptions in a concrete case. In the event of armed hostilities the interpretation of these provisions may vary and lead to abuse. Accordingly, the exception for 'military necessity' in the 1954 Hague Convention was seen as a fundamental flaw in the system of protection for cultural property provided under the Convention.

3. Developments since 1954

A significant development was the adoption in 1977 of the Additional Protocols to the 1949 Geneva Conventions, which in Article 53 in Additional Protocol I and Article 16 of Additional Protocol II, strengthened the rules of international law concerning the protection of cultural property in armed conflict.

In addition, Article 52 (1) of Additional Protocol I set out in clear terms the principle that civilian objects must not be the object of attack and civilian objects were defined as all objects which are not military objectives as defined in Article 52(2). Article 52(2) defined 'military objectives' as 'objects which by their nature, location, purpose or use make an effective contribution to military action and whose total or partial destruction, capture or neutralisation, in the circumstances ruling at the time, offers a definite military advantage'. The definition of military objective in Article 52(2) contains two criteria which have to be fulfilled cumulatively before objects can be destroyed, captured or neutralised. Firstly, the objects must be objects which by their nature, location, purpose or use make an 'effective contribution to military action'. Secondly, their total or partial destruction, capture or neutralisation must, 'in the circumstances ruling at the time', offer 'a definite military advantage'. The definition of military objective in Article 52(2) of Additional Protocol I was one of the major achievements of the Diplomatic Conference that adopted the Protocol I. Even States not party to Additional Protocol I, such as the United States, Turkey and India, confirmed the customary law nature of this provision during the 1999 Diplomatic Conference that adopted the Second Protocol.

Article 57(3) of Additional Protocol I 1977, further laid down the precautions that must be observed before an attack is launched. An attacking force must do everything feasible to ensure that the objectives to be attacked are not civilians or civilian objects and not subject to special protection but are military objectives. All feasible precautions must be taken to avoid, and in any event minimise, incidental damage and to refrain from an attack, or cease an attack if incidental damage would be excessive in relation to the concrete and direct military advantage anticipated. When a choice is possible between several military objectives for obtaining a similar military advantage, the objective to be selected shall be that the attack on which may be expected to cause the least danger to civilian lives and to civilian objects.

The effectiveness of the 1954 Hague Convention became a subject of general concern in the early nineties, during the first Gulf War and the war in the former Yugoslavia. It was clear that any revision of the 1954 Hague Convention would need to take into account the developments in International Humanitarian Law brought in by the Additional Protocols. The time was therefore ripe for a review of the 1954 Convention and its Protocol to see what improvements could be made to these instruments in the light of these developments. This resulted in the review by Professor Patrick Boylan of the Convention and it Protocol. This review made a number of recommendations to improve the effectiveness of these instruments.

4. The new conditions for invoking military necessity under the Second Protocol

One of the recommendations for amending the 1954 Hague Convention made by Patrick Boylan in his Review of the Convention was that the 'military necessity' exemption in Article 4(2) of the Convention should be discarded on the grounds that it was already inappropriate by the time of the 1954 Convention. As expected, this aim proved unrealistic. As was the case at the 1954 Diplomatic Conference, there was a tension between those who favoured the removal of the military necessity exception and those representing the interests of the military who favoured its retention. All agreed however that a major difficulty with the notion of imperative military necessity was that it was too vague to constitute an effective limitation on warfare. Even military lawyers at the Diplomatic Conference admitted that it was difficult to teach their troops how to interpret and work with the concept. The goal of the Diplomatic Conference was therefore to give content to the notion of imperative military necessity with a view to enhancing its meaning and effect. The resulting text of Article 6 of the Second Protocol represents a compromise between these two views.

Article 6, paragraph (a) sets out two conditions that must be present cumulatively before the waiver of 'imperative military necessity' under Article 4, paragraph 2 of the Convention can be invoked to direct an act of hostility against cultural property: firstly, the property has by its function been made into a military objective (as defined in Article 52(2) of Additional Protocol I to the 1949 Geneva Conventions and reproduced in identical terms in Article 1(f) of the Second Protocol) and secondly, there is no feasible alternative available to obtain a similar military advantage to that offered by directing an act of hostility against that objective. The words 'when and so long as' in the opening sentence of paragraph (a) mean that both conditions must be present at the time that the attack is launched and that the right to invoke the waiver continues only for as long as both conditions are fulfilled.

As regards the first condition, the property must 'by its function' have been made into a military objective. It is the *function* to which the cultural property is put in the circumstances prevailing at the time, rather than the inherent nature of the property that determines whether it has been made into a military objective. Thus the mere location of cultural property could never turn it into a military objective. Some positive action should be required from the holder of the property before it could become a military objective. One example commonly cited at the Diplomatic Conference was that of a historic bridge. The existence of such a bridge could confer a military advantage on the enemy. Would it therefore be permissible as a pre-emptive move to destroy the bridge and thus deprive the enemy of the possibility of using the bridge to its military advantage? Under the old regime of the 1954 Hague Convention it could be argued that in some circumstances this was a case of 'imperative military necessity'. But under the Second Protocol such action must be ruled out, since it is really the use of a site that turns it into a military objective. Support for this can be found in Article 27 of the 1907 Hague Regulations which stipulates: 'in sieges and bombardments all necessary steps must be taken to spare, as far as possible, buildings dedicated to religion, art, science, or charitable purposes, historic monuments, hospitals, and places where the sick and wounded are collected, *provided they are not being used at the time for military purposes*' (emphasis added). This text confirms that it is their use at the time which makes these objects lose their protection.

The second condition in paragraph (a) is that there is no feasible alternative available to obtain a similar military advantage to that offered by directing an act of hostility against that military objective. This condition in effect clarifies the requirement of the 1954 Hague Convention that the military necessity has to be 'imperative', namely, that no other feasible alternative is available. This means that when there is a choice between several military objectives and one of them is a cultural property, the latter shall not be attacked.

The effect of this provision is to add cultural property to the military objectives which, under Article 57(3) of Additional Protocol I, should only be attacked where the attack would constitute the lesser of two or more evils. However, neither Article 6, paragraph (a)(ii), nor Article 57(3) of Additional Protocol I, resolve the difficulty of what happens where the choice is between civilian casualties and the destruction of cultural property. The dictates of conscience require that in such cases human life must take precedence over property, however valuable. This would be included within the concept that 'no feasible' alternative is available.

Paragraph (b) concerns the conditions under which imperative military necessity can be invoked to justify the use of cultural property for purposes which are likely to expose it to destruction or damage in the event of armed conflict. Such use is only permitted when and for as long as no choice is possible between such use of the cultural property and another feasible method for obtaining a similar military advantage. Similar considerations apply to this requirement as they do to the requirement in paragraph (a)(ii) that no feasible alternative exists to obtain a similar military advantage as that obtained by directing an act of hostility against cultural property that has become a military objective. In other words, where a choice exists between a number of measures to secure a similar military advantage, the choice that favours the least risk of damage or destruction to cultural property should be preferred.

Paragraph (c) is a further safeguard against abuse of the military necessity exemption, which does not feature in the 1954 Hague Convention, at least as regards cultural property under general protection. It is intended to ensure that the decision to invoke military necessity is not taken lightly. Such decision must be taken sufficiently high up in the chain of command. Paragraph (c) states that this decision must be taken at least at the level of the officer commanding a battalion or larger. However, the decision can be taken at a lower level of command 'where circumstances do not permit otherwise'. Although this provides some flexibility it is important to recall that the purpose of requiring that the decision be taken at a sufficiently high level is to ensure that the decision is taken responsibly and with a degree of objectivity. It would therefore be rare for the decision to be taken at the level of the officer actually leading the attack since it is unlikely that he (or she) would be in a position to exercise the necessary degree of objectivity.

Paragraph (d) needs little explanation. The need to give an effective advance warning is qualified by the words, 'whenever circumstances permit'. In cases where the element of surprise is crucial to the success of an attack, then it would clearly not be practicable to give an advance warning. This situation is catered for by the words 'whenever circumstances permit'.

5. Precautions to be observed in attack

Article 6 also needs to be read in conjunction with Article 7. This requires Parties to the conflict, (a) to do everything feasible to verify that the objects to be attacked are not cultural property protected under Article 4 of the Convention, (b) to take all feasible precautions in the choice of means and methods of attack to avoid, and in any event minimise, incidental damage to cultural property, (c) to refrain from launching an attack which may be expected to cause incidental damage to cultural property which would be excessive in relation to the concrete and direct military advantage anticipated, and (d) to cancel an attack if it becomes apparent that the objective is cultural property protected under the Convention, or if the attack may be expected to cause incidental damage which would be excessive in relation to the concrete and direct military advantage anticipated. This Article is modelled on Article 57 of Additional Protocol I and applies the obligation in that Article to avoid incidental damage to civilian property specifically to cultural property.

6. Cultural property under enhanced protection

Under the 1954 Hague Convention the immunity of property under special protection could only be withdrawn 'in exceptional cases of unavoidable military necessity'. The wording implied a stricter standard than for other cultural property, where a waiver on the basis of 'imperative military necessity' was in place. In practice, however, it was not clear what 'exceptional cases of unavoidable military necessity' were and what was the difference between that expression and 'imperative military necessity'. The Second Protocol has clarified the law by establishing more clearly when cultural property under enhanced protection loses its protection. Firstly, a Contracting Party seeking enhanced protection must undertake not to use the cultural property for military purposes or to shield military sites. Secondly, the Parties to a conflict are under an obligation not to use the property, or its immediate surroundings in support of military action. Finally enhanced protection will only be lost if the protection is suspended or cancelled by the Committee for the Protection of Cultural Property in the Event of Armed Conflict or 'if, and for as long as, the property has, *by its use*, become a military objective'. It is therefore the *use* to which the property is put by the Party having control over the property, rather than its location, that determines whether the property loses its enhanced protection and thus would be liable to attack by the opposing Party.

Even where cultural property under enhanced protection has lost its immunity because those holding such property have used it in a way that it has become a military objective, the right of an opposing party to launch an attack remains subject to a number of strict conditions. Under Article 13 cultural property may only be the object of an attack if: (a) there is no feasible alternative to terminating the use of the property as a military objective; (b) all feasible precautions in the choice of means and methods of attack are taken in avoiding, or in any event minimising, damage to the cultural property; and (c) the attack is ordered at the highest level of operational command, effective advance warning is given to the other party requiring the termination of military use, and reasonable time is given to that party to redress the situation.

7. Conclusion

In an ideal world it would have been a significant achievement if the Diplomatic Conference in 1999 had succeeded in removing the military necessity exemption but that aim was always unrealistic. Nevertheless what has been achieved is undoubtedly a significant improvement over the undefined exemptions for 'imperative military necessity' and 'exceptional cases of unavoidable military necessity'. As a result of the Second Protocol cultural property can only be attacked if those holding such property have by their action turned it into a military objective (as defined in the Protocol and Additional Protocol I) and there is no feasible alternative to obtaining a similar military advantage. Those holding cultural property for purposes which are likely to expose it to attack can only invoke 'imperative military necessity' if there is no choice between such use and obtaining a similar military advantage by another feasible method. Parties to a conflict are now under an obligation to avoid incidental damage to cultural property that would be excessive in relation to the anticipated military advantage, and to cease an attack if it becomes apparent that such incidental damage would be excessive. Cultural property under the new regime of enhanced protection has complete immunity from attack. Such immunity can only be lost if those holding such property take steps, contrary to the undertakings they have given not to do so, to use the property as a military objective. Even then an attack can only be launched subject to stringent conditions being fulfilled. Finally, any attack on cultural property must be taken at the appropriate level of command.

Of course the new regime is not free of problems. For example, the new provisions on the obligation to avoid incidental damage, although to be welcomed, do impose an impossible decision on a force commander when it comes to assessing whether an attack that would be likely to cause incidental damage to cultural property that would be excessive in relation to the concrete and direct military advantage anticipated. Article 57(2) of Additional Protocol I already requires a commanding officer to make a difficult judgement by balancing the loss of civilian lives or objects against the anticipated military advantage. That is a choice that the military are likely to be faced in any conflict and should be capable of striking the right balance. However, the choice becomes far more difficult when it is between the value of cultural property and military advantage. While the military are of course capable of assessing the military advantage, one must question whether they are capable of assessing the cultural value of an object, far less being able to weigh that benefit against the military advantage. One can only express the hope that with greater awareness among the military of the importance of protecting cultural property and with more intensive training, such choices, if they ever have to be made, will become easier.

Chapter 4

Enhanced Protection: A new form of protection under the 1999 Second Protocol

*Nout van Woudenberg**

1. Introduction

The 1999 Second Protocol supplements the 'special protection' offered by the 1954 Convention for the Protection of Cultural Property in the Event of Armed Conflict ('the 1954 Hague Convention') with a system of 'enhanced protection'.[1] The reason was that virtually no country was able to meet the conditions for eligibility for special protection in the 1954 Hague Convention, mainly because of the practical requirements listed in Article 8.[2] And as there was a need for a system to provide extra protection for cultural property of exceptional importance, it was necessary to set up a new system: that of enhanced protection. But what is enhanced protection? In the following I will address the nature and scope of enhanced protection.

2. From special protection to enhanced protection

The 1954 Hague Convention established a system of special protection. As Jean-Marie Henckaerts explains[3], this system was designed to cover a limited number of refuges intended to shelter movable cultural property, centres containing monuments and other immovable cultural property of very great importance. Special protection is granted by entry of the property in the International Register of Cultural Property under Special Protection.

The distinctive emblem of the 1954 Hague Convention, a blue shield[4], repeated three times may be used to identify immovable cultural property under special pro-

* Nout van Woudenberg is a legal counsel at the International Law Division of the Dutch Ministry of Foreign Affairs. This article was written in his personal capacity. The views expressed are entirely his own and do not necessarily bind the Ministry.

1 It should be noted that this enhanced protection also applies to non-international armed conflicts (see article 22 of the Protocol).

2 Article 8 of the 1954 Hague Convention: Granting of special protection.

3 *New rules for the protection of cultural property in armed conflict: the significance of the Second Protocol to the 1954 Hague Convention for the Protection of Cultural Property in the Event of Armed Conflict*, at pp. 21-41 of this book.

4 Article 16 (1) of the 1954 Hague Convention describes the distinctive emblem of the Convention.

Nout van Woudenberg and Liesbeth Lijnzaad (eds.) Protecting Cultural Property in Armed Conflict
© *2010 Koninklijke Brill NV. Printed in The Netherlands.* *ISBN 978 9004 18377 3 pp. 51-58.*

tection.[5] This should be done in a triangular formation (one shield below).[6] If used alone, the distinctive emblem can be used as a means of identification for cultural property not under special protection.

Both Henckaerts and Toman[7] explained that the system of special protection was a weak point in the 1954 Hague Convention. Only a few States applied for special protection,[8] while others announced that a request for registration was being considered, without ever actually making such a request.

Both authors explained that there were practical difficulties to be met in the application of Article 8 of the 1954 Hague Convention, in particular with regard to cultural property in the heart of large cities close to large urban, political, and industrial centres. States did not always seem to be committed to diverting transportation routes, or to not using ports close to cultural property in need of special protection in the event of conflict. Besides, entry in the list is conditional on the property being situated at an adequate distance from any large industrial centre or important military objective.

It is almost impossible to meet this condition, as much valuable cultural property is located in city centres and surrounded by potential military objectives. In addition, there is no agreement on what constitutes an adequate distance and, as a result, it is difficult to prepare an application for registration or to assess a request. Finally, both Henckaerts and Toman point out that political motives have also stood in the way of registration. States can object to the entry in the Register and have done so on grounds such as the fact that the requesting authority was not the legitimate representative of the country in question.[9] The increased politicisation resulting from the Cold War and the tensions in relations between the States were further obstacles to success. Many States feared that the registration of refuges would reveal their location, making them an easy target.

Both the community of States and UNESCO learnt their lesson, and since it seemed that there was a need for a system of extra protection for cultural property of exceptional importance, a new system was set up in the 1999 Second Protocol, without a distance criterion, and without a broad scope for lodging objections. In fact, a whole new system was necessary as the 1999 Second Protocol does not set the 1954 Hague Convention aside but is additional to it.[10] The system of special protection had therefore to be left untouched. This means that the 1954 Hague Convention and the 1999 Second Protocol provide for a total of three forms of protection: general protection, as provided for under the Convention and Protocol, special protection as provided for under the Convention, and the enhanced protection set up under the Protocol.

---

5 Article 17(1)(a) of the 1954 Hague Convention.

6 Article 16 (2) of the 1954 Hague Convention.

7 Jiří Toman, *The Road to the 1999 Second Protocol*, at pp. 1-19 of this book.

8 Austria, the Federal Republic of Germany, the Khmer Republic, the Netherlands and the Holy See.

9 Jiří Toman, *The Protection of Cultural Property in the Event of Armed Conflict*, Dartmouth/Unesco, Aldershot/Paris, 1996, pp. 108-109.

10 See Article 2: Relation to the Convention.

Henckaerts argues in this book[11] that in fact there is no real difference in the levels of protection afforded to cultural property under general and enhanced protection: in other words, there is no lower or higher level of protection. He explains that the difference does not lie in the obligations resting on the attacker but in those resting on the holder of the cultural property. Henckaerts therefore considers the term 'enhanced protection' misleading and states that the essence of the system is that it concerns some form of 'registered' or 'certified protection'. The holder of the property registers or certifies his promise that the property will never be used for military purposes. As a result, the property may never become the object of an attack.

3. Enhanced Protection under the 1999 Second Protocol

In its definition of enhanced protection, the 1999 Second Protocol merely refers to the system as established by Articles 10 and 11 of the same Protocol. Article 12[12] gives more substance to the term by emphasising that making such property the object of attack or using the property or its immediate surroundings in support of military action is clearly prohibited. So, in contrast to cultural property under the regime of general protection, States cannot rely on the 'imperative military necessity' in the case of property under enhanced protection. The system of enhanced protection in the 1999 Second Protocol involves the obligation to make the intentional violation of the Protocol a criminal offence. This addition may also be seen as an important development in the law on the protection of cultural heritage in the event of armed conflict.[13]

Article 10 states that cultural property may be placed under enhanced protection provided that it meets the following three conditions:

a. it is cultural heritage of the greatest importance for humanity;
b. it is protected by adequate domestic legal and administrative measures recognising its exceptional cultural and historic value and ensuring the highest level of protection;
c. it is not used for military purposes or to shield military sites and a declaration has been made by the Party which has control over the cultural property, confirming that it will not be so used.

The term 'greatest importance (for humanity)' is intended to distinguish the property from that which is of 'great importance', the term under the general regime, and from that which is of 'very great importance', used for the regime of special protection. This formulation is to some extent reminiscent of the World Heritage Convention,[14] which uses the term 'outstanding universal value' for World Heritage sites.

11 See footnote 3.

12 Article 12: Immunity of cultural property under enhanced protection.

13 See my other contribution to this book: Elaboration and legal implementation of the 1999 Second Protocol: the Dutch finger on the pulse, at pp. 107-115 of this book.

14 Convention concerning the Protection of the World Cultural and Natural Heritage, Paris, 16 November 1972, 1037 UNTS 151.

Implicit in the phrase 'cultural heritage of the greatest importance for humanity' is that the property in question has exceptional cultural significance. That significance may be deduced from the following indicative criteria:[15]

- it is an exceptional cultural property bearing testimony to one or more periods of the development of humankind at the national, regional or global level;
- it represents a masterpiece of human creativity;
- it bears an exceptional testimony to a cultural tradition or to a civilization which is living or which has disappeared;
- it exhibits an important interchange of human achievements, over a span of time or within a cultural area of the world on developments in arts and sciences;
- it has a central significance to the cultural identity of societies concerned.

The term 'greatest importance for humanity' also implies uniqueness. Cultural property may be considered unique if there is no other comparable cultural property that is of the same cultural significance. Influential criteria include age, history, scientific or aesthetic value, artistic craftsmanship, shape or design, location and context.[16]

Each Party is entitled to submit to the Committee for the Protection of Cultural Property in the Event of Armed Conflict[17] ('the Committee') requests[18] for the granting of enhanced protection to cultural property under its jurisdiction or control.[19] The Committee may also decide to invite a Party to apply for enhanced protection.[20] Article 27, paragraph 1(b) of the 1999 Second Protocol gives the Committee the competence to grant, suspend or cancel enhanced protection for cultural property.[21] The Committee evaluates, on a case by case basis, the exceptional cultural significance of the property, and/or its uniqueness, and/or whether its destruction would lead to an irretrievable loss for humanity.[22] The Committee decides in each particular case whether the criteria set out in Article 10 have been met; a decision to grant or deny enhanced protection may only be made on the basis of those criteria. In addi-

15 Guidelines for the Implementation of the 1999 Second Protocol to the Hague Convention of 1954 for the Protection of Cultural Property in the Event of Armed Conflict, CLT-09/CONF/219/3 (dated 24 November 2009), paragraph 33.

16 See for the list of indicative criteria: Guidelines for the Implementation of the 1999 Second Protocol, *supra* footnote 15, paragraph 34.

17 Established by Article 24 of the 1999 Second Protocol.

18 The Secretariat of UNESCO has developed an enhanced protection request form.

19 See Article 11 (1) and (2): The granting of enhanced protection.

20 This may be done when other Parties, the International Committee of the Blue Shield or other non-governmental organisations with relevant expertise recommend specific cultural property to the Committee. See Article 11(3).

21 Article 27: Functions.

22 It is presumed that the Committee, subject to other relevant considerations, will consider that immovable cultural property inscribed on the World Heritage List satisfies the condition of greatest importance for humanity. See: Guidelines for the Implementation of the 1999 Second Protocol, *supra* footnote 15, paragraph 36. See also the article of Ariel Gonzalez, *Great expectations? Towards an effective application of the regime of enhanced protection in the Second Protocol to the Hague Convetnion on the Protection of Cultural Property in the Event of Armed Conflict*, at pp. 59-67 of this book.

tion, any objections by other Parties can only be made on the basis of these criteria, and such objections must be specific and related to the facts.[23] These rules are an attempt to depoliticise the whole procedure. The Committee decides by a majority of two-thirds of its members present and voting whether cultural property is to be granted enhanced protection.[24] If objections have been lodged by Parties earlier in the process with regard to inclusion in the List, the Committee decides by a majority of four-fifths of its members present and voting.[25] In exceptional cases, when the Committee has concluded that the requesting Party which has control or jurisdiction over the cultural property cannot meet the criteria laid down in Article 10 (b), the Committee may still decide to grant the enhanced protection, on the condition that the Party concerned submits a request for international assistance under Article 32 of the 1999 Second Protocol.[26]

Article 11, paragraph 9, of the 1999 Second Protocol provides for an emergency procedure. Upon the outbreak of hostilities, a Party to the conflict may request, on an emergency basis, provisional enhanced protection of cultural property under its jurisdiction or control. A decision on an emergency request to grant provisional enhanced protection is also taken by a majority of four-fifths of the members of the Committee present and voting.[27]

Cultural property receives the status of enhanced protection through inscription on the List of Cultural Property under Enhanced Protection, as provided for in Article 27, paragraph 1(b) of the 1999 Second Protocol ('the List').[28] The procedure for submission and inscription is fairly similar to the procedure under the World Heritage Convention for inscription on the World Heritage List, except that Article 11, paragraph 3, explicitly states that other Parties may also recommend specific cultural property to the Committee.[29] The advantage of the List is that it is tangible evidence, in particular for the opposing forces, that the property bears the status of enhanced protection, and that any attack on the property will have far-reaching consequences. The List should not be confused with the list mentioned in Article 11, paragraph 1. The latter should be seen as a 'tentative list': a list of cultural property for which a Party intends to request the granting of enhanced protection.[30] Such a list can facilitate the work of the Committee.

23 Article 11 (5).
24 Article 26 (2).
25 Article 11 (5).
26 Article 11 (8).
27 Article 11 (9).
28 Article 11 (10).
29 Article 11 (3).
30 Guidelines for the Implementation of the 1999 Second Protocol, *supra* footnote 15, paragraph 52.

4. Losing enhanced protection; loss, suspension or cancellation

Under the 1999 Second Protocol there are three ways in which enhanced protection can be lost: loss,[31] suspension or cancellation.[32] This differs slightly from the system of losing special protection under the 1954 Hague Convention. Article 11 of the Convention speaks of 'withdrawal of immunity'. Whereas the 1954 Hague Convention has one article on losing special protection, the 1999 Second Protocol has two: Article 13 concerns the loss of enhanced protection, whereas Article 14 concerns the suspension or cancellation of the enhanced protection status. It would seem that Article 56, paragraph 2, of the 1977 Additional Protocol I to the 1949 Geneva Conventions served as a source of inspiration.[33]

Article 13 determines the circumstances in which cultural property loses enhanced protection status. The first possibility is that such protection is suspended or cancelled in accordance with Article 14. In such cases, a procedure must be followed by the Committee.[34] The second possibility envisages loss of enhanced protection by operation of law, which means automatically and without a specific procedure, namely if and for as long as the property has, by its use, become a military objective. The term 'use' instead of 'function'[35] is used deliberately, and it means that for the loss of enhanced protection on the basis of Article 13, paragraph 1(b) of the 1999 Second Protocol, concrete activities must have been performed. Another reason why the term 'use' has been chosen is to illustrate the special system of protection, and to remain in line with Article 10, paragraph 1(c), where it says that the cultural property should not be used for military purposes or to shield military sites. Cultural property lacks the status of enhanced protection as long as it is a military objective: as soon as it cannot be considered as such any longer, the regime of enhanced protection revives automatically.

The loss of status does not mean that there is no protection anymore for the cultural property in question. Article 13, paragraph 2, lists the specific circumstances in which cultural property which has by its use become a military objective and has lost enhanced protection status may be the object of an attack. The paragraph tries to

---

31 Article 13: Loss of enhanced protection.

32 Article 14: Suspension and cancellation of enhanced protection.

33 Article 56 AP I: Protection of works and installations containing dangerous forces

2. The special protection against attack provided by paragraph 1 shall cease:
   (a) for a dam or a dyke only if it is used for other than its normal function and in regular, significant and direct support of military operations and if such attack is the only feasible way to terminate such support;
   (b) for a nuclear electrical generating station only if it provides electric power in regular, significant and direct support of military operations and if such attack is the only feasible way to terminate such support;
   (c) for other military objectives located at or in the vicinity of these works or installations only if they are used in regular, significant and direct support of military operations and if such attack is the only feasible way to terminate such support.

34 Guidelines for the Implementation of the 1999 Second Protocol, *supra* footnote 15, paragraphs 89-89 describe this procedure.

35 In Article 6, the term 'function' is used.

strike a balance between, on one hand, the military necessity to attack cultural property which has lost enhanced protection status, and on the other, the preservation of that property. In situations where cultural property had previously enjoyed enhanced protection, that second element is of more weight than in situations where the property only enjoyed 'general' protection. After all, property which has been granted enhanced protection status is property which has been deemed to be part of the cultural heritage and of the greatest importance for humanity. This is reflected in the stricter conditions of Article 13, paragraph 2, governing attacks on cultural property which had previously enjoyed enhanced protection compared to the conditions set out in Article 6.[36] Generally speaking, the wording of Article 13, paragraph 2, makes it clear that the attack concerned has to focus on terminating the use of the cultural property that made it a military objective.

Article 14 explains when enhanced protection status can be suspended or cancelled. Suspension is a provisional measure, which does not result in the permanent loss of enhanced protection, but in an interruption of protection when the criteria for granting it are no longer met. Once the property meets the criteria again, the Committee has to make a decision on the resumption of enhanced protection. Cancellation, however, is a definitive measure which leads to the permanent loss of enhanced protection. It is therefore expected that cancellation will only take place in exceptional circumstances. It is fair to say that the conditions for suspension or cancellation of enhanced protection are linked to the criteria of Article 10 and 12 of the 1999 Second Protocol.

When cultural property under enhanced protection no longer meets one of the criteria laid down in that Article 10, the Committee may suspend its enhanced protection status.[37] In practice, circumstances can occur under which the cultural property is no longer of the greatest importance for humanity, for instance if it has been severely damaged. It is also possible that adequate domestic protection, or the criterion of not using the property for military purposes are not met for a certain period of time, but the situation is reversed later. If the Party concerned can prove that the criteria in Article 10 are again being fulfilled, the Committee may decide to re-establish the enhanced protection status. The Committee may only cancel the enhanced protection (thereby following the more definite route) if the criteria laid down in Article 10, which are no longer met, cannot be fulfilled at a later date.[38]

In case of a serious violation of Article 12 in relation to cultural property under enhanced protection arsing from its use in support of military action,[39] the Committee may suspend its enhanced protection status until the Party concerned can prove that

36 Article 6: Respect for cultural property.

37 The Committee decides by majority of two-thirds of its members present and voting whether the status of enhanced protection needs to be suspended or cancelled; see Article 26 (2).

38 Guidelines for the Implementation of the 1999 Second Protocol to the Hague Convention, *supra* footnote 15, paragraph 87.

39 Article 12 of the 1999 Second Protocol states that the Parties to a conflict shall ensure the immunity of cultural property under enhanced protection by refraining from making such property the object of attack or from any use of the property or its immediate surroundings in support of military action.

the property is no longer being used in support of military action. But where such violations are continuous,[40] the Committee may exceptionally cancel the enhanced protection status by removing the cultural property from the List.[41]

The distinction between 'use as a military objective' and 'use in support of military action' should be kept in mind. If the cultural property is being used as a military objective, it will lose enhanced protection on the basis of Article 13; suspension or cancellation is not an option. However, when the cultural property is used in support of military action, the decision of the Committee to suspend or cancel enhanced protection can be seen as a sanction, and as a warning to the Party concerned not to proceed any further on this path by using the property as a military objective.

5. Closing remarks

This article describes the system of enhanced protection established by the 1999 Second Protocol. The hope is that it will work better in practice than the system of special protection under the 1954 Hague Convention. However, its establishment in the Protocol is only the first step. It is now time to implement and use it.

The Committee has therefore developed Guidelines[42] – to which this article sometimes refers – for the implementation of the 1999 Second Protocol. It had been asked to do so under Article 27, paragraph 1(a) of the Protocol. One of the chapters of these Guidelines concerns the enhanced protection system, providing an explanation of the system and how Parties can apply for such protection. The Guidelines have been endorsed by the Third Meeting of the Parties to the 1999 Second Protocol on 24 November 2009.[43] Let us hope that these Guidelines will serve as a tool for the proper implementation of that system. The protection of the cultural property of one State is the protection of the cultural property of humanity, especially when the property in question is eligible for enhanced protection status, since it has been deemed to be part of the cultural heritage and of the greatest importance for humanity.

40 The Committee has stated that the criterion of 'continuity' is met if the use exceeds six months and if there is no evidence that such use will end.

41 In the case of suspension, there is no removal from the List, but it is duly noted on the List.

42 CLT-09/CONF/219/3, dated 24 November 2009.

43 The Resolution of the Third Meeting of the Parties states: "5. ENDORSES the Guidelines for the Implementation of the Second Protocol (Annex I) and INVITES the Committee to report on their implementation to the next ordinary Meeting of the Parties."

Chapter 5

Great expectations? Towards an effective application of the regime of enhanced protection in the Second Protocol to the Hague Convention on the Protection of Cultural Property in the Event of Armed Conflict

*Ariel W. Gonzalez**

1. By way of introduction: Freeing Dr Jekyll

In my professional experience, classic literature is often a valuable resource in understanding and explaining the significance and complexities of a legal instrument. In the case of the system of norms for the international protection of cultural property in the event of armed conflict, I have found a most appropriate literary reference in *The Strange Case of Dr Jekyll and Mr Hyde*.[1]

The major tensions inherent in the 1954 Hague Convention are reminiscent of the inner struggle of Robert Stevenson's famous character. Over the course of the past century, a good number of Doctors Jekyll have devoted themselves to raising awareness of the importance of protecting cultural property in times of armed conflict, and to promoting legal instruments setting limits to military action that may pose a threat to cultural property. At the same time, these efforts have been undermined by caveats and exceptions that permit overstepping those same limits. These caveats and exceptions could be seen as an omnipresent Mr Hyde.[2]

The 1954 Convention for the Protection of Cultural Property in the Event of Armed Conflict – the 1954 Hague Convention for short – bears poignant witness to these tensions. This is the instrument that, for the first time in history, was designed as an international safeguard protecting cultural property *per se*. It recognised the value of cultural property as the common heritage of humanity, and did not regard it as just a corollary of the overall protection that international humanitarian law

* Counsellor, Permanent Mission of Argentina to the United Nations (Vienna). Written text of the presentation made to the symposium commemorating the tenth anniversary of the adoption of the Second Protocol to the 1954 Hague Convention on the Protection of Cultural Property in the Event of Armed Conflict (The Hague, 26 March 2009). The opinions expressed in this presentation are the exclusive responsibility of the author.

1 Robert Louis Stevenson, *The Strange Case of Dr Jekyll and Mr Hyde*, 1886.

2 This should of course not be construed as an indictment of any particular country or organisation. As Stevenson's portrayal of Dr Jekyll's twisted counterpart suggests, results may not always directly reflect intentions. Specifically, those placing the attainment of a military objective before the protection of cultural heritage are not necessarily opposed to such protection. Nonetheless, the end result is that cultural heritage becomes vulnerable to destruction.

Nout van Woudenberg and Liesbeth Lijnzaad (eds.) Protecting Cultural Property in Armed Conflict
© *2010 Koninklijke Brill NV. Printed in The Netherlands.* *ISBN 978 9004 18377 3 pp. 59–67.*

provides in an international conflict. Yet this same Convention in too many cases provides only nominal protection in practice, because it allows the destruction of cultural property when 'imperative military necessity', defined largely on the basis of subjective considerations, so dictates.[3]

Almost half a century after the adoption of the 1954 Hague Convention, those committed to the protection of cultural heritage, who viewed this instrument with a mixture of satisfaction and resignation, found renewed hope in the negotiations held once more in The Hague that led in 1999 to the Second Protocol to the Convention. One major source of hope was the regime of enhanced protection for cultural property whose destruction would be a loss to humanity – a loss that the international community by then seemed simply unwilling to accept.

The Second Protocol seemed to allow Dr Jekyll to triumph in his combat with his alter ego Mr Hyde. To all intents and purposes, it gave the cultural heritage a sanctuary from destruction in armed conflicts. Military necessity that would justify such destruction is subjected to strict and clear procedures, detailed in Chapter 3 of the Protocol. Those claiming military necessity have to consider their actions very carefully, since they may incur criminal responsibility under Chapter 4 if they are found not to have followed the proper procedures. Churches, monuments and architectural masterpieces of great importance to humanity thus acquire an aura that almost puts them on the same level as persons, and almost endows them with their own form of human rights.

Yet four years after the Second Protocol's entry into force, the regime of enhanced protection has still to prove its effectiveness. In particular, its operation may be hindered if, as is happening, the institutions responsible for implementing the Protocol appear indifferent to the ways and means of identifying cultural property that qualifies for inclusion under this regime. There is, in other words, a growing uneasiness that the expectations generated by enhanced protection may have been too great, and that Mr Hyde is as much with us as ever.

As we commemorate the tenth anniversary of the Second Protocol's adoption, this article attempts to address this uneasiness by advancing some ideas on how to set the regime of enhanced protection to work and thus reach another milestone on the 'long and winding road' towards protecting cultural property in the event of armed conflict.[4]

---

3 See Art. 4.2. of the Hague Convention, which provides that the obligation of respect for cultural property in armed conflict 'may be waived only in cases where military necessity imperatively requires such a waiver'. The Convention does not complement this major exception to its core provisions with any clear and objective definition of 'military necessity', or even with a set of criteria circumscribing the cases to which it may apply.

4 The expression 'long and winding road' was first used by the author in 2005 to describe the challenges in setting up an effective criminal jurisdiction to combat the destruction of cultural property in armed conflict. See 'Un camino largo y escarpado (y a veces frustrante): la búsqueda de una jurisdicción penal *efectiva* por actos contra los bienes culturales en caso de conflicto armado', presented at the Regional Seminar organised by the Government of Argentina with the support of UNESCO and the ICRC, Buenos Aires, 2-3 March 2005.

2. The regime of enhanced protection in the Second Protocol: A critical assessment

It is not surprising that Chapter 3 of the Second Protocol, which establishes the regime of enhanced protection, was one of the two areas on which the negotiations ten years ago were the most intense – the other being individual criminal responsibility and jurisdiction.[5]

It would exceed the scope of this article to reproduce or describe the provisions resulting from those negotiations. I prefer instead to recall one of their most interesting features: they concentrated on what could be called the 'procedural aspects' of enhanced protection. There were detailed, painstaking and often lively discussions, in particular, on the procedure for the granting, loss and suspension or cancellation of enhanced protection, as well as the conduct of States vis-à-vis the cultural property on their territory subject to that protection. This is, in essence, what became Articles 11, 13, 14 and 10, paragraphs (b) and (c), of the Second Protocol, respectively.

Little consideration was given, by contrast, to the *substantive* side of enhanced protection – in other words, to what kind of cultural property inherently qualifies for accession to this regime. The only provision in Chapter 3 on this matter, Article 10, paragraph (a), requires, somewhat laconically, that such cultural property is 'cultural heritage of the greatest importance for humanity'.

This requirement is, however, central to the functioning of the enhanced protection regime. It is an important step forward in the protection of cultural heritage in the event of armed conflict, by comparison with the regime of special protection set out in the Hague Convention. It replaces the earlier regime's relative standard of geographical proximity to military objectives[6] with an absolute one. It also substitutes importance to humanity for the national interest as a criterion for qualifying cultural property for protection; the old special protection regime had led to the criticism that it provided an attacker with a 'hit list' of properties whose destruction would weaken its opponent's morale.

The great significance of Article 10 (a) makes the limited extent of the debate on it at the Diplomatic Conference where the Second Protocol was adopted seem all the stranger, particularly at a time when experts were already reflecting on the contribution that the World Heritage List, established by Article 11, paragraph 2[7] of the Convention Concerning the Protection of the World Cultural and Natural Heritage – the 1972 World Heritage Convention for short –, would make in practice to the Second Protocol's regime of enhanced protection.[8]

5 As mentioned above, Chapter 4 of the Protocol.

6 Article 8, paragraph 1(a) of the Convention.

7 Article 11, paragraph 2: On the basis of the inventories submitted by States in accordance with paragraph 1, the Committee shall establish, keep up to date and publish, under the title of "World Heritage List," a list of properties forming part of the cultural heritage and natural heritage, as defined in Articles 1 and 2 of this Convention, which it considers as having outstanding universal value in terms of such criteria as it shall have established. An updated list shall be distributed at least every two years.

8 See, for example, Jean-Marie Henckaerts, 'New rules for the protection of cultural property in armed conflict: the significance of the Second Protocol to the 1954 Hague

Yet the development of this substantive definition continued to be conspicuously absent from subsequent interpretations of or complements to the Second Protocol. For instance, none of the conclusions of the meeting of experts coordinated in Geneva by the International Committee of the Red Cross (ICRC) in October 2000, little more than a year after the adoption of the Convention, addressed this matter. The Practical Advice by the ICRC Advisory Service, which was prepared before the meeting and modified to reflect the experts' deliberations, also dealt only with the procedural aspects of enhanced protection.[9]

An opportunity arose to fill this gap when work began in June 2007 on the Draft Guidelines for the implementation of the Second Protocol. This process began, three years after the Protocol's entry into force, with the first meeting of the Protocol's implementing body, the Committee for the Protection of Cultural Property in the Event of Armed Conflict – the 1999 Committee for short. In her opening statement at that meeting, UNESCO's Assistant Director-General for Culture called attention to the 'synergy between the World Heritage List and the List of Cultural Property under Enhanced Protection.'[10]

This statement was in line with the concerns expressed by some States Parties to the Protocol in comments they submitted on the Draft Guidelines. They expressed the hope that the Guidelines would explain 'more in detail the relationship between the Second Protocol and the 1972 World Heritage Convention as well as the co-existence of different protection regimes.' In particular, they proposed that the Guidelines 'elaborate the common position with regard to the notion of "cultural heritage of the greatest importance for the humanity"[11] and those of "culture heritage" under Article

---

Convention for the Protection of Cultural Property in the Event of Armed Conflict', in María Teresa Dutli et al. eds., *Protection of Cultural Property in the Event of Armed Conflict: Report on the Meeting of Experts (Geneva, 5-6 October 2000)* (Geneva, February 2002), pp. 27-55. It is particularly instructive to reproduce the relevant part of Dr Henckaerts' reasoning, as follows (p. 43): '*The fact that the World Heritage List established under the 1972 Paris Convention concerning the protection of the world cultural and natural heritage is widely used [...] constituted an incentive to try and make the International Register of Cultural Property under Special Protection work. But past efforts showed that this could only happen if the conditions and procedures were adjusted to redress previous shortcomings. The usefulness of such a list lies in its world-wide renown: its mere existence should constitute an effective tool of prevention and protection.* UNESCO would remind warring parties of the list and point out that any military use of or attack against any property on the list would constitute a serious war crime [...]. The commission of such acts would also have severe negative political implications. When no wartime list was available, as in the case of the attacks on Dubrovnik, UNESCO availed itself of the World Heritage List, which had not necessarily been established for wartime purposes. As a result, Dubrovnik was more or less spared. This example has strengthened *the conviction that it would be useful to have a list of exceptionally valuable cultural property to be protected in time of armed conflict.* This conviction was clearly articulated by the States represented at the Preparatory Meeting in Vienna in May 1998.' (emphasis added)

9 Ibid. See respectively Chapter IV and Part Two of the report.

10 First Meeting of the Committee for the Protection of Cultural Property in the Event of Armed Conflict: Final Report, CLT-07/CONF/210/3 (20 June 2007), p. 2, par. 6 (emphasis added).

11 Cf. Article 10 (1) of the Second Protocol [sic].

1 of the 1972 World Heritage Convention [and] elaborate precise criteria for eligibility of cultural property for enhanced protection'.[12] In the same spirit, other States Parties commented that 'the condition "cultural heritage of the greatest importance for humanity" [...] need[s] further clarification' and even 'suggested a "fast track" inscription procedure for cultural sites which are already inscribed in the World Heritage List.'[13]

The need to give 'priority attention' to the relationship between the World Heritage Convention and the List of Cultural Property under Enhanced Protection was consistently among the issues highlighted in the debate at the June 2007 meeting.[14] It was one of the 'core issues' that the Committee recommended focusing on in redrafting the Draft Guidelines.[15]Yet surprisingly, there was no concrete follow-up on these calls either at the Committee's second meeting in December 2007 nor at the third meeting – the latest to date – in June 2008.[16] The Draft Guidelines, meanwhile endorsed by the Meeting of the Parties, are still lacking of any conclusive mechanism or course of action allowing cultural property inscribed in the World Heritage List – which, by definition, are of the "greatest importance to humanity" – to be covered by the regime of enhanced protection.

3. The progressive interpretation of Article 10(a) in other forums

The lack of a proper elucidation of the definition in Article 10 (a) through the mechanisms of the Second Protocol contrasts unfavourably with the steps taken in other forums, both treaty bodies and international tribunals, to take advantage of this provision's potential to strengthen the protection of cultural heritage in the event of armed conflict.

As suggested in the previous section, this potential lies in the links that can be made between the concept of 'cultural heritage of the greatest importance for humanity' in Article 10 (a) and the terminology used to define World Heritage in the 1972 World Heritage Convention. According to that Convention, World Heritage comprises cultural and/or natural manifestations that are of 'outstanding universal value.'[17] In explaining this concept, the Operational Guidelines for the Implementation of the 1972 Convention refer to the 'common importance [of the heritage] for present and future generations of all humanity' and considers that 'the permanent protection of this heritage is of the highest importance to the international community as a whole.'[18]

12 Ibid., Annex I, pp. 6-7.

13 Ibid., p. 7.

14 Ibid., p. 3, par. 10 (iv).

15 Ibid., Annex II, p. 9.

16 Documents CLT-07/CONF/214/4 of 4 April 2008 and CLT-07/CONF/204/4 of 15 September 2008.

17 Convention concerning the Protection of the World Cultural and Natural Heritage, adopted on 16 November 1972, 1037 UNTS 151. See in particular Arts. 1 and 2.

18 See Operational Guidelines for the Implementation of the World Heritage Convention, par. 49, in *Basic Texts of the 1972 World Heritage Convention* (Paris: UNESCO, 2005),

As the Operational Guidelines also state, the World Heritage Committee 'recognises the benefits of closer coordination of its work with other UNESCO programmes and relevant Conventions', including the Second Protocol.[19] In 2004, the Committee expressly confirmed this connection when, noting the Second Protocol's entry into force, it expressed its awareness 'of the *importance of identifying appropriate links* between the 1972 Convention and the Protocol.[20]

Other international instruments also promote better coordination between the 1972 World Heritage Convention and the Second Protocol. For instance, the Declaration Concerning the Intentional Destruction of Cultural Heritage, adopted by the UNESCO General Conference at the end of 2003 on the recommendations of a group of experts that had met in Brussels a year earlier, proclaims it a moral obligation of States that they should promote 'a coordinated application of the existing and future instruments relevant to the protection of cultural heritage'.[21]

Perhaps more interesting arguments for a reinforced link between the 1972 Convention and the Second Protocol can be found in the case law of the International Criminal Tribunal for the former Yugoslavia. Particularly relevant in this regard is the case *Prosecutor v. Pavle Strugar*, known as *Dubrovnik*.[22]

As may be recalled, one of the two counts for which Lt. Gen. Pavle Strugar was sentenced to eight years in prison – in a judgment that means a great deal to all those committed to the protection of cultural heritage – was the intentional destruction of part of the cultural heritage of Dubrovnik, on the Croatian coast. The Trial Chamber of the Tribunal examining the case held that Strugar's acts were a war crime. Most notably, the Chamber considered Dubrovnik's status as World Heritage as a reason to reject any justification for this act. It even viewed the World Heritage status as an aggravating factor, falling within the Tribunal's general competence regarding the 'seizure of, destruction or willful damage done to institutions dedicated to religion, charity and education, the arts and sciences, historic monuments and works of art and science'.[23]

Among the many supporting observations in its judgment that merit citation,[24] the Tribunal held that:

---

p. 46. The Operational Guidelines have been extensively updated by the governing bodies of the 1972 Convention.

19 Ibid., pars. 41 and 44, p. 43.

20 Decision 7 EXT.COM 9, adopted at the 7th Extraordinary Session of the World Heritage Committee (UNESCO, December 2004) (emphasis added).

21 Article III, par. 4(c) of the Declaration.

22 See *Prosecutor v. Pavle Strugar*, Case No. IT-01-42-T (Trial Judgment), 31 January 2005; at: http://www.icty.org/x/cases/strugar/tjug/en/str-tj050131e.pdf .
See also the "Documents"-section of this publication.

23 Updated Statute of the International Criminal Tribunal for the former Yugoslavia, Article 3(d).

24 Emphasis added to all these citations from *Dubrovnik*.

- "[...] there was extensive damage to property, *even though the Old Town* [of Dubrovnik] *was a World Heritage protected site.* [...]"[25]
- "By way of general observation, to which the Chamber attaches significant weight, the Chamber notes that by 6 December 1991 there were quite compelling circumstances against the proposition that the Croatian defenders had defensive military positions in the Old Town. *To do so was a clear violation of the World Heritage protected status of the Old Town* [...]."[26]
- "As regards the seriousness of the offence of damage to cultural property (Article 3 (d)), the Chamber observes that '*such property is, by definition, of 'great importance to the cultural heritage of every people'* [...]."[27]
- "[...] The Old Town is also legally distinct from the rest of the wider city because the Old Town, in its entirety including the medieval walls, *enjoys a World Heritage listing and the protections and immunities that are consequent on that listing.* [...]." [28]
- "[...] Some people from the wider Dubrovnik had also been able to take up temporary residence in the Old Town during the blockade *in the belief that its World Heritage listing would give them protection from military attack.* [...]"[29]

By virtue of the reasoning in *Dubrovnik* and other, similar cases, the Tribunal took an intellectual step forward that the governing bodies for the Second Protocol seem hesitant even to explore. That is, it reinforced the stability and predictability of the regime of enhanced protection by building into it the 'cultural heritage nucleus' provided by the World Heritage List.[30]

4. Concluding remarks: Putting enhanced protection to work

Ten years after the adoption of the Second Protocol, it is time to ensure that one of its greatest assets, the regime of enhanced protection, the fruit of intense negotiations by delegations at the Diplomatic Conference, does not suffer the fate of its predecessor, the special protection regime of the 1954 Hague Convention.

---

25 Par. 176.
26 Par. 183.
27 Par. 232.
28 Par. 279.
29 Par. 285.
30 ICTY case law could also set a valuable precedent for future judgments of the International Criminal Court, although the ICC's jurisdiction over the destruction of cultural heritage is more limited than the ICTY's. Article 8 of the ICC's Rome Statute defines as a war crime the act of '(ix) Intentionally directing attacks against buildings dedicated to religion, education, art, science or charitable purposes, historic monuments, hospitals and places where the sick and wounded are collected, *provided they are not military objectives*'. (emphasis added)

As suggested in the previous sections, the development of the substantive requirement in that regime through a clear and explicit link[31] to the World Heritage List may be key to the regime's success.

It would be advisable to set up a group of experts under the 1999 Committee to study the establishment of such a link. Initially the connection could take the form of an inter-institutional agreement between the World Heritage Committee and the 1999 Committee – a 'bridge Protocol' or similar instrument – including cultural heritage on the World Heritage List in the Enhanced Protection List. Preferably, this should occur with the prior agreement of the States in whose territory the sites are located, and be confirmed by a qualified majority of the members of the 1999 Committee.

In my view, a linkage between the World Heritage Convention and the Second Protocol would have several advantages. Firstly, the fact that a property is already on the World Heritage List would add to the inherent legitimacy of the request to place it on the 1999 List, thus facilitating the implementation of the procedures under Article 10 of the Second Protocol. For similar reasons, given the current, virtually universal adherence to the 1972 World Heritage Convention, it would encourage universal adherence to the Protocol, since all countries would presumably welcome the opportunity to place a World Heritage cultural property on their territory under enhanced protection.

From the perspective of the 1972 World Heritage Convention, the proposed link would underline the gravity of the World Heritage Committee's responsibility as it considers including a property on the World Heritage List. This would lead to measures to strengthen the procedures for submitting and evaluating nominations to the List. Such measures would be very welcome, as the Committee has often been criticised for viewing the evaluation process as a sort of 'beauty contest' and paying only limited attention to the objective merits of the heritage being evaluated.

Perhaps more importantly, this connection would dilute the national dimension of cultural property, which has proved to be highly detrimental to any form of protection in the event of armed conflict. In other words, the concept of 'property precious to the enemy', whose destruction in am armed conflict could even be considered a military victory would be replaced by the idea of heritage in which humanity as a whole has an interest, with corresponding consequences for the combatant Party's standing in the international community.

Naturally, making this link would require addressing a number of challenges, including:

- the limitations on introducing amendments to either the 1972 World Heritage Convention or the Second Protocol;
- the fact that the 1972 World Heritage Convention and the Second Protocol have different constituencies, and thus the need to develop a proper mechanism for coordination;

---

31 As observed at the first meeting of the 1999 Committee, 'there is consent among States that there is no automatic granting of enhanced protection to cultural sites already inscribed in the World Heritage List'. Report of the First Meeting of the 1999 Committee, document CLT-07/CONF/210/3 (June 2007), Annex I, p. 7.

- the problem of 'natural and mixed heritage',[32] which is included on the World Heritage List but is in principle alien to the Second Protocol;
- the status under the Second Protocol of a World Heritage property that has been removed from the World Heritage List and thus ceased to be 'of the highest importance to the international community as a whole';[33]
- the increased costs, mainly for identification of the property and for technical assistance, entailed by expanding the list of properties included under the regime of enhanced protection.

None of these challenges is insurmountable, however. In any event, the effort of addressing them is more than outweighed by the benefits of ensuring the successful implementation of the Second Protocol through its better integration with the other components of the system for the international protection of cultural heritage.

Mr Hyde's role in impeding the protection of cultural heritage in the event of armed conflict may well be coming to an end. This statement may sound utopian. Yet it is no more utopian than it seemed less than ten years ago to imagine the international prosecution and conviction of individuals who have committed crimes against humanity.

32 'Mixed heritage' is defined in the Operational Guidelines, par. 46 (in *Basic Texts*, p. 46) as heritage that satisfies 'a part or the whole of the definitions of both cultural and natural heritage laid out in Articles 1 and 2' of the Convention.

33 See section 3 above.

Chapter 6

Enhancing individual criminal responsibility for offences involving cultural property – the road to the Rome Statute and the 1999 Second Protocol

*Mireille Hector**

> Damage to cultural property belonging to any people whatsoever means damage to the cultural heritage of all mankind, since each people makes its contribution to the culture of the world[1]

1. Introduction

Although the need to give protection to cultural property during armed conflict has traditionally been recognized, it has taken time to create specific obligations in this regard for the parties to armed conflicts. The establishment of individual criminal responsibility for offences involving cultural property is even more recent, with the Rome Statute of the International Criminal Court and the Second Protocol to the 1954 Hague Convention establishing important benchmarks. This article explores the development of the international legal norms on the protection of cultural property in times of armed conflict, with a focus on the penal provisions therein.

2. 1899 and 1907 Hague Regulations

The 1899[2] and 1907[3] Hague Regulations respecting the laws and customs of war on land (henceforth: the Hague Regulations – annexed to the 1899 and 1907 Hague Convention respecting the laws and customs of war on land, respectively incorporate specific provisions on the protection of cultural property. Article 27 of the Hague Regulations provides that "[i]n sieges and bombardments all necessary steps must be taken to spare, as far as possible, buildings dedicated to religion, art, science, or

* Mireille Hector, J.D., LL.M, participated in all preparatory meetings leading up to the adoption of the Rome Statute, as representative of the Lawyers Committee for Human Rights (now: Human Rights First). She currently holds the position of Legal Counsel at the International Law Division of the Ministry of Foreign Affairs of the Kingdom of The Netherlands. This article was written in a personal capacity. The opinions in this essay are solely hers and do not necessarily represent those of the Ministry.

1 Preamble, 1954 Hague Convention for the Protection of Cultural Property in the Event of Armed Conflict.

2 Adopted 29 July 1899.

3 Adopted 18 October 1907.

Nout van Woudenberg and Liesbeth Lijnzaad (eds.) Protecting Cultural Property in Armed Conflict
© 2010 Koninklijke Brill NV. Printed in The Netherlands.
ISBN 978 9004 18377 3 pp. 69–76.

charitable purposes, historic monuments, hospitals, and places where the sick and wounded are collected, provided they are not being used at the time for military purposes […]."[4] As such, this Article can be seen as a major first step in the international codification of the duty to protect cultural property in the conduct of hostilities. At the same time, this provision is rather general in scope, not establishing a clear prohibition and leaving much room for interpretation, given the phrase "as far as possible" and the broad reference to "military purposes".

The 1907 Hague Regulations also contain a provision on the protection of cultural property in situations of military authority over the territory of the hostile state. According to Article 56

> "[a]ll seizure of, destruction or wilful damage done to institutions [dedicated to religion, charity and education, the arts and sciences] […], historic monuments, works of art and science, is forbidden, and should be made the subject of legal proceedings."[5]

This provision is noticeable because it specifically calls for legal proceedings in response to acts contrary to this prohibition. At the same time, the Regulations do not further stipulate any obligation for state parties to incorporate this prohibition in their domestic legislation.

Notwithstanding the – albeit rudimentary – provisions in the Hague Regulations, it was clear from the two World Wars that parties to armed conflict showed great disregard for cultural property, and extensive damage to some. While the subsequent Nuremberg Charter of the International Military Tribunal contained an article on war crimes that included "plunder of public or private property",[6] this article was considered to constitute "only a very imperfect and incomplete penal sanction when compared with the manifold means by which attacks may be and have been made on the cultural heritage of the international community."[7]

---

4 Article 27 of the 1899 Hague Regulations contains similar language.

5 Article 56 of the 1899 Hague Regulations contains similar language.

6 Article 6(b) of the Nuremburg Charter (8 August 1945):

> The Tribunal established by the Agreement referred to m Article 1 hereof for the trial and punishment of the major war criminals of the European Axis countries shall have the power to try and punish persons who, acting in the interests of the European Axis countries, whether as individuals or as members of organizations, committed any of the following crimes.
>
> (a) crimes against peace: […]
>
> (b) war crimes: namely, violations of the laws or customs of war. Such violations shall include, but not be limited to, murder, ill-treatment or deportation to slave labor or for any other purpose of civilian population of or in occupied territory, murder or ill-treatment of prisoners of war or persons on the seas, killing of hostages, plunder of public or private property, wanton destruction of cities, towns or villages, or devastation not justified by military necessity;
>
> (c) crimes against humanity: […]

7 Georges Berlia, Report of the international protection of cultural property, by penal measures, in the event of armed conflict, 8 March 1950, MUS/CONF.1/20 (rev.), 5C/PRG/6/ANNEXI-II, page 11.

3. 1954 Hague Convention

The drafters of the 1954 Hague Convention for the protection of cultural property in the event of armed conflict (henceforth: the 1954 Hague Convention)[8] attempted to address the shortcomings in the international regulation of the protection of cultural property in times of armed conflict. Article 4 of the 1954 Hague Convention obliges High Contracting Parties to refrain from any use of cultural property, and its immediate surroundings, for purposes which are likely to expose it to destruction or damage in armed conflict. Similarly, High Contracting Parties have to refrain from any act of hostility, directed against cultural property. However, at the same time these obligations may be waived in cases where *military necessity imperatively* requires such a waiver. While it can be observed that the concept of 'imperative military necessity' seems narrower to some extent than the general reference to "military purposes" in the 1907 Hague Regulations, this concept still leaves ample room for interpretation, in light of the lack of a clear definition of the term.[9]

An important step taken by the 1954 Hague Convention is the broadening of its scope to situations of non-international armed conflict.[10] As a minimum, all parties to a conflict taking place on the territory of a High Contracting Party are bound to apply the provisions in the Convention that relate to the respect for cultural property. Another elaboration in the Convention concerned the establishment of clearer procedural norms. According to Article 28, High Contracting Parties have to "undertake to take, within the framework of their ordinary criminal jurisdiction, all necessary steps to prosecute and impose penal or disciplinary sanctions upon those persons, of whatever nationality, who commit or order to be committed a breach of the present Convention." While this is an important improvement over the Hague Regulations, this provision is still rather general and has "largely remained a dead letter".[11]

8 Adopted 14 May 1954, 249 UNTS 240.

9 The possibility of waiving in light of imperative military necessity does not affect the obligation to "prohibit, prevent and, if necessary, put a stop to any form of theft, pillage or misappropriation of, and any acts of vandalism directed against, cultural property" or the duty to "refrain from any act directed by way of reprisals against cultural property", as incorporated in art. 4 paragraphs 3 and 4 of the 1954 Hague Convention.
See also the article of Kevin Chamberlain, *Military necessity under the 1999 Second Protocol*, pp. 43-49 of this book.

10 1954 Hague Convention, article 19.

11 Jean-Marie Henckaerts, *New rules for the protection of cultural property in armed conflict: The significance of the Second Protocol to the 1954 Hague Convention for the Protection of Cultural Property in the Event of Armed Conflict*, at pp. 21-41 of this book.

4. 1977 Additional Protocols to the 1949 Geneva Conventions

While the four Geneva Conventions[12] had been silent on the protection of cultural property as such,[13] the 1977 Additional Protocols[14] made a step forward in strengthening the protection of cultural property in the conduct of hostilities, both in international and non-international armed conflict, in addition to its general protection as a civilian object. Under the First Additional Protocol only military objectives, i.e. objectives that meet the twofold criteria of article 52,[15] may be attacked. Article 53 builds on this general protection of cultural property as a civilian object and specifies that, without prejudice to the 1954 Hague Convention, it is prohibited: (a) to commit any acts of hostility directed against the historic monuments, works of art or places of worship which constitute the cultural or spiritual heritage of peoples; (b) to use such objects in support of the military effort; (c) to make such objects the object of reprisals. While in comparison with the 1954 Hague Convention, the 'imperative military necessity' waiver is absent in this provision, it is obvious that cultural property that is used as a military objective looses it protection under the First Additional Protocol.

The Second Additional Protocol contains a comparable provision,[16] absent a reference to the prohibition of reprisals against cultural property.

In terms of the individual criminal responsibility for offences against cultural property, the First Additional Protocol considers as a 'grave breach', when committed wilfully:

"making the clearly-recognized historic monuments, works of art or places of worship which constitute the cultural or spiritual heritage of peoples and to which special protection has been given by special arrangement, for example, within the framework of a competent international organization, the object of attack, causing

---

12 1949 Geneva Conventions, adopted 12 August 1949:

Convention (I) for the Amelioration of the Condition of the Wounded and Sick in Armed Forces in the Field;

Convention (II) for the Amelioration of the Condition of Wounded, Sick and Shipwrecked Members of Armed Forces at Sea;

Convention (III) relative to the Treatment of Prisoners of War;

Convention (IV) relative to the Protection of Civilian Persons in Time of War.

13 However, Article 53 of the Fourth 1949 Geneva Convention has relevance to cultural property. It reads: "Any destruction by the Occupying Power of real or personal property belonging individually or collectively to private persons, or to the State, or to other public authorities, or to social or cooperative organisations, is prohibited, except where such destruction is rendered absolutely necessary by military operations."

14 Protocol I and II Additional to the Geneva Conventions of 12 August 1949, and relating to the Protection of Victims of International Armed Conflicts and of Non-International Armed Conflict, respectively. Both Protocols were adopted 8 June 1977.

15 "[...] In so far as objects are concerned, military objectives are limited to those objects which by their nature, location, purpose or use make an effective contribution to military action and whose total or partial destruction, capture or neutralization, in the circumstances ruling at the time, offers a definite military advantage."

16 Second Additional Protocol, art. 16.

as a result extensive destruction thereof, where there is no evidence of the violation by the adverse Party of Article 53, subparagraph (b), and when such historic monuments, works of art and places of worship are not located in the immediate proximity of military objectives."[17]

The recognition of this offence as a grave breach is an important one, because it outlines the elements of the violation that entail individual criminal responsibility. In addition, the High Contracting Parties are under an obligation to repress graves breaches and to search for suspects of such breaches on their territory, in order to prosecute or extradite them.[18] Compared to the 1954 Hague Convention, this is a step forward in the enforcement of the penal provisions, as its provides the basis for the exercise of universal jurisdiction over this offence. At the same time, it can be observed that the qualification of 'grave breach' is only reserved to attacks that have created "extensive damage" to an object that has been given "special protection".

In the period following the adoption of the 1977 Additional Protocol, particularly in the 1990's, more attention was given to the need for enhanced protection of cultural property in armed conflict as well as individual accountability for offences related to such property. This was triggered by the devastation to cultural property during the armed conflict in the former Yugoslavia. The Statute of the International Criminal Tribunal for the Former Yugoslavia (henceforth: ICTY)[19] contains specific war crimes that are relevant to cultural property. Article 3 lists, inter alia, as a war crime the "seizure of, destruction or wilful damage done to institutions dedicated to religion, charity and education, the arts and sciences, historic monuments and works of art and science."[20] This provision stems from the Hague Regulations.[21]

5. 1998 Rome Statute of the International Criminal Court

The Rome Statute of the International Criminal Court[22] constitutes a landmark treaty on the individual criminal responsibility for international crimes. While, in the process of adopting the Rome Statute, offenses related to cultural property did not receive major attention, the Statute nevertheless contains important provisions in this respect. Under two sections in Article 8, "[i]ntentionally directing attacks against buildings dedicated to religion, education, art, science or charitable purposes, historic monuments, hospitals and places where the sick and wounded are collected"[23] is considered a war crime within the jurisdiction of the International Criminal Court

17 First Additional Protocol, art. 85 paragraph 4 d.

18 Id., art. 85 paragraph 1, and Sandoz et al. (eds.), *Commentary on the Additional Protocols of 8 June 1977 to the Geneva Conventions of 12 August 1949*, ICRC, Geneva, 1987, p. 975.

19 ICTY has been established by UN SC Resolution S/Res/827 (2003), dated 25 May 1993. The Statute can be found at: http://www.icty.org/sections/LegalLibrary/StatuteoftheTribunal

20 ICTY Statute, art. 3 paragraph d.

21 Article 56 of the 1899 and 1907 Hague Regulations

22 Adopted 17 July 1998; 2187 UNTS 90.

23 Rome Statute, art. 8 paragraph 2 b (ix) and art. 8 paragraph e (iv), on international and non-international armed conflict, respectively.

in both international and non-international armed conflicts, provided they are not military objectives.

Notably, the requirement of actual damage resulting from such attack, as contained in the grave breach provision of the First Protocol, is not included here. Also, there is no limitation to attacks on cultural property under special protection. The Rome Statute thus makes an important improvement towards widening the category of prohibited conduct that generates individual criminal responsibility. At the same time it has been observed that the drafters of the Rome Statute missed the opportunity to make more specific reference to cultural property as such.[24] Also, the prohibition on the use of cultural property as a military objective is not included in the list of crimes, nor the seizure, destruction or wilful damage of cultural property as such.

Unlike the ICTY, which has rendered judgements in a number of cases relating to cultural property,[25] the ICC has so far not brought any charges against persons suspected of involvement in deliberate attacks on cultural property. In this regard it is important to highlight that, under the principle of complementarity, the International Criminal Court can only exercise jurisdiction when States are unable or unwilling to investigate and prosecute crimes under the Rome Statute. Therefore, it is of critical importance for the State Parties to have or, where necessary, to adopt legislation that allows for the domestic investigation and prosecution of such crimes. According to ICC Registrar Arbia, so far this effort has been "very disappointing",[26] as only 39 of the 110 State Parties have adopted implementing legislation.

6. 1999 Second Protocol the 1954 Hague Convention

The 1999 Second Protocol is the most recent international instrument on the protection of cultural property in times of armed conflict, with 55 States Parties so far. The Second Protocol addresses some of the shortcomings of the previous instruments. The Protocol limits the scope of the notion of "imperative military necessity" to the framework of military objective in the First Additional Protocol. Hence, under the 1999 Protocol, no cultural property may be attacked unless it has, by its function, been made into a military objective. Additionally, the Second Protocol requires state parties to establish that there is no feasible alternative available to obtain a similar military advantage to that offered by directing an act of hostility against that objective.

Importantly, the Second Protocol further establishes individual criminal responsibility over five specific offences in relation to cultural property, differentiating between cultural property under enhanced protection and cultural property in

24 Gabriella Venturini, War Crimes in International Armed Conflicts, in: *The Rome Statute of the International Criminal Court. A challenge to Impunity*, edited by Mauro Politi and Giuseppe Nesi, 2001, page 99.

25 For example *Strugar*, (IT-01-42) Dubrovnik (See also Susan Somers, *Investigation and prosecution of crimes against cultural property*, at pp. 77-80 of this book) and *Kordić and Cerkez* (IT-95-14/2) Lašva Valley.

26 Remarks by Silvana Arbia, ICC Registrar at the "Roundtable on Implementing Legislation", Rome, Italy, 17 July 2009, at http://www.icc-cpi.int.

general.[27] The Protocol lists as serious violations, when committed intentionally and in violation of the 1954 Convention or the Protocol:

> "a. making cultural property under enhanced protection the object of attack;
> b. using cultural property under enhanced protection or its immediate surroundings in support of military action;
> c. extensive destruction or appropriation of cultural property protected under the Convention and this Protocol;
> d. making cultural property protected under the Convention and this Protocol the object of attack;
> e. theft, pillage or misappropriation of, or acts of vandalism directed against cultural property protected under the Convention."[28]

In addition, in order to give practical effect to this provision, States Parties are obliged to adopt such measures as may be necessary to establish these offences as criminal offences under its domestic law and to make them punishable by appropriate penalties.[29] The Second Protocol also obliges State Parties to take the necessary legislative measures to establish jurisdiction over these offences, including universal jurisdiction for the first three offences.[30] Furthermore, the Second Protocol contains detailed obligations for State Parties with regard to prosecution, extradition and mutual legal assistance in relation to these offences.[31] States Parties to the Second Protocol are regularly encouraged to adopt and effectively implement relevant national legislation.[32]

As such, the Protocol has made a significant contribution to both an enhanced specificity in the description of violations that entail individual criminal responsibility, as well as to a more elaborate system of prosecution, extradition and mutual legal assistance in relation to such offences.

7. Concluding remarks

The period 1899 – 1999 has shown important developments with respect to the protection of cultural property in times of armed conflict. In the course of time, general obligations to spare and respect cultural property have been complemented by much stricter prohibitions and by clearly established offences that entail individual criminal responsibility, both on a national and international level. At the same time,

27 See also Roger O'Keefe, *National Implementation of the Penal Provisions of Chapter 4 of the Second Protocol of 26 March 1999 to the Hague Convention of 1954 for the Protection of Cultural Property in the Event of Armed Conflict*, 29 March 2002; available at UNESCO and on file with the author.

28 Second Protocol, art. 15 paragraph 1.

29 Id., art. 15, paragraph 2.

30 Id., art. 16, paragraph 1

31 Id., arts. 17-19.

32 For example, in a resolution adopted at the Third Meeting of Parties to the Second Protocol, 23-24 November 2009.

much remains to be done in obtaining universal acceptance and implementation of the instruments underlying these improvements. The Rome Statute and the 1999 Second Protocol are still in need of more ratifications as well as implementing legislation that gives effect to the obligations contained in these instruments. Thus, while the road to the Rome Statute and the 1999 Second Protocol has been very important, it is one in need of further paving and strengthening, in order to provide cultural property with all the protection it deserves, particularly in times of armed conflict.

Chapter 7

Investigation and prosecution of crimes against cultural property

*Susan Somers**

1. Introduction

Various considerations and issues that have been addressed during the investigation and prosecution of cases involving cultural property will be discussed in the following account, and possible preventative measures that may be taken in light of this experience will be examined.

Among the egregious violations directed against cultural property in our time are the unlawful attacks against the Old Town of Dubrovnik, the destruction of the Buddhas in Afghanistan, the destruction of Stari Most in Mostar and the destruction of numerous mosques in Bosnia during the conflicts in the 1990's. Equally shocking was the widespread looting of museums during the second conflict in Iraq.

I would like bring to your attention certain relevant provisions from the 31 January 2005 ICTY Trial Chamber Judgment of Prosecutor v. Pavle Strugar. General Strugar was the overall commander of the military forces (Yugoslav People's Army or JNA) which conducted a campaign of unlawful shelling against the Old Town of Dubrovnik in 1991. General Strugar was convicted after a full trial and the conviction was upheld on appeal. The *Strugar* case addressed the infamous 6 December 1991 shelling of Old Town which resulted in loss of life and widespread destruction of cultural property. The 1954 Hague Convention for the Protection of Cultural Property in the Event of an Armed Conflict is cited throughout this case.

As lead counsel in the *Strugar* case, I will present some highlights from the preparation of the case and from the *Strugar* Trial Chamber Decision. This specifically concerns the following parts of the *Strugar* decision (see the "Documents"-section of this publication): paragraphs 223-233, 290-312 and 316-322 which contain certain points which I want to bring to your attention and which may be useful in your work.[1]

* Researcher and Former Senior Prosecuting Trial Attorney, United Nations International Criminal Tribunal for the Former Yugoslavia, The Hague, the Netherlands.

1 See *Prosecutor v. Pavle Strugar*, Case No. IT-01-42-T (Trial Judgment), 31 January 2005; at: http://www.icty.org/x/cases/strugar/tjug/en/str-tj050131e.pdf.

Nout van Woudenberg and Liesbeth Lijnzaad (eds.) Protecting Cultural Property in Armed Conflict
© *2010 Koninklijke Brill NV. Printed in The Netherlands.* ISBN *978 9004 18377 3 pp. 77-80.*

First, as to the source of the evidence relied upon, paragraph 316 of the decision indicates that the Court relied on evidence principally from citizens of Dubrovnik as well as persons visiting the Old Town during or immediately after the attack.

Identification of witnesses and obtaining their statements and other physical evidence that may be available close in time to the event is crucial. Memorializing their statements, photographing or videotaping the crime scene should be done. Prosecution of multiple accused who could be held responsible for the destruction (such as military and political officials) should go hand in hand with careful witness management. After all, witness burnout, which can occur when people who are often still traumatized are asked repeatedly to testify for different cases, must be prevented.

In the case of Dubrovnik, though having been withdrawn during some of the heavy fighting over the months, international monitors had been present during the 6 December attack, The real-time media coverage also served to document the intensity and scope of the unlawful attack.

Identifying military commanders from both sides who could provide evidence of attacking and defending positions was crucial both to determine origin of fire, and to determine location of possible military objectives which were claimed by the JNA to have been the object of the attack. Artillery and weapons experts provided evidence of range and power of weaponry. Senior military commanders both from NATO forces (a British general) and ex-Warsaw Pact (an ex-JNA general) provided evidence of doctrine and discipline. The Prosecution was able to obtain the first-hand testimony of one of the senior JNA commanding officers in the Dubrovnik campaign who provided inside information as to JNA positions, weaponry and range capability actually in place on December 6.

Military forces must be trained to distinguish civilian objects from military objectives. Practitioners can look not only to international sources but to domestic laws which should reflect international obligations. Domestic laws were cited by the Prosecution in the *Strugar* case as well as the range of sources under International Humanitarian Law (IHL). Military manuals should be examined, where available, as well as records of disciplinary proceedings against members of armed forces, to determine the level of discipline enforced and the type of violations prosecuted by these forces in military tribunals.

In *Strugar*, the command climate within the JNA had been one of impunity with respect to attacks against the Old Town. This atmosphere of impunity emboldened the troops, with the result seen on 6 December. Therefore, training as to the law on cultural property and a command climate which fosters discipline are essential.

Paragraph 224 discusses an important legal decision by the *Strugar* Trial Chamber, finding that

> "[...] despite the lack of a provision similar to Article 52 in Additional Protocol II, the general rule prohibiting attacks on civilian objects also applies to internal conflicts."

While the *Strugar* decision did not turn on the characterization of the armed conflict, the principle advanced by the Prosecution and upheld by the Court was important to the development of IHL.

It should be noted that in paragraph 327, the Court was "[...] of the view that all the property within the Old Town, *i.e.*, each structure or building, is within the scope of Article 3(d) of the Statute. The Chamber therefore concludes that the attack launched by the JNA forces against the Old Town on 6 December 1991 was an attack directed against cultural property within the meaning of Article 3(d) of the Statute, insofar as that provision relates to cultural property."

2. Investigation: A multi-disciplinary effort

Investigating violations of IHL is a multi-disciplinary exercise which may involve, *inter alia*, military analysts, lawyers, historians, police investigators, criminal analysts, forensic experts, including ballistics experts, forensic anthropologists, medical experts, artillery and weapons system experts, architects, sociologists, demographers and economists. The list is not exhaustive and depends on the facts.

Marking a structure with a 1954 Hague Convention symbol may serve as additional evidence of its status as protected cultural property, but it is the structure itself which puts it in that category. The protection may be lost by reason of improper use of cultural property. An example would be that a protected museum used as an ammunitions depot can lose its protected status. Further, with modern sanitized high-tech air attacks and weapons systems, marking structures may become less relevant, since targets should be identified and approved in advance and forces are expected to know through intelligence and satellite imagery where cultural objects are found. Educating forces to know what is where is a key goal and obligation. The presence of cultural property would be a factor in proportionality determinations.

Having a plan in place in advance of armed conflict may serve to protect cultural property. Overall identification of structures and objects, photographing or video recording objects prior to conflict to memorialize their appearance assists in assessing damage done during conflict – a crucial aspect of any prosecution. Cataloguing and inventorying these records should be done and should be available for assessment after the cessation of hostilities. This would also assist in investigating looting. Identifying in advance potential locations to which objects may be relocated and safely stored pending cessation of hostilities, may reduce loss and may assist in assessing damage afterward. This may also assist in recovery from black market activities.

Constituting a "cultural swat team" of forensic experts, architects, art historians – just to mention a few – who can perform investigative work such as crater analysis or other forensic examinations, as well as the identification of damaged or destroyed objects would greatly assist the investigation and potential subsequent prosecution. Again, before and after comparisons to show the damage done during armed conflict will be developed in court, and the more advance preparation, the better. The Dubrovnik crime scene did not have the same degree of forensic evaluation as was found in the Siege of Sarajevo, where the international forces present joined in with the local police in doing forensic assessments such as crater analyses after shelling incidents, and ballistics analyses after sniper attacks.

3. Conclusion

The legal framework within national systems should include prosecution of crimes against cultural property. This is not the exclusive domain of international courts and domestic jurisdictions must be encouraged to take responsibility for matters within their jurisdictions. Countries rich with cultural heritage, including World Heritage designations, should particularly be looking at how to protect these objects and prosecute those who harm them. The expertise reflected on the agenda for this Symposium may perhaps be harnessed to train military forces, governments and NGOs in methods calculated to protect cultural property in the event of armed conflict.

Chapter 8

The protection of cultural property in non-international armed conflicts

*Jean-Marie Henckaerts**

1. Introduction

This contribution will look at the protection of cultural property in non-international armed conflicts in the light of the adoption of the Second Protocol to the Hague Convention of 1954 for the Protection of Cultural Property in the Event of Armed Conflict ('the 1999 Second Protocol'). The preamble to the 1999 Second Protocol indicates the intention of the Protocol 'that the rules governing the protection of cultural property in the event of armed conflict should reflect developments in international law'. These developments include the increasing regulation of non-international armed conflicts, both in treaty law and in customary law. This regulation started in earnest with the adoption of common Article 3 to the Geneva Conventions in 1949 and continues to this day. The purpose of this regulation is to limit the suffering and destruction caused by non-international armed conflicts which now constitute the most prevalent form of armed conflict. The Second Protocol is part and parcel of the development over the last sixty years of increasing regulation of non-international armed conflict.

This contribution will focus on three elements of this historic development:

1. the extension of the application of the rules protecting cultural property to non-international armed conflicts;
2. the extension of the rules on the conduct of hostilities to non-international armed conflicts and their application to cultural property; and
3. the enforcement of the rules applicable to cultural property in non-international armed conflicts.

* Jean-Marie Henckaerts is a legal adviser in the Legal Division of the ICRC and head of the ICRC's project on customary international humanitarian law. He followed, on behalf of the ICRC (which had observer status at the Diplomatic Conference in The Hague), the negotiation and adoption of the Second Protocol. This article reflects the views of the author and not necessarily those of the ICRC.

Nout van Woudenberg and Liesbeth Lijnzaad (eds.) Protecting Cultural Property in Armed Conflict
© *2010 Koninklijke Brill NV. Printed in The Netherlands.* *ISBN 978 9004 18377 3 pp. 81–93.*

2. The extension of the application of the rules protecting cultural property to non-international armed conflicts

2.1 The 1954 Convention

Although the special protection due to cultural property was recognised as early as 1899,[1] it was only in 1954 that a more elaborate, specific regime for the protection of cultural property in armed conflict was created.[2] This was less than 5 years after the adoption of the Geneva Conventions, including its groundbreaking Article 3. Article 3, common to the four Geneva Conventions of 1949, constitutes the first treaty rule that formally applies to an armed conflict 'not of an international character'.[3] The approach adopted in common Article 3 is to apply a minimum of basic rules to all conflicts which are not of an international character. This 'minimal' approach is supplemented by the encouragement for the parties to an armed conflict to conclude 'special agreements' that extend all or further parts of the Geneva Conventions to their conflict. Another important element is the explicit recognition that the application of common Article 3 does not affect the legal status of the parties to the conflict.

With respect to the protection of cultural property in non-international armed conflicts, the 1954 Convention followed the model of common Article 3 of the Geneva Conventions. As a result, the 1954 Convention extends as a minimum the

---

1 Regulations concerning the Laws and Customs of War on Land, annexed to Convention (II) with Respect to the Laws and Customs of War on Land, The Hague, 29 July 1899, Article 27 ('In sieges and bombardments all necessary steps should be taken to spare as far as possible edifices devoted to religion, art, science, and charity, [...] provided they are not used at the same time for military purposes.') and Article 56 ('All seizure of and destruction, or intentional damage done to [religious, charitable, and educational] institutions [and those of arts and science], historic monuments, works of art and science, is prohibited, and should be made the subject of proceedings.') See also Regulations concerning the Laws and Customs of War on Land, annexed to Convention (IV) respecting the Laws and Customs of War on Land, The Hague, 18 October 1907, Articles 27 and 56.

2 Convention for the Protection of Cultural Property in the Event of Armed Conflict, The Hague, 14 May 1954. For a detailed commentary, see Jiří Toman, *The Protection of Cultural Property in the Event of Armed Conflict. Commentary on the Convention for the Protection of Cultural Property in the Event of Armed Conflict and its Protocol, signed on 14 May 1954 in The Hague, and on other Instruments of International Law Concerning Such Protection*, Paris/Aldershot, Unesco/Dartmouth, 1996. It should be noted, however, that prior to the 1954 Hague Convention a regional convention was developed in the Americas, the so-called 'Roerich Pact', i.e. Treaty on the Protection of Artistic and Scientific Institutions and Historic Monuments, Washington, 15 April 1935.

3 For more detailed commentary on common Article 3, see Eve La Haye, 'Common Article 3', in Antonio Cassese (ed.), *The Oxford Companion to International Criminal Justice*, Oxford University Press, 2009, p. 274; Lindsay Moir, *The law of internal armed conflict*, Cambridge University Press, 2002, pp. 30–88; Djamchid Momtaz, 'Le droit international humanitaire applicable aux conflits armés non internationaux', *Recueil des cours*, Vol. 292, 2001, pp. 9–146.

rules on 'respect' for cultural property to non-international armed conflicts.[4] In addition, the 1954 Convention encourages the parties to the conflict to conclude 'special agreements' to extend all or parts of the Convention to the conflict. Whereas common Article 3 provides that an impartial humanitarian organisation, such as the International Committee of the Red Cross (ICRC), may offer its services to the parties to the conflict, Article 19 of the 1954 Hague Convention provides that the United Nations Educational, Scientific and Cultural Organisation (UNESCO) may offer its services to the parties to the conflict.

2.2 The 1999 Second Protocol

When in 1999 the Second Protocol was negotiated, 50 years after the adoption of the 1949 Geneva Conventions and 45 years after the adoption of the 1954 Hague Convention, it could be expected that the Second Protocol would apply to non-international armed conflicts, although this was not a foregone conclusion.[5] The novelty is that the entire Protocol as such is declared applicable to non-international armed conflicts. This is a significant departure from the minimalist approach which marked the Geneva Conventions of 1949 (common Article 3) and the Hague Convention of 1954 (Article 19). The relevant provision of the Second Protocol is Article 22

Paragraph 1 of this provision declares that the Protocol as such applies to any non-international armed conflict occurring within the territory of one of the Parties. However, the provision does not spell out to whom the obligations applicable in a non-international armed conflict are addressed – to States only or to non-State armed groups as well? The problem with the Second Protocol is that the term 'Party to the conflict' is used alongside the term 'party to the conflict' and that the term 'Party' is defined as 'a State Party to this Protocol'.[6] A literal interpretation of the Second Protocol would therefore imply that those provisions which apply to each 'party to the conflict' would cover non-State armed groups, whereas provisions addressed to each 'Party to the conflict' would be limited to States Parties to the Protocol.

However, it is argued that an interpretation 'in good faith in accordance with the ordinary meaning to be given to the terms of the treaty in their context and in the light of its object and purpose' would suggest that all the relevant provisions of the Second Protocol – whether they use the term 'Party' or 'party' to conflict – apply to both State and non-State parties to a non-international armed conflict.[7] This was also clearly acknowledged at the final plenary. The understanding during the negotiation was that throughout the text the term 'Party to the conflict' includes armed groups operating in States Party to the Second Protocol but does not include third

4 The relevant provision is Article 4 on 'Respect for Cultural Property' (see *infra* Section 2(a)).

5 Roger O'Keefe, *The Protection of Cultural Property in Armed Conflict*, Cambridge University Press, 2006, p. 246.

6 This definition is contained in Article 1(a) of the 1999 Second Protocol.

7 See Vienna Convention on the Law of Treaties, Vienna, 23 May 1969, Article 31 (General Rule of Interpretation); 1155 UNTS 332.

States which have not ratified the Second Protocol.[8] The reasoning was that armed groups involved in a non-international armed conflict in a State Party to the Protocol are bound by the Protocol through the ratification of the State concerned. This interpretation makes sense in the light of the evolution from the 1954 Hague Convention to the 1999 Second Protocol as well as other developments in international humanitarian law applicable to non-international armed conflicts. It should also be noted that Article 3 common to the 1949 Geneva Conventions and Article 19 of the 1954 Convention itself already used the term 'Party to the conflict' to cover non-State armed groups. Furthermore, a literal interpretation would lead to a manifestly absurd result of declaring a treaty applicable to non-international armed conflicts and at the same time eliminating most of its practical relevance in such conflicts.[9]

As a result, a number of provisions apply to all parties to a conflict in non-international armed conflicts – notwithstanding the fact that some are addressed to each 'Party to the conflict'.[10] On the other hand, a number of provisions which are relevant to non-international armed conflicts are addressed to States only, in particular provisions related to the implementation and enforcement of the Protocol.[11]

It was unfortunate that the potential confusion of the definition of 'Party' and the use of the term 'Party to the conflict' alongside the term 'party to the conflict' was only recognised in the last hours of the Diplomatic Conference. As a result, there was no discussion on whether the general understanding that the Second Protocol applies to governmental forces and armed groups in a non-international armed conflict also applies to Article 11(9) (Request for enhanced protection on an emergency

8 Third States which have not ratified the Second Protocol are generally referred to as 'party' (in lower case). See, e.g., Second Protocol, *supra* note 6, Article 3(2) and Article 32(2) and (4).

9 See Vienna Convention on the Law of Treaties, Vienna, 23 May 1969, Article 32(b) (Supplementary Means of Interpretation).

10 These are in particular: Article 6 (Respect for cultural property); Article 7 (Precautions in attack); Article 8 (Precautions against the effects of hostilities); Article 12 (Immunity of cultural property under enhanced protection); Article 13 (Loss of enhanced protection); Article 32 (International assistance); Article 33 (Assistance of UNESCO – if offered in accordance with Article 22(7)); Article 34 (Protecting Powers); Article 35 (Conciliation procedure) and Article 36 (Conciliation in absence of Protecting Powers). Article 15(1) (Serious violations) applies on an individual basis, including to members of armed groups.

11 These are in particular: Article 5 (Safeguarding of cultural property); Article 15(2) (Serious violations of the Protocol – obligation to establish criminal offences under domestic law); Article 16 (Jurisdiction); Article 17 (Prosecution); Article 18 (Extradition); Article 19 (Mutual legal assistance); Article 20 (Grounds for refusal of extradition); Article 21 (Legislative, administrative or disciplinary measures to suppress other acts); Article 23 (Meeting of the Parties, e.g. paragraph 3(e) to discuss any problem related to the application of the Protocol, including in non-international armed conflicts); Articles 24–28 (Committee for the Protection of Cultural Property, e.g. Article 27 on the functions of the Committee to develop Guidelines for the implementation of the Protocol, including in non-international armed conflicts); Article 29 (Fund for the Protection of Cultural Property in the Event of Armed Conflict, can be used to protect cultural property in non-international armed conflicts); Article 30 (Dissemination); Article 31 (International cooperation); Article 32(1) (International assistance – request by States); Article 37 (Translation and reports).

basis). It is difficult to say whether this was indeed the intention of States as the Working Group on Chapter 3 (Enhanced Protection) did not discuss the issue. On the other hand, on the basis of the above considerations, there is nothing to suggest the contrary, particularly in the light of the object and purpose of the Second Protocol and the fact that its application does not affect the legal status of the parties to the conflict.[12]

The Protocol only applies to non-international armed conflicts, not to situations which do not constitute an armed conflict. Paragraph 2 of Article 22 defines this lower threshold as situations of internal disturbances and tensions, such as riots, isolated and sporadic acts of violence and other acts of a similar nature. This definition is inspired by the same definition provided for in Additional Protocol II.[13] Although it defines the lower threshold, the 1999 Second Protocol does not attempt to give a precise definition of the notion of non-international armed conflict and, as a result, shares the definitional problems that arise under other treaties.[14]

Paragraph 3 of Article 22 provides that the Second Protocol may not be invoked for the purpose of affecting the sovereignty of a State or the responsibility of the government, by all legitimate means, to maintain or re-establish law and order in the State or to defend the national unity and territorial integrity of the State. This underlines the 'neutral' character of the Second Protocol. As with other treaties of international humanitarian law, the Second Protocol is intended to protect property in armed conflicts, regardless of which side it belongs to, regardless of where it is located and regardless of the political motives for the conflict. Therefore the Second Protocol cannot be invoked to address political questions related to sovereignty, national unity and territorial integrity. A related provision is paragraph 5 of Article 22 which provides that the Second Protocol cannot serve as a pretext to vio-

---

12 See Second Protocol, Article 22(6).

13 Protocol Additional to the Geneva Conventions of 12 August 1949, and Relating to the Protection of Victims of Non-International Armed Conflicts, Geneva, 8 June 1977, Article 1 (2) ('Additional Protocol II').

14 On the definition of non-international armed conflict, see, e.g., Anthony Cullen, *The Concept of Non-International Armed Conflict in International Humanitarian Law*, Cambridge University Press, 2010; Anthony Cullen, 'The Definition of Non-International Armed Conflict in the Rome Statute of the International Criminal Court: An Analysis of the Threshold of Application Contained in Article 8(2)(f)', *Journal of Conflict & Security Law*, Vol. 12, 2007, p. 419; Anthony Cullen, 'Key Developments Affecting the Scope of Internal Armed Conflict in International Humanitarian Law', *Military Law Review*, Vol. 183, 2005, p. 65; Anthony Cullen, 'The Parameters of Internal Armed Conflict in International Humanitarian Law', *University of Miami International and Comparative Law Review*, Vol. 12, 2004, p. 189; How is the Term 'Armed Conflict' Defined in International Humanitarian Law?, International Committee of the Red Cross (ICRC), Opinion Paper, March 2008, available on www.icrc.org/eng/ihl (last visited on 17 September 2009); Jelena Pejic, 'Status of armed conflicts', Elizabeth Wilmshurst and Susan Breau (eds.), *Perspectives on the ICRC Study on Customary International Humanitarian Law*, Chatham House, British Institute of International and Comparative Law and Cambridge University Press, 2007, p. 77; Sylvain Vité, 'Typology of armed conflicts in international humanitarian law: legal concepts and actual situations', *International Review of the Red Cross*, Vol. 91, No. 873, 2009, p. 75.

late the principle of non-intervention in the internal or external affairs of the Party in the territory of which that conflict occurs.

The phrase in paragraph 4 of Article 22 that nothing in the Protocol shall prejudice 'the primary jurisdiction' of a State in whose territory a non-international armed conflict occurs over the serious violations of the Protocol was added at the request of China and India. This means that the territorial State has the primary responsibility to exercise jurisdiction over such violations: to investigate, prosecute and punish the offenders. But it implies that if such jurisdiction is not exercised, jurisdiction may be exercised by other States or by international criminal tribunals.

Paragraph 6 of Article 22 reiterates the text of the 1954 Hague Convention to the effect that the application of the Protocol does not alter the legal status of the parties to the conflict. Paragraph 7, finally, reiterates the text of the 1954 Hague Convention that UNESCO may offer its services to the parties to the conflict. It should be noted that Article 33 of the Second Protocol specifies that UNESCO may offer technical assistance in organising the protection of cultural property, such as preventive and organisational measures for emergency situations.

3. The extension of the rules on the conduct of hostilities to non-international armed conflicts and their application to cultural property

At the outset, international humanitarian treaty law offered only a rudimentary framework for the regulation of non-international armed conflicts, in particular with respect to the conduct of hostilities. Common Article 3 of the 1949 Geneva Conventions does not even deal with the conduct of hostilities as such. The following overview puts the 1999 Second Protocol in a historical perspective that aims to illustrate the importance it has had in consolidating the extension of rules on the conduct of hostilities to non-international armed conflicts.

3.1 The 1954 Hague Convention

The 1954 Hague Convention pioneered a change by introducing in Article 4 basic rules on the conduct of hostilities aimed at protecting cultural property, including in non-international armed conflicts.[15] That provision was the first treaty provision extending the application of rules on the conduct of hostilities to non-international armed conflicts. The High Contracting Parties undertake to respect cultural property situated within their own territory as well as within the territory of other High Contracting Parties by refraining from any use of the property and its immediate surroundings or of the appliances in use for its protection for purposes which are likely to expose it to destruction or damage in the event of armed conflict; and by refraining from any act of hostility directed against such property. These obligations may be waived only in cases where military necessity imperatively requires such a waiver.

15 The extension to non-international armed conflicts is based on the 1954 Hague Convention, Article 19.

3.2 Additional Protocol II

Although it was meant to supplement common Article 3, Additional Protocol II does not deal with the conduct of hostilities in much detail. For example, unlike Additional Protocol I, Additional Protocol II does not provide for the obligation to distinguish between military objectives and civilian objects. As a result, it does not contain any specific rule on the protection of civilian objects in general, nor does it define civilian objects and military objectives. Additional Protocol II lacks other key provisions on the conduct of hostilities, such as the prohibition and definition of indiscriminate attacks and the obligation to take precautions in attack and against the effects of attack.

Detailed provisions on the conduct of hostilities can be found in Additional Protocol I but not in Additional Protocol II, even though the draft of the protocol did contain them. In fact, the original drafts of both protocols submitted by the ICRC to the diplomatic conference that led to the adoption of the Additional Protocols were very similar.[16] Even during the diplomatic conference that led to the adoption of the Additional Protocols, Committee III, which worked on the draft of Protocol II, accepted a substantial number of the draft provisions submitted by the ICRC, often with consensus, although sometimes with minor changes. But in the final weeks of a four-year negotiation process many parts of draft Protocol II were simply deleted. The main reason for this was that it transpired during the diplomatic conference that consensus could only be reached on a much simplified text, not on the version elaborated by Committee III on the basis of the ICRC draft. This simplification process consisted, in particular, of removing or revising all articles that referred to the 'parties to the conflict'. A good example of this diplomatic manoeuvre is the provision on dissemination in the Additional Protocols. Whereas Additional Protocol I imposes an obligation on all 'High Contracting Parties' to disseminate the Conventions and the Protocol as widely as possible;[17] Additional Protocol II summarily requires that '[t]his Protocol shall be disseminated as widely as possible' without specifying to whom this obligation is addressed.[18] At the time, a number of States could not accept that armed groups as 'parties to the conflict' would have specific rights and obligations under international law, e.g. the obligation to disseminate humanitarian law.

This reluctance was based on the reasoning of then newly independent States that recognition of such rights and obligations and, in general, detailed regulation of non-international armed conflicts would encourage rebellion and secession, threatening their frail sovereignty. However, this reasoning was misleading as recognition of rights and obligations of armed opposition groups under international law predated Protocol II by at least 30 years. Indeed, as indicated above, common Article 3 of the

---

16 ICRC, Draft Additional Protocols to the Geneva Conventions of August 12, 1949, Geneva, June 1973, published in Official Records of the Diplomatic Conference on the Reaffirmation and Development of International Humanitarian Law Applicable in Armed Conflicts, Geneva, 1974–1977, Volume I.

17 Protocol Additional to the Geneva Conventions of 12 August 1949, and Relating to the Protection of Victims of International Armed Conflict, Geneva, 8 June 1977, Article 83(1) (hereinafter 'Additional Protocol I').

18 Additional Protocol II, *supra* note 13, Article 19.

Geneva Conventions already imposed obligations on 'each Party to the conflict' not of an international character and even encouraged the parties to 'further endeavour to bring into force, by means of special agreements, all or part of the other provisions of the present Convention' and so went further than Additional Protocol II.

The simplification process of Additional Protocol II has, unfortunately, left the Protocol with an awkward structure. The basic rules on the distinction between military objectives and civilian objects and their definition are missing, but detailed rules on specific objects, namely objects indispensable to the survival of the civilian population, works and installations containing dangerous forces and cultural objects and places of worship, were left in the Protocol.[19] As a result, the protection of cultural property again spearheaded the extension of the rules on the conduct of hostilities to non-international armed conflicts. The relevant provision of Additional Protocol II is Article 16 and states that without prejudice to the provisions of the 1954 Hague Convention, it is prohibited to commit any acts of hostility directed against historic monuments, works of art or places of worship which constitute the cultural or spiritual heritage of peoples, and to use them in support of the military effort.

Nevertheless, aside from the material scope of application, this provision merely corresponds to Article 4 of the 1954 Hague Convention prohibiting attacks on cultural property, as well as their use for military purposes.

3.3 Convention on Certain Conventional Weapons (CCW)

The next treaty to explicitly extend its application to non-international armed conflicts after the adoption of Additional Protocol in 1977 was the Protocol on Prohibitions or Restrictions on the Use of Mines, Booby-Traps and Other Devices, as amended on 3 May 1996 (CCW Amended Protocol II).[20] Unlike the original CCW Protocol II, the CCW Amended Protocol II was made applicable to non-international armed conflicts and includes a number of basic rules on the conduct of hostilities.[21] The CCW Amended Protocol II provides that its application 'to parties to a conflict, which are not High Contracting Parties […] shall not change their legal status or the legal status of a disputed territory, either explicitly or implicitly'.[22]

19 Additional Protocol II, *supra* note 13, Article 14 (objects indispensable to the survival of the civilian population), Article 15 (works and installations containing dangerous forces) and Article 16 (cultural objects and places of worship).

20 Convention on Prohibitions or Restrictions on the Use of Certain Conventional Weapons Which May be Deemed to be Excessively Injurious or to Have Indiscriminate Effects, Geneva, 10 October 1980, 1342 UNTS 137, (hereinafter 'CCW'), Protocol on Prohibitions or Restrictions on the Use of Mines, Booby-Traps and Other Devices, as Amended, Geneva, 3 May 1996 ('CCW, Amended Protocol II').

21 These include in particular: the prohibition against attacking civilian objects in Article 3(7); the definition of military objectives in Article 2(6); the definition of civilian objects in Article 2(7); the prohibition and definition of indiscriminate use of weapons in Article 3(8); the principle of proportionality in Article 3(8)(c); the prohibition of so-called 'area bombardments' in Article 3(9); the obligation to take all feasible precautions to protect civilians in Article 3(10); and the obligation to give an effective advance warning in Article 3(11) of CCW, Amended Protocol II, *supra* note 20.

22 CCW, Amended Protocol II, *supra* note 20, Article 1(6).

In December 2001, Article 1 of the Convention on Certain Conventional Weapons (CCW) was modified to extend the scope of application of all then existing Protocols to non-international armed conflicts, as defined in common Article 3 of the Geneva Conventions. As explained above, until then only Amended Protocol II had applied to non-international armed conflicts. Since then, Protocols I-IV have been applicable to non-international armed conflicts for States that have ratified the amendment of Article 1. This means that the provisions in the Protocols related to the conduct of hostilities which were hitherto limited to international armed conflict became applicable to non-international armed conflict as well.[23]

3.4 ICC Statute

The adoption of the Rome Statute of the International Criminal Court ('ICC Statute') in 1998 was the next important step in the development of treaty law governing non-international armed conflict. Although the ICC Statute constitutes a giant step forward in the recognition of individual criminal responsibility for serious violations of international humanitarian law in non-international armed conflicts, it was a rather hesitant step in terms of the substantive law applicable in such conflicts. Indeed, the list of war crimes for non-international armed conflicts is considerably shorter than the list for international armed conflicts and omissions related to the conduct of hostilities include, in particular, attacks against civilian objects and attacks which cause excessive incidental injury, loss of life or damage to civilians and civilian objects.[24] This is all the more surprising since the list of war crimes in non-international armed conflicts considers it a war crime to direct attacks against installations, material, units or vehicles involved in a humanitarian assistance or peacekeeping mission 'as long as they are entitled to the protection given to [...] *civilian objects* under the international law of armed conflict' and, thereby, recognises the protection of civilian objects in such conflicts.[25] It can be argued that the war crime of destruction of the property of an adversary unless such destruction be imperatively demanded by the necessities of the conflict could cover cases of attacks against civil-

23 These include: the prohibition against attacking civilian objects in CCW, Protocol on Prohibitions or Restrictions on the Use of Incendiary Weapons, Geneva, 10 October 1980, Article 2(1) ('Protocol III'); the definition of military objectives in CCW, Protocol on Prohibitions or Restrictions on the Use of Mines, Booby-Traps and Other Devices, Geneva, 10 October 1980, Article 2(4) ('Protocol II') and in Protocol III, Article 1(3); the definition of civilian objects in CCW, Protocol II, Article 2(5) and in Protocol III, Article 1(4); the prohibition of indiscriminate use of weapons in CCW, Protocol II, Article 3(3); the definition of indiscriminate attacks in CCW, Protocol II, Article 3(3)(a)–(c); the principle of proportionality in CCW, Protocol II, Article 3(3)(c); the obligation to take all feasible precautions to protect civilians in CCW, Protocol II, Article 3(4), in Protocol III, Article 2(3) and in Protocol (V) on Explosive Remnants of War, Geneva, 28 November 2003, Articles 3–5; and the obligation to give an effective advance warning in CCW, Protocol II, Articles 4(2)(b) and 5(2).

24 These violations are listed as war crimes in international, but not in non-international armed conflicts. See Statute of the International Criminal Court, Rome, 17 July 1998, 2187 UNTS 90, Article 8(2)(b)(ii) and (iv).

25 Statute of the International Criminal Court, *supra* note 24, Article 8(2)(e)(iii).

ian objects.[26] It is also remarkable that while a significant advance in the substantive law on non-international armed conflicts was made in the area of weapons (CCW, as explained above), the ICC Statute does not explicitly criminalise the use of any prohibited weapons in non-international armed conflicts.

Notwithstanding these gaps in the ICC Statute, attention was given to the protection of cultural property. Under the ICC Statute 'intentionally directing attacks against buildings dedicated to religion, education, art, science or charitable purposes, historic monuments, [...] provided they are not military objectives' constitutes a war crime in non-international armed conflicts. This wording is derived from Article 27 of the 1899 and 1907 Hague Regulations updated with a reference to 'military objectives' taken from the 1977 Additional Protocol I. However, it must be noted that the Hague Regulations (and Additional Protocol I) do not as such apply to non-international armed conflicts. Nevertheless, it is not disputed that this crime, as applicable to non-international armed conflicts, is a codification of customary international law.

3.5 The 1999 Second Protocol

When a year later, in 1999, the Second Protocol to The Hague Convention for the protection of cultural property was negotiated, a significant advance was made in the application of the rules on the conduct of hostilities in non-international armed conflicts. Indeed, by then it had become more widely accepted that a number of provisions on the conduct of hostilities apply in non-international armed conflicts, in particular on the basis of customary international law.[27] As a result, during the negotiations on the Second Protocol, the inclusion of the following rules on the conduct of hostilities, and their application to non-international armed conflicts, was largely uncontroversial:

- the prohibition against attacking civilian objects;[28]
- the definition of military objectives;[29]
- the obligation to take all feasible precautions in attack;[30]
- the obligation to give an effective advance warning whenever circumstances permit;[31] and
- the obligation to take all feasible precautions against the effects of hostilities.[32]

---

26 Statute of the International Criminal Court, *supra* note 24, Article 8(2)(e)(xii).

27 See Jean-Marie Henckaerts and Louise Doswald-Beck, *Customary International Humanitarian Law*, Volume I: Rules, Cambridge University Press, 2005, pp. 3–76.

28 Second Protocol, Article 6(a)(i) (*a contrario*).

29 Second Protocol, Article 1(f).

30 Second Protocol, Article 7 (containing a list of detailed precautionary measures very similar to those listed in Article 57(2) of Additional Protocol I).

31 Second Protocol, Article 6(d).

32 Second Protocol, Article 8 (containing a list of detailed precautionary measures very similar to those listed in Article 58(a) and (b) of Additional Protocol I).

These provisions are commented on in more detail by this author elsewhere in this volume.[33]

It seems, therefore, that after the consolidation of many States that were newly independent in the 1970s, it was possible in the 1990s to gradually extend the treaty rules on the conduct of hostilities to non-international armed conflicts, culminating in the adoption of the Second Protocol in 1999 and the amendment of Article 1 of the CCW in 2001.

4. The enforcement of the rules applicable to cultural property in non-international armed conflicts

Although the 1954 Hague Convention contains some provisions that are relevant to its enforcement in non-international armed conflicts, the 1999 Second Protocol took the issue of enforcement in such conflicts substantially further.

4.1 The 1954 Hague Convention

Article 19 of the 1954 Hague Convention declares only the provisions which relate to respect for cultural property – set out in Article 4 – explicitly applicable in non-international armed conflicts. Nevertheless, other provisions of the 1954 Hague Convention also have a potential effect on non-international armed conflicts. The provision on sanctions, for example, seems to be a case in point. The relevant provision, Article 28, would require States to cover violations of Article 4 of the 1954 Hague Convention in their national legislation, including in non-international armed conflicts.

4.2 The 1999 Second Protocol

The Second Protocol takes a more comprehensive approach based on developments since the adoption of the 1954 Hague Convention. Whereas Additional Protocol I of 1977 establishes a coherent system of criminal repression, this system is limited to international armed conflicts. Additional Protocol II of 1977, on the other hand, does not provide a system of criminal repression with respect to non-international armed conflicts. This gap as regards non-international armed conflicts was filled in part by the ICC Statute.[34] Although the war crime against cultural property in the ICC Statute refers back to the 1899 and 1907 Hague Regulations, rather than to the 1954 Hague Convention, it does apply to both international and non-international armed conflicts.[35]

33 See Jean-Marie Henckaerts, *New rules for the protection of cultural property in armed conflict: The significance of the Second Protocol to the 1954 Hague Convention for the Protection of Cultural Property in the Event of Armed Conflict,* in this book pp. 21-41.

34 For an in-depth analysis, see Eve La Haye, *War Crimes in Internal Armed Conflicts*, Cambridge University Press, 2008.

35 See *supra* section 3.4.

It is of particular importance, therefore, that the entire Second Protocol, including the section on criminal repression, applies to non-international armed conflicts. This probably explains the choice of language in Article 22(1).[36] This extension reflects a modern tendency as more and more national legislations, for example, no longer distinguish between international and non-international armed conflict when it comes to repression of violations of humanitarian law. In addition, as pointed out above, the ICC also has jurisdiction over war crimes committed against cultural property in both international and non-international armed conflict.

As a result, the Second Protocol contains a substantial part on criminal responsibility and jurisdiction (Chapter 4), applicable in both international and non-international armed conflicts. As a result, the Second Protocol can be said to be an instrument of international humanitarian law, cultural property law, as well as international criminal law. Chapter 4 of the Second Protocol deals with:

- Serious violations of the Second Protocol (Article 15)
- Jurisdiction (Article 16)
- Prosecution (Article 17)
- Extradition (Article 18)
- Mutual legal assistance (Article 19)
- Grounds for refusal (Article 20)
- Measures regarding other violations (Article 21)

These provisions are commented on in more detail elsewhere in this volume.[37]

5. Conclusion

The above overview has tried to show the extent to which the Second Protocol reflects developments in international law, as stated in its preamble. In doing so, it has focused on developments in the law governing non-international armed conflicts. This area of international humanitarian law has significantly expanded since 1949, including the rules on the conduct of hostilities and the rules on enforcement. These developments are necessary as most armed conflicts today are of a non-international character.

The Second Protocol is therefore a modern instrument that is at the crossroads of international humanitarian law, cultural property law and international crimi-

---

36 The Second Protocol, Article 22(1) declares that 'This Protocol shall apply in the event of an armed conflict not of an international character, occurring within the territory of one of the Parties' rather than stating that 'each party to the conflict' has to abide by the Protocol's provisions. The provisions of Chapter 4, in particular, apply to non-international armed conflicts but are not addressed to 'each party to the conflict', only to States, i.e. States have to implement the rules on criminal responsibility and jurisdiction in Chapter 4.

37 See Jean-Marie Henckaerts, *New rules for the protection of cultural property in armed conflict: The significance of the Second Protocol to the 1954 Hague Convention for the Protection of Cultural Property in the Event of Armed Conflict*, in this book, pp. 21-41. See also Nout van Woudenberg, *Elaboration and legal implementation of the 1999 Second Protocol: the Dutch finger on the pulse*, in this book, pp. 107-115.

nal law. It is to be hoped that it will be widely adhered to and implemented as soon as possible. The world's cultural property deserves the protection of the Second Protocol.

Chapter 9

Dissemination of the 1954 Hague Convention and the 1999 Second Protocol: Embedding cultural property protection within the military

*Joris D. Kila**

All truth passes through three stages. First, it is ridiculed. Second, it is violently opposed. Third, it is accepted as being self-evident.[1]

1. Introduction

Preceding the symposium organised by the Dutch Ministries of Foreign Affairs, Education, Culture & Science and Defence to mark the tenth anniversary of the Second Protocol to the 1954 Hague Convention, the Ministry of Defence organised a seminar on 'Cultural property protection in the event of armed conflict'.[2] This can be considered as a contribution to the Netherlands' obligation concerning dissemination of the 1954 Hague Convention[3] and the 1999 Second Protocol.[4] Organised by the Operational Preparedness Department (DAOG), the Ministry emphasised the importance and relevance of cultural property protection (henceforth: CPP) for military operations. The seminar's overall theme was the legal basis for and different aspects of CPP (and cultural property as such) as seen from both Dutch and international military perspectives. Participants concluded that it is vital to diffuse CPP expertise throughout the armed forces, as otherwise military organisations and

---

* Lieutenant-Colonel (reserve); adviser to the Dutch Ministry of Defence on the protection of cultural property and member of the International Military Cultural Resources Working Group (IMCRWG). This article was written in his personal capacity. The opinions in this essay are solely his and do not necessarily represent those of the Kingdom of the Netherlands.

1 Arthur Schopenhauer.

2 Internationally renowned experts from different countries, such as Austria, the Netherlands, the United Kingdom and the United States, presented the activities and views of their countries' militaries on the subject. Other participants included military and civilian representatives from China, Denmark, France, Germany, Iran, Israel, Japan and Poland. Topics discussed and analysed ranged from the origins of the growing interest in cultural property protection (CPP) to the increasing awareness of its importance. The seminar adopted several recommendations.

3 Article 25, Dissemination of the Convention.

4 Article 30: Dissemination.

Nout van Woudenberg and Liesbeth Lijnzaad (eds.) Protecting Cultural Property in Armed Conflict
© *2010 Koninklijke Brill NV. Printed in The Netherlands.* *ISBN 978 9004 18377 3 pp. 95–105.*

commanders cannot make sound judgments in the situations described in the 1954 Hague Convention and the 1999 Second Protocol.

To grasp the complex issues surrounding CPP, such as the wide range of interests at stake, different cultural backgrounds, types of expertise, and religious, scientific, social, ethnographic, political, historical, philosophical, legal, ethical, sociological and linguistic considerations, a number of key issues will be identified and addressed:

- The importance of CPP , especially for military organisations;
- The relationship between CPP and the Comprehensive Approach;
- The advantages of implementation of CCP by the armed forces;
- The activities of national and international organisations and countries in this field.

2. The importance of CPP, especially for military organisations

At present nations, peoples and groups seem increasingly driven to define or reaffirm themselves as distinctive entities. This creates a complex of tensions, in which a sense of identity is central and conflicting processes of identity formation and maintenance by other nations and groups also play a role. Protection and destruction of cultural property[5] are both part of these processes. Recent armed conflicts (as in Yugoslavia, Iraq and Afghanistan) and especially intrastate conflicts have the feature in common that they are culturally conditioned or even determined. In some cases the parties deliberately try to destroy or damage their opponents' material or other expressions of identity. We have seen clear examples of this in former Yugoslavia – the destruction of the Mostar bridge and of the Sarajevo library, for instance – and in Afghanistan. Such acts are sometimes referred to as a kind of rape. The term 'rape' is often used in contemporary literature on CPP and looting, as in 'the rape of Europe' (the destruction of cultural property during the Second World War) and 'the rape of Mesopotamia' (Iraq).

This explains why military organisations should deal with CPP. The fact that cultural property can be a driving force behind human identity, history, progress and in some cases economies makes CPP a matter of strategic importance for belligerents and subsequently for military peacekeeping and stabilisation operations. As mentioned above, many conflicts have a cultural dimension: one side aims to destroy its opponent's cultural heritage as a means of undermining its identity. Looting, stealing and trafficking in cultural artefacts during a conflict or in its immediate aftermath, as seen in World War II, has re-emerged as a side-effect of conflict in countries such as Iraq and Afghanistan. Accordingly archaeological sites and premises like museums, archives, libraries and monuments must be protected. Cultural property can be more effectively protected during conflicts through military channels and with military logistics and tools, especially when the security situation does not allow civilian experts to be deployed and civilian agencies like the police are no longer able to act.

CPP in time of conflict requires prior national and international preparation in peacetime. Apart from the peacetime obligations laid out in the 1954 Hague

5 The term 'cultural property' is used here as defined in Article 1 of the 1954 Hague Convention.

Convention[6] and the 1999 Second Protocol, however, CPP means protecting cultural property during military operations. During such operations cultural property can be exposed to possible damage inflicted by a country's own forces or by plunder and theft by local populations, criminal networks or opposing militant forces (OMF).[7]

The use of Hescos[8] without consulting a CPP expert is an example of how damage can be inflicted, sometimes unintentionally, by a country's own forces. Hescos are large containers filled with sand or rubble that serve as barriers for military camps and fortifications. There are cases known in which Hescos were filled with deposits from archaeological sites containing pottery fragments, bones etcetera, possibly in violation of the 1954 Hague Convention or the 1999 Second Protocol.[9] The soil in an archaeological site contains a range of data that is only useful when extracted by experts from their original context. For instance, layers of earth can yield information through stratigraphic data; pottery pieces in particular are an important dating tool. When Hescos are filled with such deposits, the context of the site is disturbed and it becomes very difficult or even impossible to do archaeological research. Even worse are situations where, after a complaint is made about the use of archaeological deposits, these deposits are replaced and dumped on another archaeological site, thus disturbing the context at a second location.[10]

As mentioned above, trafficking in and looting (often commissioned) of artefacts in war-stricken areas and the plunder of archaeological sites are often practised by OMF. Just as often, however, these practices are driven by economic motives. In the case of Uruk,[11] the economic incentive was neutralised by Dutch military experts' offering modest payments to local guards.[12] The whole complex of looting, theft

6 See Articles 3 and 4 of the 1954 Hague Convention on safeguarding and respecting cultural property and on preparing in peacetime to safeguard cultural property within a country's own territory as well as within the territory of other States Parties.

7 Sometimes referred to as insurgents.

8 Also known as Concertainer™ barriers, these were originally produced by the UK company Hercules Engineering Solutions Consortium (HESCO).

9 See Articles 3 (Safeguarding of cultural property), 4 (Respect for cultural property), 5.2 (Occupation) and 7 (Military measures) of the 1954 Hague Convention, and Articles 5 (Safeguarding of cultural property) and 9 (Protection of cultural property in occupied territory) of the 1999 Second Protocol.

10 John Curtis, Keeper of the Department of the Ancient Near East at the British Museum, gives examples in his Report on Meeting at Babylon 11-13 December 2004.

11 Uruk – its modern name is Warka – is situated in the former area of responsibility of the Dutch military forces in the province of Al Muthanna It is one of the oldest cities of South-Mesopotamia situated at a branch of the Euphrates River approximately halfway between Baghdad and Basrah in Iraq. Uruk appears in the Bible as Erech. Already from 5000 BC people inhabited the site. The most important period in Uruk's history was the era between approximately 3400 and 2800 B.C, the time of the so-called 'high civilisation' .The site of Uruk was discovered in 1849 and excavations have meanwhile exposed part of the city.

12 Joris D. Kila, 'Utilizing Military Cultural Experts in Times of War and Peace: An Introduction – Cultural Property Protection within the Military, Experience in Theatre, Different Perceptions of Culture and Practical Problems', in *Culture and International Law*, ed. Paul Meerts (The Hague: Hague Academic Press, 2008), pp. 183-229.

and smuggling of artefacts is market-driven and based on the rising international demand for antiquities. Since there is a finite supply of objects offered for trade, any increase can only come from illicit sources.[13] Buying objects from such sources encourages more theft and pillaging and helps finance the conflict. In this context, CPP is a way of denying resources to the opposing forces.

The 1999 Second Protocol is much more concrete in addressing a range of military-related aspects as well as dissemination. This makes proper training and awareness-raising for armed forces with regard to the 1954 Hague Convention and its Protocols even more indispensable.

In an effort to improve the protection of cultural property, the US currently uses a small pocket guide with instructions on how to recognise certain cultural and archaeological objects. There is also a Civil Affairs Arts Monuments and Archives Guide issued by the US Department of the Army.[14] The Netherlands, like the US, has given out decks of CPP playing cards as a tool in training military personnel for peacekeeping or peace enforcement missions abroad.

The first on-site training for military personnel took place June 2009 in Saqqara, Egypt, and was a joint Dutch/US initiative. More such training exercises are planned in Egypt during Bright Star[15] and in Petra, Jordan.

3. The relation between cultural property protection and the Comprehensive Approach

The aim of a military operation is to reach the 'end state', which generally means the establishment of a sustainably safe and secure environment. Economic, legal and political systems that can function without external military assistance are indispensable elements of such an end state. Realising it demands a 'Comprehensive Approach'.

What is the Comprehensive Approach? To quote former NATO Secretary-General Jaap de Hoop Scheffer: 'A comprehensive approach fosters cooperation and coordination between international organisations, individual States, agencies and NGOs, as well as the private sector. Developing such a culture of cooperation is not going to be easy. We are all attached to our own ways.'[16]

The Dutch Joint Doctrine Bulletin on Provincial Reconstruction Teams states that the essence of the Comprehensive Approach is the realisation that conflicts cannot be resolved by military means alone. Since most conflicts have non-military causes, the use of different types of intervention is necessary. As development and security are closely interconnected, safety, reconstruction and good governance must be approached in tandem. Development cooperation and military and diplomatic

13 Patrick O'Keefe, *Trade in Antiquities: Reducing Destruction and Theft* (Paris, UNESCO: 1997).

14 US Department of the Army, Civil Affairs Arts Monuments and Archives Guide, March 2005.

15 A major military exercise that takes place in Egypt every two years.

16 Speech held during the "Defence Leaders Forum", Noordwijk aan Zee, the Netherlands, 23 April 2007; file in possession of the author.

activities should be integrated. This means that the military contribution to crisis management operations must be combined with diplomatic efforts and development cooperation, in the so-called '3D strategy' (Development, Defence and Diplomacy). The Dutch armed forces are currently using a second generation of this 3D concept, focusing on four areas of concern: security, politics, and social and economic well-being.

Due to its complexity, CPP can by definition only be effectively implemented in a multidisciplinary and consequently joint, inter-agency manner. An effective CPP strategy stimulates reconstruction efforts in a conflict zone as well as stability in the post-conflict phase. In general, local populations have special ties with their country's cultural property, which often symbolises for them the glorious past or at least better times. In addition, cultural property is frequently an economic factor, which has a positive effect on political, social and commercial (e.g. tourism-related) aspects of reconstruction, thus furthering local stability.

4. Advantages of the implementation of cultural property protection by the armed forces

Little attention was paid to CPP in the immediate aftermath of World War II. The expertise developed by the Allies during the Second World War had been allowed to be dispersed. The subject had no priority within their respective defence organisations. CPP in the event of armed conflict only resurfaced on the Dutch agenda in 1958, when the 1954 Hague Convention was ratified. Obligations for State Parties to this Convention range from organising risk preparedness and training to actual protection of cultural property during operations. The 1999 Second Protocol widened these obligations.

After the Bamiyan Buddhas were destroyed by the Taliban in 2001, the protection of cultural heritage and its legal and ethical mainsprings gained renewed international attention. When the National Museum in Baghdad was looted in 2003 following the invasion of Iraq, the US experienced not only how important CPP can be as a 'force multiplier'[17] but also how lack of CPP can strengthen the opposing military forces and generate negative PR for the occupying force, thus undermining public acceptance of its presence. The only positive effect of the 2003 cultural debacle in Iraq[18] was an increase in international attention to CPP. If implemented correctly, preferably as part of a comprehensive approach, CPP can be an impediment to illicit traffic in artefacts and a stimulus for economic growth, stability and public acceptance of a military presence.

17 'A capability that, when added to and employed by a combat force, significantly increases the combat potential of that force and thus enhances the probability of successful mission accomplishment.' US Department of Defence, Dictionary of Military and Associated Words, 2003.

18 Thousands of archaeological sites and several monuments, museums, archives and libraries were looted and in some cases destroyed.

The seminar in The Hague and recent publications[19] support the thesis that from a military perspective, CPP can contribute substantially to an operation's success. Its multi-agency and multidisciplinary character makes it highly suitable for implementation within the Dutch Comprehensive Approach (3D) or any other comprehensive strategy. It should be noted that experience shows that CPP is necessary during all phases of a conflict or operation; most of the damage is done at the beginning of a conflict.

When Dutch troops are involved in conflicts or deployed for peacekeeping or peace enforcement missions, they generally have to work in areas where the culture is different from their own. Their operational environment will in such cases include these cultures' material representations. The military have to be prepared for this on all levels, both individually and as a group. The 1954 Hague Convention and the 1999 Second Protocol can only be correctly interpreted by a commander who has some understanding and knowledge of these legal instruments and of CPP. This knowledge can also be provided through special CPP advisers or officers, providing the armed forces have such capabilities or are willing to create them. Under all circumstances continuous research and training is needed, since CPP is not a static subject; new developments take place and should be monitored and analysed. Sufficient financial means should be available for this in the defence budget and in the state budget more generally.

5. Cultural property protection from an international perspective

Internationally no doctrine has been developed concerning CPP in times of armed conflict. NATO has laid out some provisions and procedures through its Joint Doctrine for Environmental Protection during NATO-led Military Activities but these are not embedded or codified in any domain or Operational Planning Process. It has however become clear that international cooperation is necessary. Both financial and human resources are too scarce for any individual country to be able to provide a solution on its own. Cooperation is more efficient and less costly. Training and lecturing, the development of training tools, joint exercises, special training *in situ* and joint assessments are all areas in which cooperation yields shared benefits.

CPP can strengthen the international rule of law and contribute to a positive image of the country implementing it. On the other hand, a poor CPP policy can create or reinforce a negative image. The fact that international public opinion (rightly or wrongly) has identified the US as the party most responsible for the destruction of cultural property in Iraq, and condemned it for violating international instruments on CPP, is a clear example. Images broadcast by CNN showing the looting of the National Museum in Baghdad had a great impact on international

19 Lawrence Rothfield, *The Rape of Mesopotamia: Behind the Looting of the Iraq Museum* (Chicago: University of Chicago Press, 2009); Peter G. Stone, 'The Identification and Protection of Cultural Heritage during the Iraq Conflict: A Peculiarly English Tale', in *The Destruction of Cultural Heritage in Iraq*, ed. Peter G. Stone and Joanne Farchakh Bajjaly (Woodbridge: Boydell Press, 2008); Joris Kila, 'The Role of NATO and Civil Military Affairs', part II chapter 16 in *Antiquities under Siege: Cultural Heritage Protection after the Iraq War*, ed. Lawrence Rothfield (Lanham, MD: AltaMira Press, 2008).

opinion, giving the US a reputation as a destroyer of cultural property; it will take years to change this image.

Since the US ratified the 1954 Hague Convention in September 2008, however, many CPP activities are being conducted by it. Currently the possibilities are being studied of expanding activities like training and of embedding capabilities in the Department of Defence (DoD), starting from its existing environmental and legacy programmes and the archaeologists and other experts it already employs. Civil Affairs training courses focusing on museums and art are also being given. CPP experts can already be found in all the services. Examples of CPP activities include the DoD Legacy Resource Management Programme, the Cultural Resources Programme in the Environmental Division, and the Integrated Training Area Management Programme in the Directorate of Plans, Training, Mobilisation and Security. The Central Command has a Historical/Cultural Technical Working Group and the US is represented in the newly established International Military Cultural Resources Working Group (IMCRWG) . The DoD works closely with the University of Colorado, and the US aims to join in international cooperation on CPP. Currently a CPP *in situ* training course is being conducted in Egypt in cooperation with an expert from the Dutch Ministry of Defence.

Other states are also active in the field of CPP. The UK has expressed the intention to ratify the 1954 Hague Convention and its Protocols in the near future. The British Ministry of Defence is now preparing to create military CPP capabilities, and has asked the Netherlands for advice. A first major project of the British Ministry is supporting the creation of a museum in Basra, Iraq. Professor Peter Stone[20] is advising the Culture, Media and Sport Committee of the British Parliament and will draw on the outcomes of the seminar held in The Hague before the symposium on the 1999 Second Protocol.

In Austria the subject of CPP is already firmly on the agenda. Cultural Property Protection Officers (CPPO) are deployed in all branches of the armed forces. CPP is fully integrated into training and planning. The highest ranked CPPO is a Brigadier General in the Ministry of Defence. Currently civil and military experts are preparing to establish a scientific institute in Vienna dedicated to research and PhD programmes on CPP in time of conflict. The newly founded Association of National Committees of the Blue Shield (ANCBS), though it has its main office in The Hague, is also represented in Austria.

In the 1960s the Italian Ministry of Education secured the establishment of a special unit of the Carabinieri (military police) charged with the defence of the country's palaeontological, archaeological, artistic and historic heritage. This unit, later known as the Comando Carabinieri Tutela Patrimonio Culturale, has been very active in Iraq. Rome also hosts the World Association for the protection of Tangible and intangible Cultural Heritage in times of armed conflict (WATCH),[21] an NGO with an extensive network of stakeholders in the Middle East and Mediterranean countries.

---

20 Chairman of the seminar on CPP and military operations held in The Hague.

21 See www.eyeonculture.net.

Estonia organised a major conference on CPP in February 2008 in Tallinn. A Memorandum of Cooperation on CPP has been signed by the Estonian Ministries of Culture and Defence.[22]

In the Netherlands, following the seminar organised by the Dutch Ministry of Defence in The Hague, a report was prepared containing recommendations for the way ahead. This report, advocating a dedicated CPP capability within the Ministry of Defence, has been presented to the Chief of the Dutch Defence Staff. A response is expected towards the end of 2009. CPP playing cards for Dutch troops deployed abroad have been developed by the Ministry of Defence in cooperation with the National UNESCO Committee, the Cultural Heritage Inspectorate and the Ministry of Education, Culture and Science.

6. The distinction between cultural property protection and 'cultural awareness', including Human Terrain Systems

The process of raising awareness of the 1954 Hague Convention and of getting CPP implemented by the military involves facing multiple organisational, bureaucratic, political, corporate, cultural and ethical challenges.

Currently there is an international discussion developing about ethical issues raised by anthropologists, archaeologists and art historians' working within or with the military. The discussion regards the so-called Human Terrain Systems (HTS), a United States Army program which embeds anthropologists and other social scientists within combat brigades to help tacticians in the field understand local cultures. The goal of HTS is to give commanders insight into the population and its culture in order to enhance operational effectiveness and reduce military and civilian conflict.[23] Opponents of scholarly engagement with the military are using the involvement of anthropologists in HTS as an excuse to reject all cooperation by social scientists with the military, specifically on CPP. In some people's view, "social scientists in the Human Terrain System teams embed within the military, ostensibly to improve cultural awareness of the populations in Afghanistan and Iraq. However, this 'cul-

22 The publication of this conference can be found online on: http://www.muinsuskaitse.ee/failid/156_est_haagi_konvents.pdf

23 Wikipedia states the following with regard to HTS (1 December 2009): "The Human Terrain System (HTS) is a United States Army program which embeds anthropologists and other social scientists within combat brigades (currently in Iraq and Afghanistan) to help tacticians in the field understand local cultures using Human Terrain Mapping (HTM). Between July 2005 and August 2006, the US Army put together HTS as an experimental counterinsurgency program. [...] HTS utilizes experts from social science disciplines (anthropology, sociology, political science, geography), regional studies, lingustics, and intelligence. HTS provides military commanders and staff with an understanding of the local population by conducting research, interpreting, and archiving cultural information and knowledge. The goal of the HTS is to give commanders insight into the population and its culture in order to enhance operational effectiveness and reduce military and civilian conflict [...]." (See: http://en.wikipedia.org/wiki/Human_Terrain_System)

tural awareness' is used to formulate strategies for killing and destruction."[24] Many experts also oppose the 'hearts and minds' strategy of counterinsurgency (COIN).[25] [26] Especially from the UK, a small number of archaeologists and anthropologists are spreading confusion. Even if this is done unintentionally and is merely the result of inappropriate research and insufficient knowledge, damage is being done. What is contributing to the problem is the use of the term 'cultural awareness',[27] which is often unjustly seen as forming part of CPP.[28]

It undermines the process of making the military aware of their obligations under the 1954 Hague Convention and the 1999 Second Protocol. The anthropologists working for US HTS teams should not be confused with CPP experts who work with the military in accordance with the 1954 Hague Convention and 1999 Second Protocol or other international legal instruments.

CPP differs from cultural awareness: contrary to CPP, cultural awareness is not mandatory under international conventions and is primarily meant as a tool for troops that are about to be deployed on foreign soil. Knowledge of cultural backgrounds and local habits should help them to reach the end state of a mission easier and faster. There are cases where cultural awareness intentionally or non-intentionally has been used as an excuse not to implement any projects dealing with CPP. Often, organisations state that they are already dealing with culture, while in fact they do something regarding cultural awareness and not CPP. They are of course related, but only in the sense that a dentist is related to a cardiologist because both work in the field of medicine. Contrary to the situation with cultural awareness and HTS, there are no known cases of CPP involvement in COIN; COIN and cultural awareness are both practised by different experts than CPP. In theory, there could only be a link through illicit traffic in artefacts by OMF. Nevertheless, it would be worthwhile for legal experts specialising in the 1954 Hague Convention and other cultural heritage instruments to research the implications of possible CPP involvement with COIN (e.g. in the fight against illicit trafficking). Recent discussions[29]

---

24 Dahr Jamail, 'Engineering "Trust of the Local Population": How Some Anthropologists Have Learned to Stop Worrying and Start Loving the Army', 16 May 2009, www.truthout.org/051609Z . See also David Price, 'The Leaky Ship of Human Terrain Systems', *Counterpunch* Weekend Edition, 12/14 December 2008. [counterpunch.org]

25 The ultimate goal of counterinsurgency (COIN) warfare is to "build (or rebuild) a political machine from the population upward." David Galula, *Counterinsurgency Warfare: Theory and Practice* (New York: Frederick A. Praeger, 1964, 2006), p. 95.In itself, COIN is a tool that has been in military use for some time. International humanitarian law, and sometimes national restrictions apply to this type of operation.

26 Dahr Jamail, op.cit. quotes US anthropologist David Price as saying:"The problem with anthropology being used in counterinsurgency isn't just that anthropologists are helping the military to wear different cultural skins; the problem is that it finds anthropologists using bio power and basic infrastructure as bargaining chips to force occupied cultures to surrender."

27 Awareness of local customs, tribal behaviours, etc.

28 There is now a tendency to involve cultural awareness, and especially HTS, in COIN.

29 For example at the World Archaeological Congress in Dublin in 2008.

and publications[30] have made clear that in Europe these two concepts are still being mixed up. Information and training are therefore necessary, particularly to underline the need for CPP officers to function separately from cultural awareness experts.

7. Conclusions of the cultural property protection seminar in The Hague[31]

At the beginning I referred to the seminar that has been held prior to the symposium on the occasion of the tenth anniversary of the 1999 Second Protocol. The participants in that seminar adopted the following conclusions about CPP:

- CPP expertise and capabilities developed during and immediately after the Second World War have been allowed to be dispersed, with the result that many State Parties to the 1954 Hague Convention and its Protocols are not meeting their obligations as laid out in these instruments;
- CPP has been forced back onto the political and military agenda by the catastrophic theft and looting of cultural property in Iraq since 2003. This is not a new development, however; there have been numerous examples of such activity since World War II;
- CPP is a military 'force multiplier'. It should never be regarded as an unnecessary burden that has been legally imposed but is militarily problematic or useless;
- Military success can no longer be defined in terms of battlefield victory alone, but has to take into account the long-term, post-conflict political, social, and economic stability of the countries involved (the Comprehensive Approach). CPP is critical to the Comprehensive Approach;
- While CPP relates to the issue of general cultural awareness, it is actually a separate issue involving specific concerns. It requires specialised skills that are different from those needed for general cultural awareness.

Various participants in the seminar expressed the desire to begin international military cooperation on CPP. As a first initiative, the International Military Cultural Resources Working Group (IMCRWG) was founded in Phoenix, Arizona, USA on 13 August 2009. The IMCRWG comprises cultural heritage professionals working in the military context in order to:

- enhance military capacity to implement CPP across the full range of operations;
- provide a forum for international cooperation and networking for those working in a military context;
- identify areas of common interest;

30 E.g. Umberto Albarella, 'Archaeologists in Conflict: Empathizing with which Victims?' *Heritage Management* 2.1 (Spring 2009). See also Robèrt Gooren, 'Cultuur, cultuurinformatie en cultuurtraining: De Sectie CAI en het human terrain van het missiegebied', http://www.nov-officieren.nl/Nieuwesite/Carre/2009//juli%20en%20aug/Carrejuliaug.html.

31 This Chapter has been written in cooperation with Peter Stone, Chairman of the Dutch MoD seminar in The Hague.

- share best practices and lessons learnt;
- raise awareness of and publicise the military commitment to the protection of cultural property and of cultural heritage, both tangible and intangible.

The IMCRWG is not intended to replace any existing organisation working in this field. Rather, it can be pro-active in developing partnerships and networks between the military and existing non-military organisations and groups, working within the framework of the 1954 Hague Convention and the 1999 Second Protocol and addressing issues related to archaeological sites, historic buildings, museums, libraries, galleries and archives.

Chapter 10

Elaboration and legal implementation of the 1999 Second Protocol: The Dutch finger on the pulse

*Nout van Woudenberg**

1. Introduction

During the last decade of the 20th century, it became evident that the UNESCO Convention for the Protection of Cultural Property in the Event of Armed Conflict,[1] with Regulations for the Execution of the Convention and the First Protocol (the 1954 Hague Convention for short), needed to be updated and supplemented. After various meetings and several rounds of negotiations, the Second Protocol to the 1954 Hague Convention was adopted in The Hague in March 1999.[2] This is an account of Dutch involvement in the Second Protocol: not only in the Protocol's conclusion, but also in efforts to implement its provisions as effectively as possible and to keep it in the centre of international attention.[3]

2. Dutch involvement in developing a Second Protocol to the 1954 Hague Convention

The 1954 Hague Convention, with Regulations for the Execution of the Convention and the First Protocol, was adopted in The Hague on 14 May 1954. It is indisputably the main multilateral instrument for the protection of cultural property during armed conflicts. It creates a legal regime intended to protect cultural property against the effects of an armed conflict that are foreseeable in time of peace and obliges the States Parties to respect and protect cultural property during an armed conflict.

However, barely half a century after the Convention's adoption, the need for a Second Protocol to update and supplement it became apparent, partly owing to the manner in which armed conflicts are now conducted. Cultural property became the

---

* Nout van Woudenberg is a legal counsel at the International Law Division of the Dutch Ministry of Foreign Affairs. This article was written in his personal capacity. The opinions in this essay are solely his and do not necessarily represent those of the Ministry.

1 Adopted 14 May 1954, 249 UNTS 240.

2 38 ILM 769; The text can be found at http://portal.unesco.org/en/ev.php-URL_ID=15207&URL_DO=DO_TOPIC&URL_SECTION=201.html.

3 This contribution is based on my article 'Second Protocol to the 1954 Hague Convention: Dutch involvement', in: Paul Meerts, ed., *Culture and International Law*, The Hague: Hague Academic Press, 2008, pp. 167-82.

Nout van Woudenberg and Liesbeth Lijnzaad (eds.) Protecting Cultural Property in Armed Conflict
© *2010 Koninklijke Brill NV. Printed in The Netherlands.* *ISBN 978 9004 18377 3 pp. 107-125.*

target of direct attacks, and violations of the 1954 Hague Convention went unpunished in many cases. Moreover, many recent conflicts have not been international, and it was this above all which would have to be addressed in a new instrument to supplement the Convention. As it had a leading part in the conclusion of the 1954 Hague Convention and its First Protocol, the Netherlands wished to play a similar role in relation to the measures to strengthen this Convention.

At the 26th session of the General Conference of UNESCO in November 1991, the indignation among the members about the destruction of cultural heritage during the conflict in the Balkans was so great that it was decided to review the effectiveness of the 1954 Convention and make proposals for improvement. The Dutch government then took the initiative in 1992 of drawing up an Explanatory Note on ways of strengthening the Convention.[4] This Dutch proposal resulted in a preliminary discussion at the 140th session of the UNESCO Executive Board in October 1992. In close collaboration with the Director-General of UNESCO, the Netherlands organised meetings of experts in July 1993 and February 1994 to prepare the way for decisions. A similar meeting was held in Paris in late 1994. The aim of these meetings was to formulate specific recommendations for improving the 1954 Hague Convention and enhancing the effectiveness of its implementation. The first question that arose in this connection was whether the aim should be to revise the 1954 Hague Convention or conclude a second protocol. Ultimately it was decided to have a second protocol, because the unanimous decision required to amend the Convention had proved unfeasible.

A broad meeting of experts was held in Vienna in 1998. UNESCO, together with the Netherlands, set out the results of the meeting in a working document containing the draft text of a legal instrument. UNESCO and the Netherlands jointly sent this document to the individual States, the International Committee of the Red Cross and various international organisations for their comments. On the basis of these comments, UNESCO – once again with the help of the Netherlands – prepared a final draft that would serve as a basis for a diplomatic conference to negotiate the text.

Subsequently, the Second Protocol to the 1954 Hague Convention for the Protection of Cultural Property in the Event of Armed Conflict was adopted in The Hague on 26 March 1999 after two weeks of negotiation. This diplomatic conference was attended by 93 States and various international organisations. The chairman of the conference was Adriaan Bos, at that time Legal Adviser of the Dutch Ministry of Foreign Affairs.

This Second Protocol to the 1954 Hague Convention is a major step forward in the protection of cultural property under international humanitarian law. It strengthens and supplements the Convention by introducing more effective international rules.[5] In this publication, I will focus on some of the Protocol's principal and most innovative aspects:

- Non-international armed conflicts: The application of the 1954 Hague Convention in non-international armed conflicts was deficient. As conflicts of

---

4 Doc. no. 140 EX/26 of 11 September 1992.

5 See Article 2 of the Protocol.

this type are on the increase, the necessary supplementary rules are now contained in the Second Protocol (chapter 5).

- Enhanced protection: The Second Protocol supplements the 'special protection' under the 1954 Hague Convention with a system of 'enhanced protection'.[6] It was found that virtually no country was able to meet the conditions for eligibility for special protection, partly because of the practical requirements listed in Article 8 of the 1954 Hague Convention. There was however a need for extra protection for cultural property of exceptional importance, so it was necessary to set up a new system: that of enhanced protection.[7]
- Individual criminal responsibility: One of the shortcomings of the 1954 Hague Convention was the lack of a peremptory system of sanctions. Chapter 4 of the Second Protocol, on criminal responsibility and jurisdiction, provides a list of serious violations of international humanitarian law in relation to cultural property and contains provisions governing criminal responsibility and jurisdiction. It reaffirms the inviolability of cultural property in time of war or military occupation and imposes an obligation on the Parties to provide for individual criminal responsibility in the event of several different violations of the Second Protocol.[8]
- Dissemination: Knowledge of the rules is an important precondition for compliance with them. Article 25 of the 1954 Hague Convention served as a model for a new article on dissemination in the Second Protocol, but has been extended in various respects. Article 30 of the Second Protocol imposes a number of obligations on the Parties regarding the Protocol's dissemination and communication.
- The Second Protocol further defines some of the terms and provisions of the 1954 Hague Convention, whose lack of clarity stood in the way of their actual implementation. 'Preparatory measures' is one example of such a term. Military necessity is another.[9]

The Second Protocol entered into force on 9 March 2004. Currently, 55 States are Party to the Protocol. Recently the Republic of Bosnia and Herzegovina became a Party, a laudable step as the war in that country and the resulting destruction of cultural property was one of the reasons for drafting the Protocol. However, we are still working towards more geographically comprehensive ratification of the Second Protocol, particularly by States in regions of conflict. Unfortunately, the regions of Africa, Asia/Pacific and the Arab States are currently underrepresented. It must be applauded that the Third Meeting of the Parties to the 1999 Second Protocol,

6 It should be noted that this enhanced protection also applies to non-international armed conflicts (see Article 22 of the Protocol).

7 See also my article *Enhanced protection: a new form of protection under the 1999 Second Protocol*, at pp. 51-58 of this book.

8 Namely those listed in Article 15.

9 See Kevin Chamberlain, *Military necessity under the 1999 Second Protocol*, at pp. 43-49 of this book.

which took place in Paris on 23 and 24 November 2009, adopted a resolution, stating amongst others:

> '1) Encourages High Contracting Parties to the Hague Convention not yet party to the Second Protocol to promptly become party to it and to adopt and effectively implement national legislation.
> 2) Invites the Director-General to promote ratification of the Second Protocol by High Contracting Parties, in particular with a view to a more balanced geographical participation.
> [...]'

The Netherlands ratified the Protocol on 30 January 2007 and became a Party on 30 April 2007. This gap of three years after the entry into force of the Protocol was due to the Netherlands' desire to fulfil its implementation obligations to the letter. I will go a bit more into this in the last part of this account.

3. Membership of the Committee under the Second Protocol

For the Netherlands, its involvement does not end with its contribution to the drafting and adoption of the Second Protocol, or with the incorporation of the Protocol's provisions into its national legislation. These were just the first steps. The Netherlands wanted to stay active and involved. One way to do so was through membership of the Committee for the Protection of Cultural Property in the Event of Armed Conflict. At the Second Meeting of the States Parties to the Second Protocol in December 2007, chaired by the Dutch Chair of the 1999 Diplomatic Conference, the Netherlands was chosen for membership of the Committee, taking a seat in the Committee's Bureau as one of its vice-chairs.

This Committee, provided for by Article 24 and subsequent articles of the Second Protocol, can be considered as the Protocol's executive body.[10] It operates at the crossroads of international humanitarian law and the protection of cultural heritage. The Netherlands believes it has special knowledge and expertise to contribute in both fields. It has a long tradition and expertise in the field of the laws of war, manifest for example in the Hague Conferences of 1899 and 1907. In the field of cultural heritage, the Netherlands can draw on its membership of the World Heritage Committee.[11]

Since its establishment, the Committee has been in the process of developing 'Guidelines for the Implementation of the 1999 Second Protocol to the Hague Convention of 1954 for the Protection of Cultural Property in the Event of Armed Conflict', as well as 'guidelines concerning the use of the Fund for the Protection of Cultural Property in the Event of Armed Conflict', provided for by Article 29 of the 1999 Second Protocol.

---

10 Its functions are listed in Article 27 of the 1999 Second Protocol.

11 From 2004 until 2007, the Netherlands has been a member of the World Heritage Committee, the Committee under the World Heritage Convention.

On 24 November 2009, the Third Meeting of the Parties to the 1999 Second Protocol endorsed the Guidelines,[12] and adopted the guidelines concerning the use of the Fund.[13]

4. The obligation to implement

A number of the specific articles in the 1999 Second Protocol require national implementation. This applies particularly to the articles on criminal responsibility and jurisdiction in chapter 4 of the Protocol. One of the shortcomings of the 1954 Hague Convention, which imposed an obligation on the Parties to make violations of the Convention criminal offences under national law, was the lack of a peremptory system of sanctions. Chapter 4 of the 1999 Second Protocol[14] adds a more exact list of serious violations of international humanitarian law in relation to cultural property (Article 15 (1)) and contains provisions on criminal responsibility and jurisdiction; it imposes an obligation on the Parties to provide for individual criminal responsibility in the case of the violations of the Protocol listed in article 15.[15]

The question has been raised several times how the Netherlands has implemented Chapter 4 in its national legislation. The Netherlands has already arranged for the acts defined as offences in the 1999 Second Protocol to be included in the 2003 International Crimes Act,[16] through amendments to the Surrender of War Crimes Suspects Act. It can thus be said, that the Netherlands implemented the 1999 Second Protocol even before it became a Party to it. The International Crimes Act actually killed two birds with one stone, as it also served as the implementation legislation for the Rome Statute of the International Criminal Court.

---

12 Doc. CLT-09/CONF/219/3, dated 24 November 2009.
The Resolution of the Third Meeting of the Parties states:
'5. ENDORSES the Guidelines for the Implementation of the Second Protocol (Annex I) and INVITES the Committee to report on their implementation to the next ordinary Meeting of the Parties.
6. ADOPTS the guidelines concerning the use of the Fund for the Protection of Cultural Property in the Event of Armed Conflict (Annex II) and INVITES the Committee to report on their implementation to the next ordinary Meeting of the Parties.'

13 In reaction to this adoption, the Netherlands decided to be the first to making a financial contribution to the Fund, hoping that other States Parties will follow expeditiously.

14 On the basis of Article 22 of the 1999 Second Protocol, chapter 4 – like the Protocol as a whole – applies to armed conflict of both international and non-international character.

15 See also Roger O'Keefe, *National Implementation of the Penal Provisions of Chapter 4 of the Second Protocol of 26 March 1999 to the Hague Convention of 1954 for the Protection of Cultural Property in the Event of Armed Conflict*, 29 March 2002; available at UNESCO and on file with the author.

16 Government Gazette 2003, No. 270. In Dutch, the Act is called: Wet Internationale Misdrijven (WIM). An English version of the Act can be found in the Documents section of this book.

What follows is an account of the Dutch implementation of later articles in the Second Protocol's chapter on criminal responsibility and jurisdiction.

Article 15: Serious violations of this Protocol

Paragraph 1 of Article 15 describes a number of acts contrary to the Protocol as serious violations and obliges the Member States to make such acts criminal offences. This applies to any acts whereby a person intentionally and in violation of the Protocol (a) makes cultural property under enhanced protection the object of attack; (b) uses cultural property under enhanced protection or its immediate surroundings in support of military action; (c) causes extensive destruction or appropriation of such cultural property; (d) makes cultural property protected under the 1954 Hague Convention and the Second Protocol the object of attack;[17] (e) commits theft, pillage or misappropriation of, or acts of vandalism directed against cultural property protected by the 1954 Hague Convention.

As far as Dutch law is concerned, these obligations in relation to offences committed in an international armed conflict have been implemented by inclusion in section 5, subsection 4 (a), (b), (c), (d) and (e) of the International Crimes Act. Although the International Crimes Act does not explicitly state that these acts are criminal offences when committed in a non-international armed conflict, they will still be criminal under the catch-all provision of section 7 of the International Crimes Act. Here too, therefore, provision is made for these acts to be criminal offences.

Article 16: Jurisdiction

Under paragraph 1, States which are Party to the Protocol are required to establish jurisdiction over the offences listed in article 15, in so far as they are committed in their territory, by one of their nationals and, in the case of the offences set out in article 15, paragraphs a), b) or c), when the alleged offender is present in its territory. The Netherlands has established jurisdiction over these offences by including them in the International Crimes Act; section 2 of the Act provides that Dutch jurisdiction over these offences is in keeping with the requirement in article 16 (1) of the Second Protocol.

Nonetheless, as is apparent from paragraph 2 (a), broader jurisdictional criteria may be applied in respect of individual criminal responsibility than those specified in paragraph 1. Similar provisions are already known from previous instruments of criminal law, for example article 6 (5) of the International Convention for the Suppression of Terrorist Bombings (STB).[18]

---

17 This provision thus does not deal with enhanced protection, which is covered under (a).

18 Adopted in New York on 15 December 1997 by UNGA Resolution 52/164.
Article 6 (5) STB: 'This Convention does not exclude the exercise of any criminal jurisdiction established by a State Party in accordance with its domestic law'.

Article 18: Extradition

This extradition provision also corresponds with previous provisions from the recent terrorism conventions, namely Article 9 STB[19] and Article 11 of the International Convention for the Suppression of the Financing of Terrorism (FTC).[20] It obliges Parties to make extradition possible for the most serious violations of Article 15 (1). These criminal offences are already deemed to be included as extraditable offences in any extradition treaty concluded between any of the Parties before the entry into force of the Protocol. Moreover, the Parties undertake to include such offences in every extradition treaty to be subsequently concluded between them. The Protocol also gives States the option of treating the Protocol itself as the legal basis for extradition between States Parties. To make this possible for the Netherlands too, a reference to this Protocol has been added to Article 1 of the Surrender of War Crimes Suspects Act. In that provision, the four 1949 Geneva Conventions, as well as the First Additional Protocol to the 1949 Geneva Conventions, had already been listed as providing a legal basis for extradition under certain circumstances. The amendment has come into force on 1 January 2010.

Article 20: Grounds for refusal

Paragraph 1 of this Article provides that for the purposes of extradition and mutual legal assistance the offences set out in Article 15, paragraphs 1 a), b) and c) are not to be regarded as political offences, nor as offences connected with political offences,

---

19 Article 9, STB:

‘1. The offences set forth in article 2 shall be deemed to be included as extraditable offences in any extradition treaty existing between any of the States Parties before the entry into force of this Convention. States Parties undertake to include such offences as extraditable offences in every extradition treaty to be subsequently concluded between them.

2. When a State Party which makes extradition conditional on the existence of a treaty receives a request for extradition from another State Party with which it has no extradition treaty, the requested State Party may, at its option, consider this Convention as a legal basis for extradition in respect of the offences set forth in article 2. Extradition shall be subject to the other conditions provided by the law of the requested State.

3. States Parties which do not make extradition conditional on the existence of a treaty shall recognize the offences set forth in article 2 as extraditable offences between themselves, subject to the conditions provided by the law of the requested State.

4. If necessary, the offences set forth in article 2 shall be treated, for the purposes of extradition between States Parties, as if they had been committed not only in the place in which they occurred but also in the territory of the States that have established jurisdiction in accordance with article 6, paragraphs 1 and 2.

5. The provisions of all extradition treaties and arrangements between States Parties with regard to offences set forth in article 2 shall be deemed to be modified as between State Parties to the extent that they are incompatible with this Convention.’

20 Adopted in New York on 9 December 1999, by UNGA Resolution 54/109.

nor as offences inspired by political motives.[21] Paragraph 1 also provides that States which are Party to this Protocol may not refuse a request for extradition or for mutual legal assistance based on the offences listed in Article 15, paragraphs 1 a), b) and c) on the sole ground that the offence in question is a political offence or an offence connected with a political offence or an offence inspired by political motives. A virtually identical de-politicisation clause can be found in Article 11 of the STB[22] and Article 14 of the FTC; the underlying idea is once again that the offences are of such a serious nature that they cannot be justified by political motives of any kind whatever.

In both these Conventions the clause in question is followed by a non-discrimination clause, with which it is closely connected.[23] This clause, which is included in paragraph 2 of Article 20, provides that there is no obligation to extradite or afford mutual legal assistance if the requested State has substantial grounds for believing that the request for extradition has been made for the purpose of prosecuting or punishing a person on account of that person's race, religion, nationality, ethnic origin or political opinion or that compliance with the request would cause prejudice to that person's position for any of these reasons.

Together, the two paragraphs of Article 20 strike a balance between the protection of two justified interests: on the one hand that a suspect should not escape prosecution or punishment for a serious violation of the Second Protocol on the sole ground that his offence was of a political nature and on the other that an individual should not be exposed to prosecution on improper grounds. Section 12 of the International Crimes Act already contains a depoliticisation clause for the serious violations of the Protocol which are to be made criminal offences and have, as mentioned above, already been included in that Act.

Article 21: Measures regarding other violations

Under Article 21 the Parties to the Second Protocol are required to adopt, in addition to the criminal sanctions prescribed by Article 15 (2) for the serious violations described in paragraph 1 of that article, such other measures as may be necessary to

21 As the Netherlands does not treat such offences as political offences, the exception for political offences is excluded in extradition law.

22 Article 11 STB: 'None of the offences set forth in article 2 shall be regarded, for the purposes of extradition or mutual legal assistance, as a political offence or as an offence connected with a political offence or as an offence inspired by political motives. Accordingly, a request for extradition or for mutual legal assistance based on such an offence may not be refused on the sole ground that it concerns a political offence or an offence connected with a political offence or an offence inspired by political motives.'

23 Article 12, STB: 'Nothing in this Convention shall be interpreted as imposing an obligation to extradite or to afford mutual legal assistance, if the requested State Party has substantial grounds for believing that the request for extradition for offences set forth in article 2 or for mutual legal assistance with respect to such offences has been made for the purpose of prosecuting or punishing a person on account of that person's race, religion, nationality, ethnic origin or political opinion or that compliance with the request would cause prejudice to that person's position for any of these reasons.'

suppress other intentional violations of the Protocol. Paragraphs a) and b) of this Article indicate when these measures must be taken.[24]

However, the Parties have greater freedom of choice in respect of these measures than in the case of the serious violations, since the measures in question need not necessarily be of a criminal law nature. Nonetheless, Dutch law already penalized a number of the acts covered by this, for example under the Cultural Heritage Preservation Act,[25] and the definitions of offences of a more general nature (such as handling stolen goods in Article 416, paragraph 1 of the Criminal Code) may be applicable in certain situations.

The application of disciplinary procedures in the armed forces is an example of a sanction that is not under the criminal law.

5. Concluding remarks

During the last decade of the 20th century the need for a Second Protocol to the 1954 Hague Convention became apparent. As described above, the Netherlands took the lead, together with UNESCO, in introducing and developing this Protocol.

It is safe to say that the Netherlands has made a great investment in the elaboration and implementation of the Second Protocol. We can only hope that the provisions of criminal liability and jurisdiction do not need to be applied too often.

The number of States Parties is growing steadily. To our satisfaction, States that were the immediate cause of the Second Protocol's elaboration are themselves becoming Parties to it. However, we are still working towards more geographically comprehensive ratification of the Second Protocol, particularly by States in regions of conflict.

24 The Geneva Conventions also have similar provisions. See for example Article 146 of the Geneva Convention relative to the protection of civilian persons in time of war, concluded on 12 August 1949: 'The High Contracting Parties undertake to enact any legislation necessary to provide effective penal sanctions for persons committing, or ordering to be committed, any of the grave breaches of the present Convention defined in the following Article.'

25 Sections 7, 14a and 14b in conjunction with section 1 of the Economic Offences Act.

Chapter 11

The Dutch Ministry of Defence and the protection of cultural heritage

*Robèrt Gooren**

1. Introduction: Underlying legal principles

All military involvement in the protection of cultural property in the Netherlands is a direct consequence of legal obligations laid down in international humanitarian law (IHL). The earliest attempts to codify the conduct of war and to protect non-belligerents resulted in two Peace Conferences held in The Hague in 1899 and 1907, though sadly, these efforts proved inadequate to prevent the destruction of cultural property during the First World War. Further initiatives to draft modern laws of war were taken in the 1930s, but real progress only came after the large-scale destruction and plunder of cultural heritage during the Second World War. While the Geneva Conventions of 1949, and the Additional Protocols of 1977, constitute a general framework for both belligerent and non-belligerent parties during times of war, the 1954 Hague Convention for the Protection of Cultural Property in the Event of Armed Conflict specifically aims to restrict the destructive impact of hostilities on cultural property. The 1954 Hague Convention was supplemented by Protocol I, which imposed further obligations on occupying forces in control of hostile territory and on other High Contracting Parties to take into custody and to return cultural property coming from occupied territories at the close of the hostilities.

However, the eruption of armed conflict in former Yugoslavia in the 1990s demonstrated the very limited effect of IHL protection. Belligerent parties deliberately targeted their enemy's cultural property, regardless of all international rules, leading to severe destruction in places like Sarajevo, Dubrovnik and Mostar. As a result of this, Protocol II to the 1954 Convention sought to impose even tighter restrictions on the impact of military operations on cultural property. It was signed on 26 March 1999 and came into force on 9 March 2004.[1]

---

* Lieutenant-Colonel Dr Robèrt Gooren is Head of the Cultural Affairs & Information Section at the Land Forces Command Support Group of the Royal Netherlands Army. This article was written in his personal capacity. The opinions in this article are solely his and do not necessarily represent those of the Kingdom of the Netherlands.

1 http://portal.unesco.org/en/ev.php-URL_ID=15207&URL_DO=DO_TOPIC &URL_SECTION=201.html

Nout van Woudenberg and Liesbeth Lijnzaad (eds.) Protecting Cultural Property in Armed Conflict
© *2010 Koninklijke Brill NV. Printed in The Netherlands.* *ISBN 978 9004 18377 3 pp. 117–121.*

The role of the Dutch armed forces in protecting cultural property will be the focus of this account.

2. Military involvement

In the final months before the outbreak of the Second World War, the General Staff of the Dutch Army participated in meetings with officials from the Ministry of Education & Culture on the need to safeguard the nation's cultural treasures should the country become involved in a full-scale war. Despite their good intentions, few preparations had actually been made by the time the Netherlands was invaded in May 1940.

From these improvised origins a more serious initiative followed after the war had ended. In 1953 the Army set up a special Bureau for Cultural Heritage as part of the military organisation. It was staffed with a number of army reserve officers who were appointed 'art protection officers'. Most of them were university-educated conscripts with a degree in art history or architecture. This position was modelled on the 'monuments, fine arts and archives officers' in the US Army, who played an important role in protecting and retrieving cultural property during the liberation of Western Europe in 1944-45.[2]

In times of armed conflict, art protection officers would be assigned to the Provincial Military Command in each of the Dutch provinces, where they would act as liaisons between the military commanders and civilian authorities responsible for the protection of cultural property in their particular geographical area of responsibility. Their duties would mainly consist of planning emergency evacuations, transport and secure storage of movable cultural objects, and taking precautions for protecting immovable monuments.

From 1953 until 1996 the Cultural Heritage Bureau was a separate unit within the army's National Territorial Command. Its officers established close links with the provincial Cultural Heritage Inspectors of the Ministry of Education and Culture. After several restructurings of the military organisation the unit, renamed the Cultural Affairs and Information Section (henceforth: CAI Section) in 2001, is now part of the Land Forces Command Support Group.

The activities of CAI Section follow from articles 7.1 and 7.2 of the 1954 Convention. The relevance of these provisions was underlined in a letter sent to parliament on 21 November 2006 by the Minister of Foreign Affairs concerning the ratification of Protocol II of the 1954 Convention.[3] In that letter, the minister emphasised the importance of disseminating information on cultural property protection among service personnel who take part in operations abroad:

> "This mainly involves the restrictions set by the Protocol on the execution of military operations, as well as the responsibility to protect cultural goods against misappropriation, theft, pillage, damage or destruction. In this respect the information

2 See Lynn H. Nicholas, *The Rape of Europe: The Fate of Europe's Treasures in the Third Reich and the Second World War* (New York: Knopf, 1995).

3 States General 2006-2007, 30 894, A and no. 1, pp. 1-18.

required will be included in basic military training, and in pre-deployment training."

Within the Dutch armed forces the implementation of these regulations has been assigned to CAI Section and 1st CIMIC Battalion.[4] In practice, the staff of CAI Section is responsible for three closely related fields:

- national operations;
- pre-deployment training for stability and peace support operations; and
- 1st CIMIC Battalion Network for Cultural Affairs and Education (henceforth: CA&E)

3. National operations

After the Cold War ended, the chances of a military conflict fought on Dutch soil seemed very remote. From the early 1990s onwards, the armed forces focused on expeditionary tasks and paid little attention to domestic responsibilities. In recent years a renewed interest in domestic affairs led to a new set of agreements, signed in 2005 and 2006 between the Minister of Defence and the Minister of the Interior. Both parties confirmed that the armed forces have an important role to play in the event of natural or man-made disasters, terrorist attacks, or a pandemic that can profoundly affect national security.[5]

The possible deployment of specialized military units and personnel under civilian authority has become an integrated aspect of emergency planning and preparations. Staff officers of Army Command National Operations Bureau coordinate military activities in support of civilian authorities. They are backed up by a number of liaison groups which are responsible for maintaining contact with civilian organisations in different sectors. One such sector is the cultural domain. The CAI Section provides a number of staff who will act as liaison officers between the military and cultural heritage institutions in times of crisis, and serve as advisors to military authorities on military assistance in safeguarding national cultural heritage. In his military capacity the Head of the CAI Section is commander of the Liaison Group for Cultural Heritage. He is in contact with the Ministry of Education, Science and Culture and various governmental and non-governmental branch organisations, and represents the Dutch Army in several institutionalised branch meetings.

4. Pre-deployment training for stability and peace support operations

The expeditionary role of the armed forces has meant that Dutch military personnel work under difficult and dangerous circumstances in different parts of the world. Preparing these troops for their tasks in a different cultural environment demanded new forms of training. Every member of the Dutch armed forces has to meet certain

4 The military unit responsible for Civil-Military Cooperation.

5 Voluntary agreement on Civil-Military Administrative Agreements (CMBA, 2005) and Intensifying Civil-Military Cooperation (ICMS, 2006).

requirements before being allowed to take part in military operations abroad. The Netherlands armed forces military directive on training (directive A-700) specifically mentions that pre-deployment training should always address the cultural heritage and cultural history of the mission area, as well as provide detailed information on local culture, religious beliefs, social customs, and do's and don'ts.

Dutch military units in the UN Protection Force (UNPROFOR) during the 1992-1995 war in Bosnia-Herzegovina witnessed the destruction of cultural property by members of the warring parties. These Dutch soldiers had to be able to identify cultural property. They also needed to be adequately informed about the legal obligations pertaining to the protection of cultural property.

Staff from the CAI Section started participating in pre-deployment training in 1993. They now take part in every general pre-deployment training programme organised by the army's School for Peacekeeping Operations. The main focus of this instruction is to make clear how knowledge of, and respect for culture in the mission area can contribute to a better understanding between the local people and Dutch troops during a military mission. Examples of cultural property such as taken from the Red List of Afghanistan Antiquities at Risk and examples of unlawful actions (e.g. damage, looting, graffiti, illicit trade) are included in every cultural awareness lesson.

5. 1st CIMIC Battalion Network for Cultural Affairs & Education (1CIMICBAT)

Within the Dutch armed forces the Commanding Officer of 1CIMICBAT is responsible for maintaining a network of some 33 reserve officers who in civilian life are experts in the fields of cultural affairs and education. Any one of them can be called out for a tour of duty with a Civil-Military Cooperation (CIMIC) team attached to a Dutch military taskforce taking part in a military operation abroad. Experts in the field of archaeology, museum management, architectural monuments and cultural heritage protection are available whenever their services are needed in the field.

The Network has close personal links with the CAI Section. From 2005 to 2008 the Head of the CAI Section served as chairman of the CA&E Network, and the Deputy Head now serves as Network Manager. Other regional experts at the CAI Section have joined the Network as well, with two of them currently serving as Cultural Advisors in Afghanistan.

CIMIC activities are an important tool for the Dutch taskforce commander in pursuing the mission objectives. These are planned in coordination with many other actors in the field: first and foremost with officials from the Ministry of Foreign Affairs, but also with representatives of international and non-governmental organisations, and with local authorities and governmental institutions. Together, these actors set priorities for planning civilian aid to the local community.

Unfortunately, cultural heritage is not always given the attention and high priority granted to other fields, like public health, education or public services. Perhaps the present concept of the 3D Approach to foreign policy (in which the instruments of Defence, Diplomacy and Development cooperation are to be combined in a comprehensive way) will offer better opportunities for cultural heritage protection in the future, when civilian organisations and experts offer assistance as well.

6. Afterword

The Dutch armed forces have long since taken a serious interest in the 1954 Hague Convention and in the 1999 Second Protocol. Firstly, by setting up a special unit responsible for implementing the provisions of this aspect of IHL within the military organisation. Secondly, by including the required knowledge in military education programmes; and, third, by maintaining a pool of experts available for foreign deployment. Unfortunately, only a few NATO or non-NATO military organisations have shown a similar commitment to culture and cultural heritage.

Chapter 12

The implementation of the Second Protocol to the 1954 Hague Convention in the Republic of Macedonia

*Lazar Sumanov and Jovan Ristov**

1. Introduction

The Republic of Macedonia was among the first countries to ratify the Second Protocol to the 1954 Hague Convention for the Protection of Cultural Property in the Event of an Armed Conflict, thus helping to fulfil the conditions for its entry into force. The Protocol was ratified by an Act adopted on 23 January 2002 and published on 18 February 2002.[1]

This contribution describes the efforts of a network of Macedonian institutions and experts to implement innovative elements of the Second Protocol, such as 'enhanced protection', 'criminal responsibility and jurisdiction' and 'protection of cultural property in an armed conflict that is not of an international character'. It also discusses the results that these efforts have produced.

2. The institutional, governmental and non-governmental environment in Macedonia

At present, there is both a governmental and a non-governmental network of institutions and organisations active in the Republic of Macedonia in the field of tangible (immovable and movable) and intangible heritage protection.

The governmental network includes:

- the Ministry of Culture;
- the Cultural Heritage Protection Office (CHPO), a body within the Ministry of Culture;
- the National Conservation Centre in Skopje;
- the Conservation Centre of the City of Skopje (a national institution);
- museums and institutes for the protection of cultural monuments in the towns of Bitola, Ohrid, Prilep, Strumica and Shtip (all national institutions);
- the Museum of Macedonia in Skopje;

* Dr Lazar Sumanov, Senior Conservator, Secretary-General, ICOMOS Macedonia; Mr Jovan Ristov, Senior Conservator, National Conservation Centre (NCC).

1 *Official Gazette of the Republic of Macedonia*, International Agreements, no. 13/02.

Nout van Woudenberg and Liesbeth Lijnzaad (eds.) Protecting Cultural Property in Armed Conflict
© *2010 Koninklijke Brill NV. Printed in The Netherlands.* *ISBN 978 9004 18377 3 pp. 123-133.*

- seven museums in the towns of Gevgelija, Kavadarci, Kratovo, Kumanovo, Negotino, Skopje and Veles.

Active within the non-governmental network are:
- the Macedonia National Committee of the International Council on Museums and Sites (ICOMOS) (since 1994);[2]
- the Macedonia National Committee of the International Council of Museums (ICOM) (since 1993);
- the Macedonian National Committee of the Blue Shield (since 2003).

3. Criminal responsibility and jurisdiction (Chapter IV of the Second Protocol)

Here we wish to highlight the steps taken by the relevant Macedonian ministries, institutions and bodies to address issues of national criminal prosecution and jurisdiction since the ratification of the Second Protocol in 2002.

The provisions of the Second Protocol have been enshrined in the Law on Protection of Cultural Heritage of 2004[3] and the 2004 amendments to the 1996 Criminal Code.[4] Certain issues were regulated in greater detail in delegated legislation adopted between 2005 and 2008 in the following areas:
- special measures to protect cultural heritage in a state of war or state of emergency;[5]
- the content and the administration of the national inventory of protected property in an event of an armed conflict;[6]
- the design and issuance of the ID template and armbands of the official inspectors for cultural heritage in an event of an armed conflict;[7]
- the use of emblems designating cultural heritage in keeping with international agreements.[8]

2 In 2002 (following the non-international armed conflict in Macedonia in 2001), ICOMOS Macedonia organised an Urgent Regional Workshop on 'Cultural Heritage at Risk in the Event of an Armed Conflict – the Case of Macedonia' in Skopje and Ohrid on 20-24 February 2002. Over 100 representatives took part from international and national, governmental and non-governmental organisations from Europe generally and Southeast Europe in particular, including UNESCO and NATO. The workshop received full financial support from the Embassy of the Kingdom of the Netherlands in Skopje and the Ministry of Culture of the Republic of Macedonia. It concluded with the adoption of the Ohrid Declaration by acclamation by all the participants. The workshop proceedings have been published in English and are available on request from ICOMOS Macedonia, P.O. Box 816, 1000 Skopje, Macedonia, email: icomosmk@mt.net.mk.

3 *Official Gazette of the Republic of Macedonia*, nos. 20/04 and 115/07, www.uzkn.gov.mk/propisi_en.html.

4 *Official Gazette of the Republic of Macedonia*, nos. 37/96 and 19/04.

5 *Official Gazette of the Republic of Macedonia*, no. 56/08.

6 *Official Gazette of the Republic of Macedonia*, no. 25/05.

7 See footnote 6.

8 See footnote 6.

Still in preparation is the last of the five planned instruments, on a special methodology for assessing damage during and caused by an armed conflict or natural disaster.

The Law on Protection of Cultural Heritage stipulates that any requisition, misuse of, or attack on cultural heritage, and any use of cultural heritage for military purposes are prohibited (Section 54). In addition, the law lays down the obligatory preparatory measures for protection in the event of armed conflict, the special protection measures to be taken in time of war, and the measures to be undertaken upon the cessation of hostilities (Sections 107-110). It designates the Cultural Heritage Protection Office, a legal entity within the Ministry of Culture, as the competent authority with respect to these measures.

The Law on Protection of Cultural Heritage makes failure to take the preparatory measures necessary for the protection and salvaging of cultural heritage from the foreseeable consequences of an armed conflict a misdemeanour, liable to a fine of €6,000 to €8,000 for legal entities, €3,000 to €4,000 for individual traders and €800 to €1,000 for other natural persons (Section 172).Serious violations of the Second Protocol (Article 15) were made offences under the Criminal Code in 2004. The chapter on crimes against humanity and international law (Chapter 34) now includes three such specific offences: war crimes against cultural property (Article 404, paragraph 2), destruction of cultural heritage or of property under temporary protection (Article 414), and illicit use of international emblems (Article 416).Paragraph 2 of the article on crimes against the civilian population (Article 404) was amended to distinguish property having the status of cultural heritage from other types of property. The amended Criminal Code also makes it an offence in time of war, armed conflict or occupation to order, in violation of international law:

- an attack on cultural property which is under enhanced protection or on other structures under special protection;
- indiscriminate strikes against structures that are protected under international law;
- long-term and extensive destruction of the natural environment that might harm cultural property under enhanced protection;
- use for the purpose of military operations of the surroundings of cultural property under enhanced protection;
- large-scale destruction or illicit appropriation of cultural property protected under international law;
- theft or expropriation of or acts of vandalism directed against cultural property protected under international law.

An offence under Article 404, paragraph 2 of the Criminal Code is liable to a term of imprisonment of at least ten years or by imprisonment for life. A person who, in violation of international law, destroys property under temporary protection during a war or an armed conflict commits an offence under Article 414, paragraph 1 of the Criminal Code and will be sentenced to a term of imprisonment of at least one year. If the property is under the special protection of international law, the perpetrator will be sentenced to a term of imprisonment of at least five years (Article 414, paragraph 2). The illicit or unauthorised use of the emblem of the 1954 Hague

Convention is an offence under Article 416, paragraph 1 of the Criminal Code, liable to a term of imprisonment varying from three months to three years. If the offence is committed in a zone of military operations, the perpetrator will be sentenced to a term of imprisonment of no less than six months but not exceeding five years.

The national legislation now in force in the Republic of Macedonia can thus be considered a solid legal basis for consistent enforcement of the Second Protocol.

4. Final remarks and suggestions

As an appendix to this contribution, the text of the Ohrid Declaration of 2002 has been appended for reference. We would like to emphasise the following. It was necessary for the Republic of Macedonia to establish an institutional and legal framework for the treatment and protection of its cultural heritage that was consistent both with our national legislation and with the international conventions and other agreements to which we are a party. Unfortunately, our country suffered both loss of human life and damage to its cultural heritage during the 2001 armed conflict. Since that time the Republic of Macedonia has fulfilled a number of its obligations at institutional level. In our opinion, however, there are necessary changes to national legislation that have still not yet been made.

We believe that the protection of cultural heritage and the implementation of all the relevant legislation and national and international recommendations should not only be the responsibility of governmental and other institutions. The owners and users of cultural heritage should also be fully involved in this process. We would stress that protection of cultural heritage should be regarded as part of a cyclical, ongoing process that includes actions taken prior to, during and after man-made or natural disasters. The Ohrid Declaration of 2002[9] recommends many measures that should be taken prior to, during and after the calamity itself. Eight years after the armed conflict in Macedonia, we are, in the words of the Ohrid Declaration, only entering 'the phase before the next disaster'. There are a great many tasks for all the stakeholders to fulfil in order to prevent another one. As the Macedonian saying goes, *podobro da se spreci, otkolku da se leci*: prevention is better than cure.

9 To be found in the appendix of this article.

Appendix

2002 Ohrid Declaration on the Protection of Cultural Heritage in the Event of Armed Conflict

The participants of the Urgent Regional Workshop 'The Cultural Heritage at Risk in the Event of Armed Conflict – Macedonia Case' held in Ohrid, Republic of Macedonia, 20 – 24 February 2002:

- expressing sincere gratitude to the organizers – the Macedonian National Committee of ICOMOS and the State Institute for Protection of the Monuments of culture for their extraordinary efforts and dedication to organize this topical, very specific regional international workshop as well as the Ministry of Culture of the Republic of Macedonia and the Embassy of the Kingdom of the Netherlands in the Republic of Macedonia for their full support of this Urgent Workshop;
- welcoming the readiness of Macedonian authorities for comprehensive presentation of the 'Macedonia Case' in conditions when certain animosities and military activities are still going on in the Republic of Macedonia and the access to the areas where damaged, looted or destroyed monuments of culture is not everywhere allowed and many sites are dangerous to visit;
- recalling the Hague Convention of May 14, 1954 on protection of cultural assets in the even of armed conflict and accompanying acts;
- aware that the protection of cultural assets in the event of armed conflict is a very complex system of measures, activities and procedures the implementation of which is conditioned by a large number of internal and external factors and considering that the international model of military – humanitarian protection does not provide always the expected results;
- being however sure that the negative impact of the military activities may be diminished by timely and systematic implementation of appropriate measures of protection and preservation of the cultural assets;
- taking the 'Macedonia Case' as a pretext;
- With the aim of stimulating the process of upgrading and implementation of national models of cultural heritage protection in the segments that are the subject of organized activity before, during and after the armed conflicts;
- based on proposals from the working groups and deliberations during the final plenary session have adopted on February 22, 2002 as a final act of the Urgent Regional Workshop have adopted the following Ohrid Declaration:

I. Activities before the Armed Conflict

1. Awareness increase

It is recommended to give a greater stress to the increase of protection awareness. Such campaigns should be directed to two main directions: (a) the general public and (b) particular target groups as the politicians, legislators, the military, law enforcement bodies and the customs. The campaign should be carried out through all relevant channels including the media. In areas where this is the feature, cultural diversity should be promoted from the aspect of cultural heritage. It is desirable that the general public sensibilisation is made through special information programs and projects while the sensitivisation of the particular target groups should be through special training programs and projects.

2. Identification of protected assets

To facilitate the identification of unmovable and movable assets being the subject of protection in case of armed conflict it has been considered that where ever this has not been done a particular stress should be given to the establishment and regular updating of the national and other inventories of protected assets. Such inventories may be kept in the classical as well as in electronic form. It is recommended that the identification of the protected assets be facilitated through topographic maps especially for the assets that are of international, national and regional significance. The topographic maps should be updated and include all possible actual changes.

3. Technical measures

At peace time, beside regular conservation – restoration works and other measures of technical protection particular importance should be given to the preparatory efforts for preservation of the cultural assets from consequences of the armed conflict. These measures include primarily planning of urgent measures for the protection of the assets from the risks of fire or destruction, preparation for evacuation of movable assets and procurement of appropriate materials for assets protection in situ. This concerns special measures of architectural nature, provision of save shelters, elaboration of evacuation plans, provision of appropriate packing materials etc.

4. Risk assessment

The risk assessment plans should be regularly updated and revised to respect all factors of risk, natural as well as those manmade. Such plans should include but not be limited to active protection of the unmovable and movable assets, evacuation and emergency planning.

5. Military measures

It is recommended that all members of the military and security agencies are familiar with the location and history of the cultural asset especially those that are of international, national and regional significance. Also, relevant military training should include special courses that will enable good knowledge of the 1954 Hague Convention and its follow up documents as well as knowledge of other international agreements on cultural heritage protection.

6. Administrative measures

To be able to manage eventual consequences of an armed conflict or natural disaster all relevant administrative structures should be strengthened. Such strengthening should reflect on the collaboration with all other actors as education and scientific institutions are and the non-governmental organizations on cultural heritage.

7. Legal measures

Having in mind that the international agreements even those that refer to the cultural heritage have legal jurisdiction only in the countries that have ratified them, namely accepted them, we appeal to the countries that have not done so yet, to become signatories to all relevant international agreements on cultural heritage protection including the Second Protocol to the 1954 Hague Convention adopted in 1999. Also it has been recommended that laws and other national regulations be adopted for the implementation of ratified international agreements on cultural heritage protection in case of armed conflict as well as for other international agreements on this topic.

8. Bilateral agreements and regional cooperation

With the aim to strengthen the existing frames of cultural heritage protection every state should make the efforts to conclude bilateral agreements with the countries in the broader region to which it belongs thus advancing regional cooperation.

II. Activities during the Armed Conflict

9. Protection implementation matrix

Relevant international agreements in the field of military and humanitarian law basically provide for immunity of the cultural assets through differentiated regime of general, special and strengthened protection. In this respect the responsibilities of the countries signatories of these agreements are clearly defined. On the other side, any national system for protection of cultural heritage regulates more or less the implementation of the cultural heritage protection in state of war through laws or regulations and other rules and the defense namely disaster emergency plans as well.

However, in practice, contrary to peacetime planning there is a need imposed for additional tasks and role determination for the various participants in relation to cultural heritage protection in armed conflict irrespective if state of war has been declared or not. In this respect it has been assessed that it is necessary to develop a generic model for determination of tasks through adoption of a matrix for the protection of the cultural heritage in time of armed conflict. This matrix may be used as a formula for checking i.e. a means of analysis.

The matrix itself indicates four categories of involved: a. civilian state authorities responsible for the cultural heritage protection (museums, libraries, archives, centers, laboratories etc.); b. parties in the conflict including 'our own forces' and the 'opposing forces'; c. peace supporting forces and d. international and non-governmental organizations. Each of these participants involved in the matrix has or may have a properly defined role and task depending on concrete circumstances. The basic tasks i.e. activities during an armed conflict as element of the matrix are listed under the headings bellow.

10. Physical safeguard

To prevent the cultural heritage becoming a legal military target but also to avoid its destruction, burning, looting or any other act of vandalism, immediately after the outburst of animosity or immediately ahead of it, physical protection of selected structures and site should be undertaken. There should be here an assessment of what kind of protection measures should be used to justify the deployment of guards.

11. Monitoring

For certain selected sites and structures for which the measure of physical protection is not applied presence of monitors should be provided. The aim of this measure is to prevent destruction, looting and vandalism.

12. Technical protection in situ

This measure is undertaken for most diverse kinds of structures and sites especially for those that have characteristically artistic and other contents. Based on previously provided appropriate materials (see Heading 3 of this Declaration) technical protection is undertaken (walling up, earth fill, paving, strengthening etc.) based on appropriate order by the competent body.

13. Dismounting

Certain composite parts of immovable cultural assets for which high degree of risk has been determined are dismounted and sheltered at an other appropriate place all in accordance with the plan and previous order by the competent body.

14. Evacuation

Evacuation is implemented according set plans and when an evacuation order has been received. This measure involves special transport within the frontiers of the country but also on the territory of an other state and strict respect for predetermined procedures.

15. Conservation measures

During the time of an armed conflict it is desirable to practice only preventive conservation and other temporary measures of direct protection to prevent further destruction. The control of the physical state of the protected assets and documentation of changes is of extraordinary importance.

16. Measure of precaution

During an armed conflict each responsible command has the responsibility to undertake measures of precaution from an attack and measures of precaution against the consequences of an attack. The first group of measures understands precaution in selecting the targets, means and methods of attack, while the second refers to dislocation of cultural assets that are found in the vicinity of military structures or provision of in situ protection if they are not dislocated and avoidance of deploying military means in the vicinity of cultural assets.

17. Cooperation of military and civilian authorities

The civilian authorities and public services on cultural heritage which continue to work in conditions of military conflict coordinate their activities with the responsible military command and in this respect collaborate with the military units and personnel appointed for the cultural assets protection.

18. Personnel identification

Civilian authorities and public services personnel for the protection of cultural heritage has to be provided with properly issued identification cards and armbands indicating applications of international identification marks set by the 1954 Hague Convention. The identity cards and armbands should be prepared in accordance with national regulations even at peacetime and distributed immediately after r the start of animosities. The identity cards and armbands are also issued to other individuals in accordance with the Convention and The Rules for its implementation.

19. Mediation, assistance

Beside the institutional frames of international control set by the Rules for Implementation of the 1954 Hague Convention the practice has indicated the need to engage other participants. Most often these are the 'Peace support forces' and a significant role may be played by the international governmental and non-governmental organizations as the UN, EU, ICRC, OSCE, the Blue Shield Organization etc. In this context the concept of 'Civilian ' military cooperation' (CIMIC) is recommended.

20. Investigations

During the armed conflict investigation and other activities in respect of discovering, apprehending and determination of criminal responsibility of perpetuators of war crimes against the cultural heritage should not be excluded as well as for the determination of other responsibilities of the perpetuators of crimes against protected assets.

III. Activities after the Armed Conflict

21. National Crisis Council

If this has not been already done during the armed conflict it is recommended that a National Crisis Council be established i.e. a body with an appropriate other name as for example – national Council for Emergency Interventions. This Council should be composed by representatives of the various ethnic and religious groups if for the respective country on the territory of which the armed conflict is taking place such a structure is necessary. The activity of such a body is significant especially in the conditions when it can not be determined with certainty if the armed conflict has ceased i.e. when the post-conflict period started.

22. Priority list

It has been recommended to elaborate and adopt a priority list of endangered cultural heritage parallel with organized activities on determination of the war damage or immediately after that.

23. Endangered cultural heritage

Efforts should not be spared to up grade the laws of the national systems on cultural heritage protection where the laws of that field do not contain provisions on endangered cultural heritage as a specific and priority category. Also, according to the Priority List of Heading 22 of this declaration, the endangered cultural heritage should be protected according to special programs or it should be given priority in financing and implementation of regular programs of the competent public services.

24. Owner information

Proprietors and other owners of protected immovable and movable assets should receive all relevant information in respect of planned activities to rehabilitate the armed conflict damage from the competent bodies and public services. These should include conditions; procedures and manner in which they can execute their rights especially in case of subsidy, loans or other forms of assistance from the state including compensation for determined damage.

25. Role of religious leaders

In countries or communities where more confessions exist and are active, if not done before or during the armed conflict, it is desirable that religious leaders advocate the strengthening of confidence and respect for the cultural heritage irrespective of the confession to which it belongs. The making of separate or joint public statements may have great effect on the sensitivisation of the believers.

IV. The 'Macedonia Case'

26. Concern, condemnation, encouragement, appeal

In respect of the destruction and damage to cultural assets in the 'Macedonia Case' the participants of the Urgent Regional Workshop:

a. express their deep concern for the state of the cultural heritage after the recent armed conflict;
b. condemn manifested vandalistic, revengeful and other acts of violence against protected sacral monuments and other religious structures, but also of their use as military objects and attack targets;
c. encourage the competent Macedonian authorities especially the governmental and non-governmental organizations in their efforts to provide greater voice to the "Case Macedonia" with all relevant information on the destruction and damage to cultural assets being distributed to interested international organizations;
d. urge the international community, at the request of the Macedonian authorities or at their own initiative, to offer financial, technical and other kinds of assistance on a non-commercial base for the rehabilitation of the war damage on the cultural heritage and its reconstruction.

27. National Blue Shield Committee

The establishment of a National Committee of the Blue Shield for Macedonia is recommended.

Chapter 13

Iraq and the Second Protocol to the 1954 Hague Convention

*Marja van Heese**

1. Introduction

Our modern Western society evolved from an earlier civilisation, which as far back as 3,200 BC had its own rulers, ministers, civil servants, wage labourers and even a care system for widows and orphans. This civilisation founded the first cities, conducted international trade over distances of more than 2,000 km and built complex irrigation works. The first legal system with laws and codified rights and obligations developed here. Cuneiform, the oldest form of writing, which marked the end of prehistoric times, also originated here. Mesopotamia is the cradle of our Western civilisation; the territory it encompassed falls largely within the borders of modern-day Iraq, though it also included part of Syria and Iran. Iraqi cultural heritage is important not only to Iraq, but to the entire world. What happens to this world heritage is therefore of concern to us all.

In 2003, during the Second Gulf War, it was not only government buildings that were looted, but also the Iraq Museum, the National Library, the National Archives and the Religious Library (Awqaf Library). With the exception of the museum, all the buildings were then set on fire.[1] In addition, considerable damage was inflicted on libraries in Basra and Mosul, the museum in Nimrud and the archaeological remains of the ancient cities of Nineveh, Babylon and Ur. A proportion of the looted property is still missing, and it is doubtful how much of it can ever be traced and returned to the institutions from which it was taken. Even if these irreplaceable works of art and artefacts are recovered, there is no way of knowing what condition they will be in. One thing is certain: many objects, particularly those stolen from archaeological sites, are deliberately stripped of any information regarding their provenance when

* Marja van Heese is an art historian and an inspector on the staff of the Cultural Heritage Inspectorate of the Ministry of Education, Culture and Science of the Netherlands. This article was written in a personal capacity. The opinions in this essay are solely hers and do not necessarily represent those of the Kingdom of the Netherlands.

1 John M. Russell, Archaeological Institute of America, 'A Personal Account of the First UNESCO Cultural Heritage Mission to Baghdad, May 16-20, 2003' (2003).

Nout van Woudenberg and Liesbeth Lijnzaad (eds.) Protecting Cultural Property in Armed Conflict
© *2010 Koninklijke Brill NV. Printed in The Netherlands.* *ISBN 978 9004 18377 3 pp. 135–145.*

they are put up for sale on Western markets, thereby depriving scholars of a great deal of essential information.[2]

Iraq is Party to the 1954 Hague Convention for the Protection of Cultural Property in the Event of Armed Conflict and its First Protocol,[3] but not yet to the Second Protocol of 1999. Article 2 of the Second Protocol states that 'this Protocol supplements the Convention in relations between the parties'. Since Iraq is already party to the Convention, it is also entitled to become party to the Second Protocol.

The Second Protocol calls, inter alia, for parties to take general provisions regarding the protection of cultural property in peacetime. The Convention says much the same thing, but the Second Protocol fleshes out this idea and makes the pertinent concepts more specific; Article 5 (safeguarding of cultural property) of the Second Protocol is thus an elaboration of Article 3 of the Convention. The Second Protocol also offers opportunities for enhanced protection,[4] international assistance[5] and financial assistance for 'emergency [...] measures to be taken to protect cultural property during periods of armed conflict or of immediate recovery after the end of hostilities [...].'[6]

If Iraq had been Party to the Second Protocol, would the situation there have been different – before, during and after the Gulf Wars? Could tangible heritage have been saved? Could certain sites have been spared? In what way could the Second Protocol have had added value for Iraq? This article is an attempt to answer these questions.

2. The situation in Iraq

2.1 Cultural situation before the war

An almost uninterrupted series of excavations were conducted in Iraq from 1840 all the way up to the 1980s, by British, French, German, Italian, American, Polish, Russian, Japanese and Iraqi archaeologists. This period was marked by international cooperation and knowledge-sharing. Until the First Gulf War broke out in the early 1990s, Iraq's cultural heritage was reasonably well protected. There were highly trained archaeologists and a well-developed Department of Antiquities, and looting of archaeological sites was rare.[7]

---

2 D. Meijer and M. van Heese, 'Illegale handel in beschermd cultureel erfgoed uit Irak', *Kunst & Antiek Journaal* 6 (June-July 2007), p. 10.

3 On 21 March 1968, Iraq ratified the 1954 Convention and its First Protocol.

4 Article 10 of the 1999 Second Protocol. Nout van Woudenberg's chapter 'Enhanced Protection: a new form of protection under the 1999 Second Protocol', at pp. 51-58 considers this concept in greater detail.

5 Article 32 (international assistance) and Article 33 (Assistance of UNESCO) of the 1999 Second Protocol.

6 Article 29 (The Fund for the protection of cultural property in the event of armed conflict) of the Second Protocol.

7 P. Gerstenblith, 'From Bamiyan to Baghdad: Warfare and the Preservation of Cultural Heritage at the Beginning of the 21st Century', *Georgetown Journal of International Law* 37.2 (Winter 2006), pp. 278-86.

But in recent years the situation has changed, due to a growing demand for Iraqi objects on the Western market and the economic sanctions imposed on Iraq by the UN Security Council in the 1990s.[8] These developments affected cultural heritage. Collections and their managers were cut off from international trends relating to registration, digital retrieval, conservation and risk management. Scholarly exchanges in the areas of information, technology and security were no longer possible; financial resources were limited, and buildings and sites were not maintained, exposing the often vulnerable objects and structures to the ravages of nature, such as erosion and groundwater problems.[9]

Iraq has 10,548 officially registered archaeological sites and other historical monuments. A conservative estimate puts the total number of archaeological sites between 20,000 and 100,000. Only 1/7 of the sites have ever been investigated, and the scope of the research is highly diverse.[10] The collections of the Iraq Museum comprised approximately 100,000 objects at one time. At the start of the Second Gulf War, as with the First, officials drew up a list of archaeological and cultural sites that had to be protected from attack, along with a list of important buildings in Baghdad. The blue shield, the symbol for marking protected cultural property and as such specified in the 1954 Hague Convention, was affixed to a number of museums.[11]

Iraq has laws to protect cultural property. These prohibit antiquities smuggling, establish a licensing system for excavations and set down rules for the registration of ancient manuscripts.[12] On 12 May 1973 Iraq ratified the 1970 UNESCO Convention on the Means of Prohibiting and Preventing the Illicit Import, Export and Transfer of Ownership of Cultural Property. At first, only one Iraqi site was placed on the

---

8 United Nations Security Council Resolution 661 (August 6, 1990) concerning the situation between Iraq and Kuwait; Resolution 986 (1995) on authorisation to permit the import of petroleum and petroleum products originating in Iraq, as a temporary measure to provide for humanitarian needs of the Iraqi people.

9 M. Olbryś, 'The Polish Contribution to Protection of the Archaeological Heritage in Central South Iraq, November 2003 to April 2005', *Conservation and Management of Archaeological Sites* 8 (2007), p. 90.

10 Ibid., p. 89. John Malcolm Russell describes some of Iraqi's most important sites on the website of the World Monuments Fund: http://www.wmf.org/pdf/ICON_2003_iraq.pdf.

11 P. Gerstenblith, op.cit., pp. 286-87.

12 Antiquities Law no. 59 of 1936 and its two Amendments (no. 120 of 1974 and no. 164 of 1975); Law Prohibiting the Smuggling of Antiquities No. 40 of 1926; Law no. 6 of 1942: Regulations regarding the Registration of Old Manuscripts. Article 3 of the Antiquities Law 1936 reads: "all antiquities in Iraq whether movable or immovable that are now on or under the surface of the soil shall be considered to be the common property of the State." Article 3 further provides that individuals and groups are prohibited from disposing of such property, or from claiming the ownership of such property, other than under the provisions of the 1936 Law. By article 4 the ownership of land does not entitle the land owner to dispose of antiquities discovered on or under the surface of that land, or to excavate for antiquities in that land. For objects removed before 1936 there is equivalent provision in the Antiquities Law 1924. In 2002 a new law entered into force in Iraq, governing archaeological sites, historic buildings and movable cultural heritage; law no. 55 of 2002 for the antiquities and heritage of Iraq.

UNESCO World Heritage List, in 1985: Hatra, a large fortified city under the influence of the Parthian Empire and the capital of the first Arab Kingdom.[13] Babylon, one of the most famous archaeological sites in the world, which was first excavated in 1935, has not, for example, been placed on the List.[14]

2.2 Situation during the war

The outbreak of the Second Gulf War in 2003 showed just how far behind the international mainstream Iraqi museums and other cultural institutions had fallen. There were no complete inventories or documentation for collections, libraries, archives, historic buildings or archaeological sites. There was no central database or any other type of computerised collection registration, and the photographic record was inadequate.[15] Only a few of the registered collections could be transported to scattered locations outside the cultural institutions. A number of objects from the national collections were brought to a place of safety (e.g. the Central Bank, nuclear shelters or various secret storage areas), while in other cases, museum staff had to take makeshift measures, such as surrounding objects with sandbags to help reduce the impact of vibrations and shocks and minimise the damage of a possible fall.[16] In this way, it was possible to safeguard a number of objects, though many buildings nevertheless suffered fire or even structural collapse, resulting in the destruction of cultural property.[17]

Even before the outbreak of the Second Gulf War, Iraqi archaeologists and international experts had warned of the possibility of widespread looting.[18] This was, of course, nothing new. In the years prior to the Second Gulf War, cultural property was illegally excavated from archaeological sites. Items could generally be spirited out of the country by organised networks via the smuggling routes that crisscross the

13 For a full description, see www.whc.unesco.org.

14 Babylon was the capital of two of the most famous kings of antiquity, Hammurabi (1792-1750 BC), who introduced the world's first law code, and Nebuchadnezzar (604-562 BC) who built the Hanging Gardens of Babylon, one of the Seven Wonders of the World.

15 M. Bogdanos, 'The Casualities of War: The Truth about the Iraq Museum, *American Journal of Archaeology* 109 (2005), pp. 477-526. In this article Bogdanos describes the problems associated with reconstructing the original catalogue of the Iraq Museum collections.

16 McGuire Gibson and Donny George Youkhanna, 'What Cultural Ministries and Heritage Sites Should Do to Prepare for Conflict', in *Antiquities under Siege: Cultural Heritage Protection after the Iraq War*, ed. Lawrence Rothfield (Plymouth, 2008), pp. 251-56. The Iraq Museum, for example, is located in one of Bagdad's most unstable areas, only two blocks west of Haifa Street, where it has regularly been subject to vibrations from gunfire and the rumbling of passing tanks.

17 The combination of a number of these factors makes it difficult to reconstruct the original inventories of cultural institutions. Attempts are now being made to do so, with the help of national and international experts.

18 Zainab Bahrani, 'Desecrating history', *The Guardian*, 9 April 2008; Mounir Bouchenaki, 'UNESCO and the Safeguarding of Cultural Heritage', in *Antiquities under Siege*, pp. 214- 218.

country's lengthy borders; once they were out of Iraq, the stolen items typically found their way to Western markets.[19] The situation worsened in the chaotic period leading up to the American invasion in 2003, when the staff of cultural institutions proved powerless against the rapacity of the local population. At the same time, archaeological sites fell victim to organised gangs, who were often heavily armed. There was little that could be done by the State Board of Antiquities and Heritage, whose personnel were poorly paid, unarmed and without access to means of transport.

Archaeological sites were also damaged during the war as a consequence of military operations and their aftermath,[20] such as the construction of barracks and landing strips, the use of HESCO barriers (large bags filled with sand or rubble to serve as barriers for military camps and fortifications),[21] oil and chemical leaks, the use of minarets as posts for snipers,[22] fighting in historic cities like Najaf, the deployment of heavy military machinery and the erection of a military camp in the vicinity of an archaeological site. Babylon, 90 km south of Baghdad, where Saddam had built one of his palaces in 1982, was hard hit during the war; from 2003 to 2004, it was used as the base for coalition forces.[23] Other sites, such as Isin, Samarra, Larsa, Ur and Nineveh, were also subjected to military action and looting.[24] In the course of the Second Gulf War, it also emerged that Saddam Hussein had placed military installations near archaeological sites, such as the Parthian site of Ctesiphon.[25]

As a result of all these factors, art and artefacts representing five millennia of human history could disappear in little over a decade. Thousands of years' worth of archaeological material, stratigraphy and historical data were lost or destroyed, permanently depriving scholars of invaluable information on the sociocultural context of material culture, occupation patterns and urban planning in the past.

19 Neil Brodie, 'The Western Market in Iraqi Antiquities', in *Antiquities under Siege*, pp. 63-72; Neil Brodie, 'The Market in Iraqi Antiquities, 1980-2008', in *Organised Crime in Art and Antiquities*, ed. S. Manacorda (Milan, 2009), pp. 63-74.

20 During the first Gulf War, damage to archaeological sites was limited, thanks to military intervention. P. Gerstenblith, 'The 2003 Gulf War, the Hague Convention and the International Response', in Patty Gerstenblith, *Art, Cultural Heritage, and the Law, Cases and Materials* (Durham, 2008), pp. 535-540.

21 Also known as Concertainer™ Barriers, these are made by the British company Hercules Engineering Solutions Consortium, hence HESCO.

22 An example is the 9th-century Malwiya minaret of the al-Mutawakkil mosque in Samarra. Gerstenblith, *Art, Cultural Heritage and the Law*, p. 539.

23 Report on meeting in Babylon, 11-13 December 2004 (www.britishmuseum.org).

24 To judge by the findings of missions by the British Museum (in June 2008) in the north (Nimrud, Nineveh, Ashur and Hatra) and UNESCO (in November 2008) in the south (Ur, Ubaid, Eridu, Warka, Larsa, Tell el-Ouelli, Lagash, Tell el-Lahm), it would seem that the looting of archaeological sites has stopped. M. Bailey, *The Art Newspaper*, 18 December 2008 and July-August 2008, pp. 1, 4. A positive note is the slow recommencement of archaeological activity in the north of Iraq, where Leiden University (the Netherlands) hopes to start excavations in the Spring of 2010.

25 Gerstenblith, p. 538.

2.3 International assistance during and after the Second Gulf war

Since the start of the 2003 war, international institutions and experts have done a great deal to attract worldwide attention to Iraq's cultural heritage. Measures were taken in a wide variety of areas: legislation, cultural protection, fund-raising and the training of site guards and staff at the Iraq State Board of Antiquities and Heritage.

The UN Security Council issued specific restrictions[26] that were subsequently adopted by the Council of the European Union in Council Regulation (EC) no. 1210/2003.[27] Each of the member states then drew up a list of authorities competent to supervise the implementation of the Regulation's provisions.[28]

A variety of Iraqi and international institutions are working together to protect cultural heritage. On 7 May 2003 the International Council of Museums (ICOM) drew up an Emergency Red List of Iraqi Antiquities at Risk.[29] Interpol launched a special database of stolen Iraqi objects,[30] as did the Oriental Institute of the University of Chicago.[31] A number of task force meetings were organised by UNESCO[32],

---

26 UN Security Council Resolution 1483, of 22 May 2003; section 7 on the protection of Iraq's heritage by establishing a ban on international trade in cultural property illegally removed from Iraq; UN Security Council Resolution 1546 (8 June 2004), which stresses the need to respect Iraq's heritage.

27 Council Regulation (EC) No. 1210/2003 of 7 July 2003 concerning certain specific restrictions on economic and financial relations with Iraq and repealing Regulation (EC) No 2465/96. Article 3 prohibits, within the EU, the import and export of and trade in Iraqi cultural property and other objects of archaeological, historical, cultural, or rare scientific and religious importance which were transported out of Iraq after 6 August 1990.

28 For instance, in the Netherlands the Cultural Heritage Inspectorate, which is part of the Ministry of Education, Culture and Science, is designated as the competent authority, while the Ministry of Foreign Affairs is in charge of the overall coordination of sanction regulations.

29 See http://icom.museum/redlist/irak/en/index.html. This list, which was drawn up by a team of international experts, contains general categories of cultural property that are popular on the illegal art market.

30 Interpol organised an international conference on cultural property stolen in Iraq in Lyon on 5-6 May 2003. See http://www.interpol.int/Public/WorkOfArt/Iraq/Minutes.asp#2. The suppression of the illicit cross-border traffic in antiquities is of course assisted by the ability of claimant States of origin to seek restitutionary legal remedies, the known availability of which should in time act as a deterrent to original removal. The prospects of recovering illicitly removed antiquities from market countries appear to have been significantly enhanced by the decision of the English Court of Appeal in *Government of the Islamic Republic of Iran v The Barakat Galleries Ltd* [2007] EWCA 1374, [2009] QB 22. This landmark decision supports the giving of effect by countries of destination to laws conferring ownership and/or the right of possession over antiquities on the country of origin.

31 See http://oi.uchicago.edu/OI/IRAQ/iraq.html.

32 Compliance with UNESCO's International Code of Ethics for Dealers in Cultural Property (endorsed November 1999) is an important aspect of the fight against the trade in cultural property with illegal origins. See http://portal.unesco.org/culture/en/files/35190/11919358451ethics.doc/ethics.doc, and the ICOM Code of Ethics for Museums (last revised on 8 October 2004) at http://icom.museum/ethics.html.

the International Centre for the Study of the Preservation and Restoration of Cultural Property (ICCROM), the International Council of Museums (ICOM), the International Council on Monuments and Sites (ICOMOS), the International Federation of Library Associations and Institutions (IFLA) and the International Committee of the Blue Shield (ICBS).[33] A similar initiative was mounted by the British Museum in London. Several missions to Iraq were organised to get a sense of the scope of the problem. In 2003 an International Coordination Committee for the Safeguarding of the Cultural Heritage of Iraq (ICC) was created under the joint auspices of the Iraqi authorities and UNESCO, to advise on measures to improve and enhance international cooperation.[34] A separate action plan has been drafted for the restoration of the Iraq Museum and the Babylon archaeological site.[35]

The Iraq Cultural Heritage Project, which is funded by the US government, will provide American resources and expertise to assist in rebuilding professional capabilities in Iraq's museums and archaeological organisations. One way it will be doing this is through grants to help protect and restore key museums, purchase necessary equipment for the Iraq Museum, restore various departments of the Museum and train personnel of the Iraq State Board of Antiquities and Heritage in Amman and Cairo on how to protect cultural heritage sites and document and catalogue objects.[36]

In 2006 and 2008 the whole of Iraq was placed on the List of the 100 Most Endangered Sites of the World Monuments Fund (WMF), an unprecedented

33 It is worth noting that in the past several years UNESCO has also contributed to the rehabilitation of cultural heritage in several countries and regions emerging from conflict, including Afghanistan, South-eastern Europe, Cyprus, Cambodia and Timor-Leste.

34 At the first plenary session of the ICC in May 2004, seven objectives were formulated: 1) institutional reform of the Ministry of Culture, capacity building and training, 2) assisting and strengthening national legislation on cultural heritage, libraries and archives, 3) drafting a museum conservation plan, 4) establishing a network of international partners to rehabilitate the National Library and Archives, 5) coordinating international action and aid, 6) protecting intangible cultural heritage, 7) instituting a national programme for recording and mapping archaeological sites.

35 Final Report on Damage Assessment in Babylon, Subcommittee on Babylon of UNESCO's International Coordination Committee for the Safeguarding of the Cultural Heritage of Iraq, UNESCO, 26 June 2009.

36 Many other institutions have also contributed to the recovery of cultural heritage through smaller initiatives, such as the Prince Claus Fund in the Netherlands with its Cultural Emergency Response project (CER). Together with the International Federation of Library Associations and Institutions, CER contributed to the reorganisation of the Central Library of Baghdad University, al-Waziriye campus (2003-04). The Packard Humanities Institute, for example, has made 20 pick-up trucks available for use by archaeological site guards and has also donated computer equipment and furniture to the Iraq Museum. The Jordanian Department of Antiquities has been holding a number of recovered objects for return to Iraq at some future date – an example of off-site, safe storage of cultural property. See the Third Plenary Session of the ICC in Paris, 13-14 November 2007 Guidelines for the establishment and conduct of safe havens are formulated in Resolution No. 2/2008: Cultural Heritage Law during the 73rd Conference of the International Law Association, held in Rio de Janeiro, Brazil, 17-21 August 2008.

move.[37] Two sites joined Hatra on the UNESCO World Heritage List, in 2003 and 2007.[38] Together with the US Department of State and with the help of local and international partners, the WMF has developed an extensive site management plan, and help has been offered in the preparations of further nominees for the World Heritage List. Along with that, the WMF jointly maintains a state-of-the-art record-keeping system for cultural heritage with the Getty Conservation Institute, a system that makes use of the latest satellite technologies in order to protect sites from future damage.[39]

During the Second Gulf War, especially its later stages, ways were devised for the military to better protect cultural heritage and raise general awareness on the subject. Thanks to the intervention of Dutch and German troops, who were able to ensure that local Bedouins continued to be paid to guard the site, the ruins of the ancient Sumerian city of Uruk (now called Warka) were spared from looting until at least 2005.[40] Spanish and Polish helicopters would regularly fly over the archaeological site at Nippur to prevent looting, and Polish and Italian service personnel trained local guards.[41] During the Second Gulf War the Americans instituted a local amnesty programme, which prompted the mass return of stolen objects to the institutions from which they had been taken.[42] The US has also invested in awareness-raising by distributing information leaflets among the general population and their own troops, and by making specially designed playing cards for American service personnel.[43] The US, the UK, Italy and Poland were particularly instrumental in protecting sites, historic buildings and movable cultural property. But despite these successes, incidents like the looting of the Iraq Museum illustrate the need to incor-

37 For more information on the World Monuments Fund and its activities to protect Iraq's cultural heritage, see http://www.wmf.org/iraq.html.

38 Ashur (Qal'at Sherqat), an ancient city with a rich history that dates back to the 3rd millennium BC (2003) and the archaeological city of Samarra, the site of a powerful Islamic capital that ruled over the provinces of the Abbasid Empire (2007). For a full description, see www.whc.unesco.org.

39 See http://www.getty.edu/conservation/field_projects/iraq/index.html.

40 G. Schwartz, 'Dutch help Bedouins guard the Sumerian site of Uruk', *The Art Newspaper*; J. Kila, 'Utilizing Military Cultural Experts in Times of War and Peace: an Introduction. Cultural Property Protection within the Military, Experiences in Theatre, Different Perceptions of Culture and Practical Problems', in P. Meerts, *Culture and International Law* (The Hague, 2008), pp. 192-200.

41 J. Kila, 'The Role of NATO and Civil Military Affairs', in *Antiquities Under Siege*, pp. 177-194.

42 Bogdanos, op.cit., pp. 495-98.

43 The Heritage Resource Preservation playing cards, which were developed in the US in 2007, are an educational and informational tool for US military personnel deployed in Iraq and Afghanistan. Because of their great success, the concept was freely shared with other parties, including the Netherlands, which produced its own version of the cards in 2009 for the purpose of disseminating the principles of the 1954 Hague Convention and its two Protocols.

porate the element of cultural property protection into the planning of military campaigns.[44]

3. What could have been the added value of the 1999 Second Protocol?

It is fair to say that the case of Iraq is an atypical one. Thanks to the exceptional importance of Iraq's cultural heritage, there was extraordinary worldwide interest in the subject, particularly at the outbreak of the Second Gulf War, and experts and institutions, both national and international, took action on extremely short notice. This level of exceptional assistance – before, during and after a conflict – will obviously not always be possible. What is more, the assistance offered was not always well coordinated and sometimes arrived at the wrong moment.

The Second Protocol can provide various kinds of framework, not only for a possible assistance mechanism, but also for structured measures that can be taken by the State itself.

For example, a substantial part of the Second Protocol's added value lies in the sphere of preventive measures: precautions taken during peacetime, such as drawing up inventories and making contingency plans (e.g. for the evacuation of collections). If States are not capable of doing this themselves, the Second Protocol offers them the option of asking for assistance. Article 32 states that 'a Party may request [...] assistance with respect to the preparation, development or implementation of the laws, administrative provisions and measures referred to in Article 10'. This type of assistance could include help in formulating regulations or safety and security plans, or in aiding museums with conservation activities and other damage-control measures during and after an armed conflict.

Article 33 states that 'a Party may call upon UNESCO for technical assistance in organising the protection of its cultural property, such as preparatory action to safeguard cultural property, preventive and organisational measures for emergency situations and compilation of national inventories of cultural property, or in connection with any other problem arising out of the application of this Protocol.' It is no coincidence that this article puts such a strong emphasis on preventive, preparatory measures: as the saying goes, prevention is better than cure. The Fund for the Protection of Cultural Property in the Event of Armed Conflict, which is provided for in Article 29 of the Second Protocol, also offers the possibility of 'financial and other assistance in support of preparatory or other measures'.

The Second Protocol has another important function when cultural property is subject to direct attack and damage is inflicted on vulnerable archaeological sites and historic locations during an armed conflict. Whenever cultural property is deemed to qualify for 'enhanced protection', the deliberate destruction of this property is subject to penalties under criminal law. The option of imposing such sanctions is an

44 Major James B. Cogbill (US Army), 'Protection of Arts and Antiquities during Wartime: Examining the Past and Preparing for the Future', in *Military Review* (January-February 2008), pp. 30-36; Conference on Protecting Cultural Heritage in Times of Armed Conflict, Tallinn, February 2008.

important principle, but even more important is the fact that eligible property has been placed on the Enhanced Protection List, which gives the belligerent parties a clear idea of the property's status and the consequences of damaging it. One of the conditions for conferring enhanced protection status is that the cultural heritage in question is of 'the greatest importance for humanity'. The above-mentioned Article 32 also offers the opportunity to request assistance for property under enhanced protection.[45]

A further point should be made on the matter of enhanced protection in this context: although sites in Iraq were not directly used as military objectives, they were often inevitably mixed up in the fighting, due to their proximity to military camps or installations or government buildings and sometimes used in support of military action. Under Article 12 of the Second Protocol, this is not permitted if the cultural property is under enhanced protection, and in this example, the Committee would be within its rights to suspend enhanced protection under Article 14.

Finally, if Iraq had been Party to the Second Protocol and had endeavoured to implement Article 30, by disseminating information, conducting educational programmes for the general public and cultural institutions, and incorporating guidelines and instructions on protection in military rules, if necessary in collaboration with UNESCO and similar parties, certain damage to cultural property could have been prevented. The importance of the inclusion of a reference to cultural protection in military regulations is often underestimated, but it proved to be crucial in Iraq.[46] Good communication and cooperation at the highest level can go a long way in preventing damage, as can reaching out to local tribes and making use of cultural experts (known as cultural protection officers) under the auspices of the army.

4. Concluding remarks

In the light of the level of international assistance and financial aid for measures relating to the protection of cultural property, it would almost seem as if Iraq was already party to the Second Protocol during the Second Gulf War. An emergency plan for the rehabilitation of cultural institutions in Iraq was drafted, and various experts and institutions, both national and international, were actively involved in cataloguing the damage done to Iraqi heritage and in issuing recommendations for its recovery. It is worth mentioning that this assistance was not limited to movable and immovable cultural heritage, but extended to intangible cultural heritage that was also under threat, as well as the arts and cultural industries. Thanks to all these measures, many threats to Iraqi cultural heritage were kept within limits, although a substantial proportion of that heritage is still missing and other movable heritage has been irreparably damaged.

If Iraq had truly been a Party to the Second Protocol, a number of things might have gone differently. Iraqi cultural heritage would have been even better protected if preparatory/preventive measures had been taken in peacetime, such as registering

45 Article 32(1): A Party may request from the Committee international assistance for cultural property under enhanced protection [...].

46 See Cogbill, op.cit.

the heritage, drawing up a tentative list of cultural property eligible for enhanced protection, taking photographs for documentation purposes, creating a central database for missing cultural property, formulating emergency measures in the event of fire or structural collapse (complete with risk analyses) and formally designating competent authorities responsible for safeguarding cultural property. If knowledge of the importance of Iraqi cultural heritage had been better disseminated via educational and informational programmes aimed at the public and cultural institutions, the plundering of these institutions and archaeological sites might have been less severe. And if guidelines and instructions had been incorporated into military regulations, military and civil authorities might have had second thoughts about placing military installations in the vicinity of archaeological sites.

Finally, the assistance mechanism should have occupied a more structured, and thus more secure place in the work of local, national and international authorities. For all these reasons it is to be hoped that Iraq will decide to accede to the Second Protocol. And that this move will be followed by other parties, especially States in conflict regions.

Chapter 14

Sleeping Beauty, the untold story of the (first) Protocol to the 1954 Hague Convention

*Liesbeth Lijnzaad**

1. Introduction

In the following, the Protocol to the 1954 Hague Convention (probably soon to be called the *first* Protocol) will be discussed. It is a little-known, yet far-reaching instrument that merits more attention than it has so far received. I intend to explore the substantive content of the Protocol that deals with the seizure of artefacts exported illegally from occupied territory. The role of the State on whose territory such goods are found will be analysed, as well as the problems the obligations in the Protocol cause in a national jurisdiction. Also the more general issues surrounding the implementation of this Protocol will be addressed. A domestic court case in the Netherlands triggered the drafting of implementing legislation in 2007, some fifty years after ratification. More in general, this Protocol raises issues that suggest it is time this Sleeping Beauty be awoken.

2. The (first) Protocol to the 1954 Hague Convention

The Protocol to the 1954 Hague Convention was drafted at the same time as the Convention itself. It had initially not been the intention to create a separate instrument to cover the matter of the illegal exportation in cultural property originating from occupied territories. The separation of the Protocol and the Convention took place in the final phase of the negotiations when it became clear that the provisions on the seizure of immovable property would become a major stumbling block for the future Convention.[1] At the eleventh hour it was decided to separate what are now the Convention and the (first) Protocol. It has hardly been a sophisticated separation – the Protocol bears the scars of a rough cut: it is editorially not really a self-standing instrument. For instance, O'Keefe notes that the provisions of the

* Dr E. Lijnzaad is the Legal Adviser, Head of the International Law Division, Netherlands Ministry of Foreign Affairs. This article was written in her personal capacity. The views expressed are entirely her own and do not necessarily bind the Ministry.

1 L.V. Prott, The Protocol to the Convention for the Protection of Cultural Property in the Event of Armed Conflict (The Hague Convention) 1954, in: Humanitäres Völkerrecht 1993.4, 191-194 at 194.

Nout van Woudenberg and Liesbeth Lijnzaad (eds.) Protecting Cultural Property in Armed Conflict
© *2010 Koninklijke Brill NV. Printed in The Netherlands.* *ISBN 978 9004 18377 3 pp. 147–156.*

Protocol are not called articles, but are merely numbered paragraphs.[2] Part III of the Protocol contains the Final Clauses and is twice as long as the substantive provisions in Parts I and II. Remarkably, the Protocol does not establish a formal link with the Convention, the Protocol is a distinct document and yet it barely looks like that – the close relation with the Convention is still very visible. It is probably a theoretical question, but one wonders whether it would be possible to become a Party to the Protocol without becoming a Party to the Convention.[3]

As these are separate legal instruments, the Convention and the Protocol require separate steps to express consent to be bound. When the United States finally became a party to the 1954 Hague Convention,[4] the then Legal Advisor of the State Department John Bellinger III, mentioned that the United States acceded "because nobody could remember why we were *not* a Party". Yet, the much welcomed US accession was limited to the Convention, and it was hardly noticed that the first Protocol was excluded. Today, while the Convention to date has had 123 ratifications[5], the Protocol is less endowed with a mere 100 ratifications.[6]

The subject matter of the Protocol is the protection of movable cultural objects during occupation, in particular against illegal exportation from occupied territory. These obligations are a reflection of Article 4(3) of the 1954 Hague Convention which obliges the High Contracting Parties to "prohibit, prevent and, if necessary, put a stop to any form of theft, pillage or misappropriation of, and any acts of vandalism directed against, cultural property." Moreover, High Contracting Parties "shall refrain from requisitioning moveable cultural property situated in the territory of another High Contracting Party." Thus the framework is clear, the Occupying Power itself may not take cultural property, and is obliged to protect it against the dangers created by armed conflict. In addition to the role of the Occupying State, other States will have obligations under the Protocol: most notably the State where the protected cultural goods appear.

It should be kept in mind that the law of occupation, and hence the rules on the protection of cultural property during occupation, is only applicable during international armed conflict. The majority of contemporary armed conflicts are non-international, thus limiting the potential impact of these rules.

The 1954 Convention itself also contains a specific provision on occupation in Article 5. This requires the Occupying State to co-operate with the competent authorities of the Occupied State in order to protect cultural property. Also, the Occupying State may be required to take action to protect cultural property if the national authorities are unable to do so. Though the provision does not state this specifically, one gets the impression that Article 5 has been drafted with immovable

---

2 See R. O'Keefe, Protection of cultural property in armed conflict, in: The Handbook of International Humanitarian Law; Dieter Fleck ed.; Cambridge, 2008, 433-474, footnote 106 at 466.

3 See paragraphs 6-15, 1954 Protocol.

4 The United States expressed consent to be bound on 13 March 2009.

5 November 2009.

6 November 2009.

property in mind. In general it deals with objects remaining in the occupied territory, whereas the Protocol deals with objects that have left the country.

As such, the protection of cultural property during occupation is not something that started with the (first) Protocol, earlier instruments also contained rules to that effect. In particular, the law of armed conflict referred to the obligation not to destroy or seize enemy property (presumed to also include a prohibition on the seizure of cultural property) in Article 23(g) of the Hague Regulations.[7] The Hague Regulations state that private property may not be confiscated during occupation (Article 46), and that pillage is forbidden (Article 47). Also, the occupying State must safeguard public property (Article 55) and the seizure, destruction or wilful damage to historic monuments, works of art and science is forbidden and should be prosecuted (Article 56). In the field of cultural law, the 1970 UNESCO Convention on the Illicit Import, Export and Transfer of Ownership of Cultural Property determines in its Article 11 that "[T]he export and transfer of ownership of cultural property under compulsion arising directly or indirectly from the occupation of a country [...] shall be regarded as illicit."[8]

3. Scope of the Protocol

Although it has been called a "revolutionary instrument"[9], the Protocol has led a somewhat sleepy life: it is little known, and not as well ratified as the 1954 Hague Convention. Remarkably, it has rarely been discussed in academic literature, even if the Protocol raises some important questions.[10] Perhaps this is related to the absence until recently of an academic debate about the law of occupation in general. In any case, this absence of a legal debate is striking and leads to the intriguing question whether the Protocol has indeed been implemented, which will be addressed further below.

Let us have a closer look at the obligations under the Protocol. The primary obligation lies with the Occupying State. That State has the responsibility to prevent the export of cultural property from territory occupied by it (paragraph 1). This is also reflected in the 1999 Protocol which in Article 9 states: "[A] Party in occupation of the whole or part of the territory of another Party shall prohibit and prevent in relation to the occupied territory: any illicit export, other removal or transfer of ownership of cultural property." It is a clear and unambiguous rule, which is probably part of international customary law by now. Then the (first) Protocol continues to deal with a second situation: what happens when – in spite of the obligation of the Occupying State – goods have nevertheless left the Occupied Territory. In that case, the State where the goods appear will take them into custody, either automatically or

7 Regulations respecting the laws and customs of war on land, annexed to the IVth Hague Convention (The Hague, 18 October 1907).

8 1970 UNESCO Convention on the Means of Prohibiting and Preventing the Illicit Import, Export and Transfer of Ownership of Cultural Property, 823 UNTS 231.

9 See: Prott, op.cit. at 191.

10 See also: J. Toman, La protection des biens culturels en cas de conflit armé, UNESCO 1994, at 361-378.

at the request of the authorities of the Occupied Territory (paragraph 2). This State is most likely a Third State in relation to the occupation that is taking place elsewhere in the world. It acts in the interest of the protection of cultural heritage, not necessarily in its own interest. That Third State fulfils a treaty obligation, but it does so to the benefit of the Occupied Territory (so that goods may be returned at the close of hostilities) and to the benefit of the Occupying State (which may thus have the possibility to remedy its earlier failure to prevent exportation). The Protocol thus establishes a relationship between three States: the Occupying Power, the Occupied State and the Third State in which cultural heritage originating from the Occupied State appears. It may be said that the Protocol creates a tri-partite relationship that is quite uncommon in international law.

The situation covered by the Protocol is an unusual one. The starting point in law is that each State Party needs to fulfil its treaty obligations in full and in good faith.[11] Yet, *pacta sunt servanda* may prove to be not such a simple rule with respect to this Protocol, considering that not all States in this tri-partite relationship may be Parties to the Protocol. A mere hundred States are Parties to the Protocol, and many States are still missing from the list of States Parties. So it is not unlikely that not all three States in a situation will be bound by the Protocol. The question is what that would mean for the protection of cultural property exported illegally during occupation. Or to put it otherwise, who exactly needs to be bound by the Protocol in order for the system of seizure and return of cultural heritage described in the Protocol to properly function? Is it a requirement that all three States in this situation are each Parties to the Protocol or will two of the three suffice? Is this a *si omnes* type of situation or not?

Let us look at three scenarios with respect to whether States are Parties to the Protocol or not:

1. The first situation is the simplest: all three States concerned are Parties to the Protocol. In the situation in which for whatever reason the Occupying State has been unable to prevent the export of a particular cultural object from the Occupied Territory, the Third State must take this object into custody and it will have to be returned to the relevant authorities at the end of hostilities;
2. What the situation would be when the Occupying State and the Third State are Parties to the Protocol, but the Occupied State is not. According to paragraph 1 of the Protocol, the Occupying State must prevent export of the cultural objects and the Third State must take such objects into custody following paragraph 2. It would appear that this obligation exists irrespective of whether or not the Occupied State is a Party to the Protocol.[12] This is a noteworthy situation in which the Occupied State appears to benefit from a treaty to which it is not a Party in spite of the *pacta tertiis* rule;[13]
3. Third, and perhaps most complicated, is the question what the obligations are when the Occupying State is not a Party, but the Third State and the Occupied

11 Cf. Article 26 Vienna Convention on the Law of Treaties; 1155 UNTS 332.

12 Toman, op.cit. at 373 writes: "Le paragraphe traite de l'exportation par une Haute Partie contractante des biens culturels du territoire occupé, indépendamment du fait que ce territoire appartient à une Partie contractante *ou non*." (emphasis added, LL)

13 But compare Articles.34 and 36 Vienna Convention on the Law of Treaties.

State are. Once cultural goods appear in the Third State, will there be an obligation for the Third State to take such goods into custody when the Occupying State who is not a Party to the Protocol has failed to live up to the rules in paragraph 1 of the Protocol? The mere fact that the Occupying State is not a Party to the Protocol will surely not influence the obligations agreed between the Occupied State and the Third State under the Protocol. Looking at the text of paragraph 2, it is clear that it does not qualify the notion of *"any occupied territory"* in the sense of territory occupied by a State Party only. A logical line of reasoning, and a common sense approach, would thus be that also in this particular case, the Third State is entitled to take custody of cultural property originating in territory occupied by a non-State Party. Whether this goes as far as being a legal obligation is a matter for debate. Additionally, one might argue that if indeed paragraph 1 of the Protocol – the obligation to prevent the exportation of cultural goods from Occupied Territory – would be a rule of customary international law, the authority of the Third State to take those cultural goods into custody is the natural corollary of such a rule.

These are intricate puzzles and to the best of my knowledge they have so far not been discussed in literature about the Protocol. That is surprising, considering the amount of States that are not yet Parties to the Protocol, which implies that situations in which not all three States are parties may arise from time to time.

4. Protecting the new owner

Presumably the crucial issue with the first Protocol and the lack of ratifications is that the Protocol has a scope going beyond the traditional laws of war. While the law of occupation always stressed the need for protection of cultural heritage and has prohibited looting, it has rarely dealt with the consequences of theft and looting during armed conflict. The transfer of cultural property outside of Occupied Territory may in itself be a criminal act (and thus addressed under international criminal law),[14] but that still leaves the question open as to how to deal with the objects themselves. Punishing the perpetrators – if at all feasible – does not yet address the custody over the cultural goods that have disappeared from Occupied Territory.

Paragraphs 2 and 3 on the seizure and return of cultural property imply considering the private law aspects of such steps. Issues of ownership will need to be addressed, and raise questions in the field of private law, and potentially also private international law as well as administrative law. Carducci rightly observes that the first Protocol has "inserted a private law provision in an International Humanitarian Law instrument."[15] Recuperation and seizure of cultural property originating from Occupied Territory trigger discussions about property and ownership, and how to

14 See for instance the 1998 Rome Statute for the International Criminal Court, 2187 UNTS 90, Articles 8.2.a.iv and 8.2.b.xiii.

15 G. Carducci, The protection of cultural property in the event of armed conflict: the 1954 Convention and its two Protocols 50 years after, in: Human Dignity, IIHL Proceedings 2006, 190-196 at 193.

deal with the acquisition in good faith of cultural goods that should not have left occupied territory in the first place. Related to that are questions about the desirability of far-reaching interventions by a State (Party to the Protocol) in questions of ownership. But that is what the (first) Protocol essentially requires.[16]

5. The Netherlands as a Party to the 1954 Hague Convention and Protocol

It is perhaps useful to briefly look at the domestic practice of implementing the Protocol in the Netherlands. The parliamentary papers in preparation of the ratification of the Convention and the Protocol were presented to the Dutch parliament in March 1958.[17] In the parliamentary papers, the Netherlands government expressed its regret about the separation that occurred between the Convention and the Protocol. While explaining that, as a consequence of this, both instruments required separate consent to be bound, the government also described the inevitability of the separation. This had been necessary in order to ensure that as many States as possible could become Parties to the Convention. Compared to today's parliamentary papers, the Explanatory Note is strikingly short. A mere two and a half pages present the reasons for drafting the Convention, the Regulations and the Protocol. The Convention and the Protocol did not cause much debate in parliament and by July 1958 parliamentary approval had been given, and ratification took place in October 1958.

Ordinarily, in the Dutch legal system it is obligatory for the government to indicate already in the parliamentary papers, how and through what kind of domestic legislation the implementation of a treaty is foreseen. In this case such information is missing. If there is no reference to domestic legislation there be two reasons: either the government feels that it is a treaty that will not enter the domestic legal sphere at all, that it is an instrument purely at inter-state level. Or alternatively, the treaty will create individualised rights within the domestic legal sphere and these rights do not require any specific transformation in national law as the treaty itself is sufficiently clear. A self-executing treaty can be directly invoked before a Dutch court.[18]

With respect to the Convention and the Protocol, the parliamentary papers do not contain any indication as to what would be necessary for implementation in the domestic legal system – and no proposals for legislation were included. This is understandable in the sense that most of the Convention deals with questions of the law of armed conflict, which – at the time – was considered law at inter-state level *par excellence*. Yet Article 28, the provision on the incrimination of violations of the 1954 Hague Convention requires a High Contracting Party to "take all necessary steps to prosecute and impose penal or disciplinary sanction upon those persons, of whatever nationality, who commit or order to be committed a breach of the present Convention." The parliamentary papers do not indicate either how this "grave breach" – type of obligation would be implemented. Neither was there any information on how the Protocol would be implemented.

16 Paragraph 2.

17 Kamerstukken II 1957-1958, 5110, 1-3, 19 March 1958.

18 Article 93 Dutch Constitution.

6. Genuine domestic problems: Cypriot icons

So, at the time of ratification of the Protocol in 1958 no specific implementing legislation had been drafted in the Netherlands, and this has not been an issue for a long time. As could be expected things went wrong years later. In 1995, the claimed owners of cultural goods originating from an Occupied Territory obtained an order to seize particular artefacts, which at the time belonged to a Dutch owner.[19] In this situation the Netherlands was the Third State: the goods had arrived in the Netherlands and the occupation was taking place elsewhere. This private law seizure under Dutch law had to be validated before a court as is the regular procedure with respect to seizures, and the claimed owners started a procedure before the district court of Rotterdam for the return of their property. In the court case between the claimant and the current owner, the Netherlands authorities were requested to intervene by the authorities of the Occupied State. Under Dutch law this is however not possible, as no *amicus curiae* procedure or similar interventions exist.

After a lengthy procedure, the Court determined that no implementation legislation for the Protocol existed, and determined that paragraph 4 of the Protocol could not be considered to be directly applicable in the sense of Article 94 of the Dutch Constitution.[20] Consequently the Court was unable to intervene. This decision was upheld in appeal.[21]

The State concerned also separately addressed the Netherlands as a State Party to the Protocol, requesting the intervention of the Dutch authorities. On researching this request, it proved to be impossible to comply with the Protocol in spite of the fact that in this case all three States concerned are Parties to the Protocol. Even if the Protocol (and thus international law) required the Netherlands to comply with the request, it was impossible to do so within existing national law.

The judges' view that the Protocol could not be directly invoked before a Dutch court implied that the implementation of the Protocol in the domestic legal order was incomplete, to put it mildly. In fact, it was clear that legislation needed to be drafted in order to be able to implement the Protocol.

As a consequence of the case of the Cypriot icons new legislation was drafted in the Netherlands. The Cultural Property Originating from Occupied Territory (Return) Act was adopted in March 2007.[22] The Act indicates that it is (retroactively) applicable to goods originating from territories occupied since 14 January 1959, the date on which the Protocol entered into force for the Netherlands. The Act is based on a general prohibition to import cultural goods from occupied territory into the Netherlands or to hold such goods. The Minister for Education, Culture and Science may take into custody such good, including in situations in which there is

19 Also discussing this case G. Carducci, L'obligation de restitution des biens culturels et des object d'art en cas de droit armé: droit coutumier et droit conventionnel avant et après la Convention de La Haye de 1954; in: 104 RGDIP (2000) 289-357, footnote 318 at 346.

20 District Court of Rotterdam, 4 February 1999, published in: NJ kort 1999, 37.

21 Court of Appeals of The Hague, 7 March 2002, unpublished (number 99/693)

22 Stb.2007, 123.

the suspicion of illegal import. Custody will be based on a prior ministerial decision. Payment of costs related to seizure and custody may be imposed on the holder of cultural goods, based on a ministerial decision and such determination of costs may be enforced in court. The taking of cultural goods into custody preceeds a judicial procedure against the owner or holder for the surrender of the goods to the State.

The Dutch failure to properly implement the Protocol leads to the question whether the Netherlands was the only State not to have created appropriate legislation. Informal information from UNESCO suggests that very few States have made such legislation. This would either mean that the Protocol is directly applicable in those States (which is somewhat unlikely), that situations of the import of cultural goods from occupied States have not happened (equally unlikely) or have not been brought before courts. It may in fact be that the Protocol has very much remained law on the books, missing crucial legislation to turn it into law in action.

7. The difficulty of domestic implementation

Domestic implementation of the Protocol appears to require a conceptual framework in which different conflicting principles and rules of law have been considered. Only if a State will have properly thought through all these aspects will it be possible to draft implementing legislation that satisfies the requirements of the Protocol.

It must be recognized that the Protocol, and thus its implementation, tie in with the debate on the issue of the spoils of war. At the very heart of the Protocol is the message that cultural goods need to be returned to the State of origin at the end of occupation. As paragraph 3 clearly states: "Such property shall never be retained as war reparation." So the Protocol clearly expresses contemporary thinking on the obligation to return cultural goods after armed conflict, and it may be that this aspect will reinforce efforts to establish implementing legislation.

While the origins of ownership – be it in good faith or not – are directly related to armed conflict and indeed occupation, the practical issues to address are not very different from intervening in the trade in illegally obtained artefacts in peacetime. The subject matter of the Protocol, the trade in cultural goods exported illegally from Occupied Territory, ties in with modern treaties on the trade of illegally exported goods.[23] While the difference is the Protocol's focus on illegal export from Occupied Territory, in terms of practical intervention required there may be little difference between the Protocol and these contemporary instruments. It probably means that States Parties will be able rely on implementation mechanisms developed for other cultural treaties which may in part also serve to implement this Protocol.

The discussion about the implementation of the (first) Protocol starts with what it exactly is that the Third State[24] does when a cultural object originating in occupied

23 Such as the 1970 UNESCO Convention on Illicit Import, Export and Transfer of Ownership of Cultural Property, or the 1995 UNIDROIT Convention on Stolen or Illegally Exported Cultural Objects. To be found at: http://www.unidroit.org/english/conventions/1995culturalproperty/1995culturalproperty-e.htm.

24 It should be noted that the Dutch legislation is based on the situation that the Netherlands are the Third State, that is the place were the goods from Occupied Territory appear. This perspective runs through the whole Act.

territory is taken into custody. Clearly, there is a need to address how to deal with the good faith owners of cultural property originating from Occupied Territory. Related to the protection of the good faith owner are the constitutional rules on nationalisation of property.[25] Equally relevant are rules from the field of human rights on the protection of the right to property.[26] These are important aspects, as they are key to ensuring the incorporation of the Protocol in domestic law.

It must be recognised that some of the cultural goods originating from occupied territory may in actual fact belong to a *bona fide* owner. There are situations where the owner has legitimately and unknowingly acquired an object that would fall under the protection of the Protocol. Dutch private law, belonging to the Roman law family, requires the protection of the owner in good faith of movable goods against faults in the title to property. This only covers situations of *bona fide*, and is certainly not an excuse for anyone who was aware, or should have been aware, of the tainted origins of a particular object. Yet it may not always be easy to determine whether the objects came from Occupied Territory or from a nearby non-occupied region.

Thus it may be necessary to provide for a procedure in which the *bona fide* character of ownership can be established, and necessarily a procedure must be establish to provide a legal basis for the seizure and custody by the State of the goods concerned. The consequence of ownership in good faith is that for the State to take possession of a particular object, the owner will need to be properly indemnified. While the Protocol provides that the Occupying State is obliged to pay an indemnity to holders in good faith (paragraph 4), it may in practice not be the Occupying State but the Third State who is first confronted with this issue of the protection of the owner or holder in good faith, and the potential financial implications of the seizure.

Paragraph 4 of the 1954 Protocol is the only location where the Protocol speaks about the financial aspects of the seizure of cultural goods. That is striking and one may comment that the absence of indications as to the financial implications is clearly an omission in the Protocol.

The Protocol implies that the Third State makes an effort. It is required to act as a caretaker and custodian of the movable property once it has been seized. This implies concrete steps to safeguard the integrity and the condition of the cultural object. It is a responsibility and it may be an expensive responsibility – safeguarding cultural goods can be costly. A necessary element in steps towards implementation of the Protocol will be the need to seriously consider the potential costs of the storage of goods once they have been seized. While it is necessary to store such goods, these will most likely require specialist handling and hence imply costs for the State seizing them. These costs can be substantial, and it is hardly foreseeable how long the storage and seizure will last as it is rarely clear how long an occupation will last. The Netherlands legislation provides for the possibility of payment of costs by the owner or holder, but that may not always be an available option. The Third State may thus be facing unpredictable expense under the Protocol when an Occupying State is unable to prevent illegal export.

25 Cf. Article 14 Dutch Constitution.

26 Article 17 Universal Declaration of Human Rights, Art.1 First Protocol ECHR.

Under the Protocol there is a suggestion that these efforts will be compensated at the end of the occupation, when the goods are returned to the competent authorities of the territory previously occupied. The Occupying State is under an obligation to pay an indemnity to the holder in good faith of cultural property to be returned to the competent authorities of the territory previously occupied. Presumably the State that has seized cultural property illegally exported from Occupied Territory has become a holder in good faith and will be able to rely on paragraph 4. But obtaining such compensation may not be as certain as it appears from the text. Particularly in a situation in which the Occupying State is not a Party to the Protocol, there is a risk that at the end of the occupation, the Third State may not be compensated for its efforts as there is no legal obligation for the Occupying State to do so.[27] Hence, seizing cultural property originating from Occupied Territory may be a financially risky venture for the Third State.

Indemnity and compensation are financial matters. This becomes important when discussing the scope of the obligations under the Protocol, and thus the scope of the implementing legislation. Clearly a restrictive interpretation of the group of States covered by the Protocol – the *si omnes* question – implies a limitation of the number of situations in which a Third State will have to seize goods and pay indemnity to the owners or holders as well as provide for the seizure, storage and handling of the cultural goods. Or alternatively, the broader the interpretation of the Protocol, the more situations will be covered. Thus the costs will increase, and some costs may not be recovered at the end of the occupation, particularly in cases where the Occupying State is not a Party to the Protocol.[28] That is not an attractive option for the Third State. It is clear that the financial implications of the scope of the Protocol may thus play a role in discussions about implementation of the Protocol.

8. Conclusion

In the end the conclusion must be that the implementation of the Protocol poses serious, but not insurmountable problems, as the Dutch experience shows. Given the lack of clarity surrounding the private law aspects of the role the Third State is to play under the Protocol, it is understandable that these provisions were not easily acceptable at the diplomatic conference in 1954, leading to the separation of the Convention and the Protocol. The key difficulty is the intricate relationship between the three States involved in the execution of the Protocol who are not necessarily all three Parties to the Protocol.

We cannot be complaisant, as the protection of cultural property requires our ongoing efforts. But it may require more discussion before the (first) Protocol wakes up to become well-established law in practice.

27 It is likely that there is a good faith obligation to compensate, but that is not exactly clear. Nor is it clear whether the Third State would have the right to retain the cultural goods seized until compensation has been paid.

28 On the basis of *the pacta tertiis* rule, nothing could be reclaimed from a non-State Party to the Protocol, see: Article 34 Vienna Convention on the Law of Treaties.

Documents

Convention for the Protection of Cultural Property in the Event of Armed Conflict

The High Contracting Parties,

Recognizing that cultural property has suffered grave damage during recent armed conflicts and that, by reason of the developments in the technique of warfare, it is in increasing danger of destruction;

Being convinced that damage to cultural property belonging to any people whatsoever means damage to the cultural heritage of all mankind, since each people makes its contribution to the culture of the world;

Considering that the preservation of the cultural heritage is of great importance for all peoples of the world and that it is important that this heritage should receive international protection;

Guided by the principles concerning the protection of cultural property during armed conflict, as established in the Conventions of The Hague of 1899 and of 1907 and in the Washington Pact of 15 April, 1935;

Being of the opinion that such protection cannot be effective unless both national and international measures have been taken to organize it in time of peace;

Being determined to take all possible steps to protect cultural property;

Have agreed upon the following provisions:

Chapter I. General provisions regarding protection

Article 1. Definition of cultural property

For the purposes of the present Convention, the term `cultural property' shall cover, irrespective of origin or ownership:

(a) movable or immovable property of great importance to the cultural heritage of every people, such as monuments of architecture, art or history, whether religious or secular; archaeological sites; groups of buildings which, as a whole, are of historical or artistic interest; works of art; manuscripts, books and other objects of artistic, historical or archaeological interest; as well as scientific collections and important collections of books or archives or of reproductions of the property defined above;

(b) buildings whose main and effective purpose is to preserve or exhibit the movable cultural property defined in sub-paragraph (a)
such as museums, large libraries and depositories of archives, and refuges intended to shelter, in the event of armed conflict, the movable cultural property defined in sub-paragraph (a);

(c) centers containing a large amount of cultural property as defined in sub-paragraphs (a) and (b), to be known as `centers containing monuments'.

Article 2. Protection of cultural property

For the purposes of the present Convention, the protection of cultural property shall comprise the safeguarding of and respect for such property.

Article 3. Safeguarding of cultural property

The High Contracting Parties undertake to prepare in time of peace for the safeguarding of cultural property situated within their own territory against the foreseeable effects of an armed conflict, by taking such measures as they consider appropriate.

Article 4. Respect for cultural property

1. The High Contracting Parties undertake to respect cultural property situated within their own territory as well as within the territory of other High Contracting Parties by refraining from any use of the property and its immediate surroundings or of the appliances in use for its protection for purposes which are likely to expose it to destruction or damage in the event of armed conflict; and by refraining from any act of hostility, directed against such property.
2. The obligations mentioned in paragraph 1 of the present Article may be waived only in cases where military necessity imperatively requires such a waiver.
3. The High Contracting Parties further undertake to prohibit, prevent and, if necessary, put a stop to any form of theft, pillage or misappropriation of, and any acts of vandalism directed against, cultural property. They shall refrain from requisitioning movable cultural property situated in the territory of another High Contracting Party.
4. They shall refrain from any act directed by way of reprisals against cultural property.
5. No High Contracting Party may evade the obligations incumbent upon it under the present Article, in respect of another High Contracting Party, by reason of the fact that the latter has not applied the measures of safeguard referred to in Article 3.

Article 5. Occupation

1. Any High Contracting Party in occupation of the whole or part of the territory of another High Contracting Party shall as far as possible support the competent national authorities of the occupied country in safeguarding and preserving its cultural property.
2. Should it prove necessary to take measures to preserve cultural property situated in occupied territory and damaged by military operations, and should the competent national authorities be unable to take such measures, the Occupying Power shall, as far as possible, and in close co-operation with such authorities, take the most necessary measures of preservation.
3. Any High Contracting Party whose government is considered their legitimate government by members of a resistance movement, shall, if possible, draw their attention to the obligation to comply with those provisions of the Convention dealing with respect for cultural property.

Article 6. Distinctive marking of cultural property

In accordance with the provisions of Article 16, cultural property may bear a distinctive emblem so as to facilitate its recognition.

Article 7. Military measures

1. The High Contracting Parties undertake to introduce in time of peace into their military regulations or instructions such provisions as may ensure observance of the present Convention, and to foster in the members of their armed forces a spirit of respect for the culture and cultural property of all peoples.
2. The High Contracting Parties undertake to plan or establish in peace-time, within their armed forces, services or specialist personnel whose purpose will be to secure respect for cultural property and to co-operate with the civilian authorities responsible for safeguarding it.

Chapter II. Special protection

Article 8. Granting of special protection

1. There may be placed under special protection a limited number of refuges intended to shelter movable cultural property in the event of armed conflict, of centers containing monuments and other immovable cultural property of very great importance, provided that they:
   (a) are situated at an adequate distance from any large industrial center or from any important military objective constituting a vulnerable point, such as, for example, an aerodrome, broadcasting station, establishment engaged upon work of national defence, a port or railway station of relative importance or a main line of communication;
   (b) are not used for military purposes.

2. A refuge for movable cultural property may also be placed under special protection, whatever its location, if it is so constructed that, in all probability, it will not be damaged by bombs.
3. A center containing monuments shall be deemed to be used for military purposes whenever it is used for the movement of military personnel or material, even in transit. The same shall apply whenever activities directly connected with military operations, the stationing of military personnel, or the production of war material are carried on within the center.
4. The guarding of cultural property mentioned in paragraph I above by armed custodians specially empowered to do so, or the presence, in the vicinity of such cultural property, of police forces normally responsible for the maintenance of public order shall not be deemed to be used for military purposes.
5. If any cultural property mentioned in paragraph 1 of the present Article is situated near an important military objective as defined in the said paragraph, it may nevertheless be placed under special protection if the High Contracting Party asking for that protection undertakes, in the event of armed conflict, to make no use of the objective and particularly, in the case of a port, railway station or aerodrome, to divert all traffic there from. In that event, such diversion shall be prepared in time of peace.
6. Special protection is granted to cultural property by its entry in the 'International Register of Cultural Property under Special Protection'. This entry shall only be made, in accordance with the provisions of the present Convention and under the conditions provided for in the Regulations for the execution of the Convention.

Article 9. Immunity of cultural property under special protection

The High Contracting Parties undertake to ensure the immunity of cultural property under special protection by refraining, from the time of entry in the International Register, from any act of hostility directed against such property and, except for the cases provided for in paragraph 5 of Article 8, from any use of such property or its surroundings for military purposes.

Article 10. Identification and control

During an armed conflict, cultural property under special protection shall be marked with the distinctive emblem described in Article 16, and shall be open to international control as provided for in the Regulations for the execution of the Convention.

Article 11. Withdrawal of immunity

1. If one of the High Contracting Parties commits, in respect of any item of cultural property under special protection, a violation of the obligations under Article 9, the opposing Party shall, so long as this violation persists, be released from the obligation to ensure the immunity of the property concerned. Nevertheless,

whenever possible, the latter Party shall first request the cessation of such violation within a reasonable time.

2. Apart from the case provided for in paragraph 1 of the present Article, immunity shall be withdrawn from cultural property under special protection only in exceptional cases of unavoidable military necessity, and only for such time as that necessity continues. Such necessity can be established only by the officer commanding a force the equivalent of a division in size or larger. Whenever circumstances permit, the opposing Party shall be notified, a reasonable time in advance, of the decision to withdraw immunity.
3. The Party withdrawing immunity shall, as soon as possible, so inform the Commissioner-General for cultural property provided for in the Regulations for the execution of the Convention, in writing, stating the reasons.

Chapter III. Transport of cultural property

Article 12. Transport under special protection

1. Transport exclusively engaged in the transfer of cultural property, whether within a territory or to another territory, may, at the request of the High Contracting Party concerned, take place under special protection in accordance with the conditions specified in the Regulations for the execution of the Convention.
2. Transport under special protection shall take place under the international supervision provided for in the aforesaid Regulations and shall display the distinctive emblem described in Article 16.
3. The High Contracting Parties shall refrain from any act of hostility directed against transport under special protection.

Article 13. Transport in urgent cases

1. If a High Contracting Party considers that the safety of certain cultural property requires its transfer and that the matter is of such urgency that the procedure laid down in Article 12 cannot be followed, especially at the beginning of an armed conflict, the transport may display the distinctive emblem described in Article 16, provided that an application for immunity referred to in Article 12 has not already been made and refused. As far as possible, notification of transfer should be made to the opposing' Parties. Nevertheless, transport conveying cultural property to the territory of another country may not display the distinctive' emblem unless immunity has been expressly granted to it.
2. The High Contracting Parties shall take, so far as possible, the necessary precautions to avoid acts of hostility directed against the transport described in paragraph 1 of the present Article and displaying the distinctive emblem.

Article 14. Immunity from seizure, capture and prize

1. Immunity from seizure, placing in prize, or capture shall be granted to:

   (a) cultural property enjoying the protection provided for in Article 12 or that provided for in Article 13;
   (b) the means of transport exclusively engaged in the transfer of such cultural property.
2. Nothing in the present Article shall limit the right of visit and search.

Chapter IV. Personnel

Article 15. Personnel

As far as is consistent with the interests of security, personnel engaged in the protection of cultural property shall, in the interests of such property, be re-spected and, if they fall into the hands of the opposing Party, shall be allowed to continue to carry out their duties whenever the cultural property for which they are responsible has also fallen into the hands of the opposing Party.

Chapter V. The distinctive emblem

Article 16. Emblem of the convention

1. The distinctive emblem of the Convention shall take the form of a shield, pointed below, persaltire blue and white (a shield consisting of a royal-blue square, one of the angles of which forms the point of the shield, and of a royal-blue triangle above the square, the space on either side being taken up by a white triangle).
2. The emblem shall be used alone, or repeated three times in a triangular formation (one shield below), under the conditions provided for in Article 17.

Article 17. Use of the emblem

1. The distinctive emblem repeated three times may be used only as a means of identification of:
   (a) immovable cultural property under special protection;
   (b) the transport of cultural property under the conditions provided for in Articles 12 and 13;
   (c) improvised refuges, under the conditions provided for in the Regulations for the execution of the Convention.
2. The distinctive emblem may be used alone only as a means of identification of:
   (a) cultural property not under special protection;
   (b) the persons responsible for the duties of control in accordance with the Regulations for the execution of the Convention;
   (c) the personnel engaged in the protection of cultural property;
   (d) the identity cards mentioned in the Regulations for the execution of the Convention.
3. During an armed conflict, the use of the distinctive emblem in any other cases than those mentioned in the preceding paragraphs of the present Article, and

the use for any purpose whatever of a sign resembling the distinctive emblem, shall be forbidden.

4. The distinctive emblem may not be placed on any immovable cultural property unless at the same time there is displayed an authorization duly dated and signed by the competent authority of the High Contracting Party.

Chapter VI. Scope of application of the Convention

Article 18. Application of the Convention

1. Apart from the provisions which shall take effect in time of peace, the present Convention shall apply in the event of declared war or of any other armed conflict which may arise between two or more of the High Contracting Parties, even if the state of war is not recognized by, one or more of them.
2. The Convention shall also apply to all cases of partial or total occupation of the territory of a High Contracting Party, even if the said occupation meets with no armed resistance.
3. If one of the Powers in conflict is not a Party to the present Convention, the Powers which are Parties thereto shall nevertheless remain bound by it in their mutual relations. They shall furthermore be bound by the Convention, in relation to the said Power, if the latter has declared, that it accepts the provisions thereof and so long as it applies them.

Article 19. Conflicts not of an international character

1. In the event of an armed conflict not of an international character occurring within the territory of one of the High Contracting Parties, each party to the conflict shall be bound to apply, as, a minimum, the provisions of the present Convention which relate to respect for cultural property.
2. The parties to the conflict shall endeavour to bring into force, by means of special agreements, all or part of the other provisions of the present Convention.
3. The United Nations Educational, Scientific and Cultural Organization may offer its services to the parties to the conflict.
4. The application of the preceding provisions shall not affect the legal status of the parties to the conflict.

Chapter VII. Execution of the Convention

Article 20. Regulations for the execution of the Convention

The procedure by which the present Convention is to be applied is defined in the Regulations for its execution, which constitute an integral part thereof.

Article 21. Protecting powers

The present Convention and the Regulations for its execution shall be applied with the co-operation of the Protecting Powers responsible for safeguarding the interests of the Parties to the conflict.

Article 22. Conciliation procedure

1. The Protecting Powers shall lend their good offices in all cases where they may deem it useful in the interests of cultural property, particularly if there is disagreement between the Parties to the conflict as to the application or interpretation of the provisions of the present Convention or the Regulations for its execution.
2. For this purpose, each of the Protecting Powers may, either at the invitation of one Party, of the Director-General of the United Nations Educational, Scientific and Cultural Organization, or on its own initiative, propose to the Parties to the conflict a meeting of their representatives, and in particular of the authorities responsible for the protection of cultural property, if considered appropriate on suitably chosen neutral territory. The Parties to the conflict shall be bound to give effect to the proposals for meeting made to them.
   The Protecting Powers shall propose for approval by the Parties to the conflict a person belonging to a neutral Power or a person presented by the Director General of the United Nations Educational, Scientific and Cultural Organization, which person shall be invited to take part in such a meeting in the capacity of Chairman.

Article 23. Assistance of UNESCO

1. The High Contracting Parties may call upon the United Nations Educational, Scientific and Cultural Organization for technical assistance in organizing the protection of their cultural property, or in connexion with any other problem arising out of the application of the present Convention or the Regulations for its execution. The Organization shall accord such assistance within the limits fixed by its programme and by its resources.
2. The Organization is authorized to make, on its own initiative, proposals on this matter to the High Contracting Parties.

Article 24. Special agreements

1. The High Contracting Parties may conclude special agreements for all matters concerning which they deem it suitable to make separate provision.
2. No special agreement may be concluded which would diminish the protection afforded by the present Convention to cultural property and to the personnel engaged in its protection.

Article 25. Dissemination of the Convention

The High Contracting Parties undertake, in time of peace as in time of armed conflict, to disseminate the text of the present Convention and the Regulations for its execution as widely as possible in their respective countries. They undertake, in particular, to include the study thereof in their programmes of military and, if possible, civilian training, so that its principles are made known to the whole population, especially the armed forces and personnel engaged in the protection of cultural property.

Article 26. Translations reports

1. The High Contracting Parties shall communicate to one another, through the Director-General of the United Nations Educational, Scientific and Cultural Organization, the official translations of the present Convention and of the Regulations for its execution.
2. Furthermore, at least once every four years, they shall forward to the Director-General a report giving whatever information they think suitable concerning any measures being taken, prepared or contemplated by their respective administrations in fulfillment of the present Convention and of the Regulations for its execution.

Article 27. Meetings

1. The Director-General of the United Nations Educational, Scientific and Cultural Organization may, with the approval of the Executive Board, convene meetings of representatives of the High Contracting Parties. He must convene such a meeting if at least one-fifth of the High Contracting Parties so request.
2. Without prejudice to any other functions which have been conferred on it by the present Convention or the Regulations for its execution, the purpose of the meeting will be to study problems concerning the application of the Convention and of the Regulations for its execution, and to formulate recommendations in respect thereof.
3. The meeting may further undertake a revision of the Convention or the Regulations for its execution if the majority of the High Contracting Parties are represented, and in accordance with the provisions of Article 39.

Article 28. Sanctions

The High Contracting Parties undertake to take, within the framework of their ordinary criminal jurisdiction, all necessary steps to prosecute and impose penal or disciplinary sanctions upon those persons, of whatever nationality, who commit or order to be committed a breach of the present Convention.

Final provisions

Article 29. Languages

1. The present Convention is drawn up in English, French, Russian and Spanish, the four texts being equally authoritative.
2. The United Nations Educational, Scientific and Cultural Organization shall arrange for translations of the Convention into the other official languages of its General Conference.

Article 30. Signature

The present Convention shall bear the date of 14 May, 1954 and, until the date of 31 December, 1954, shall remain open for signature by all States invited to the Conference which met at The Hague from 21 April, 1954 to 14 May, 1954.

Article 31. Ratification

1. The present Convention shall be subject to ratification by signatory States in accordance with their respective constitutional procedures.
2. The instruments of ratification shall be deposited with the Director-General of the United Nations Educational, Scientific and Cultural Organization.

Article 32. Accession

From the date of its entry into force, the present Convention shall be open for accession by all States mentioned in Article 30 which have not signed it, as well as any other State invited to accede by the Executive Board of the United Nations Educational, Scientific and Cultural Organization. Accession shall be effected by the deposit of an instrument of accession with the Director-General of the United Nations Educational, Scientific and Cultural Organization.

Article 33. Entry into force

1. The present Convention shall enter into force three months after five instruments of ratification have been deposited.
2. Thereafter, it shall enter into force, for each High Contracting Party, three months after the deposit of its instrument of ratification or accession.
3. The situations referred to in Articles 18 and 19 shall give immediate effect to ratifications or accessions deposited by the Parties to the conflict either before or after the beginning of hostilities or occupation. In such cases the Director-General of the United Nations Educational, Scientific and Cultural Organization shall transmit the communications referred to in Article 38 by the speediest method.

Article 34. Effective application

1. Each State Party to the Convention on the date of its entry into force shall take all necessary measures to ensure its effective application within a period of six months after such entry into force.
2. This period shall be six months from the date of deposit of the instruments of ratification or accession for any State which deposits its instrument of ratification or accession after the date of the entry into force of the Convention.

Article 35. Territorial extension of the Convention

Any High Contracting Party may, at the time of ratification or accession, or at any time thereafter, declare by notification addressed to the Director-General of the United Nations Educational, Scientific and Cultural Organization, that the present Convention shall extend to all or any of the territories for whose international relations it is responsible. The said notification shall take effect three months after the date of its receipt.

Article 36. Relation to previous conventions

1. In the relations between Powers which are bound by the Conventions of The Hague concerning the Laws and Customs of War on Land (IV) and concerning Naval Bombardment in Time of War (IX), whether those of 29 July, 1899 or those of 18 October, 1907, and which are Parties to the present Convention, this last Convention shall be supplementary to the aforementioned Convention (IX) and to the Regulations annexed to the aforementioned Convention (IV) and shall substitute for the emblem described in Article 5 of the aforementioned Convention (IX) the emblem described in Article 16 of the present Convention, in cases in which the present Convention and the Regulations for its execution provide for the use of this distinctive emblem.
2. In the relations between Powers which are bound by the Washington Pact of 15 April, 1935 for the Protection of Artistic and Scientific Institutions and of Historic Monuments (Roerich Pact) and which are Parties to the present Convention, the latter Convention shall be supplementary to the Roerich Pact and shall substitute for the distinguishing flag described in Article III of the Pact the emblem defined in Article 16 of the present Convention, in cases in which the present Convention and the Regulations for its execution provide for the use of this distinctive emblem.

Article 37. Denunciation

1. Each High Contracting Party may denounce the present Convention, on its own behalf, or on behalf of any territory for whose international relations it is responsible.

2. The denunciation shall be notified by an instrument in writing, deposited with the Director-General of the United Nations Educational, Scientific and Cultural Organization.
3. The denunciation shall take effect one year after the receipt of the instrument of denunciation. However, if, on the expiry of this period, the denouncing Party is involved in an armed conflict, the denunciation shall not take effect until the end of hostilities, or until the operations of repatriating cultural property are completed, whichever is the later.

Article 38. Notifications

The Director-General of the United Nations Educational, Scientific and Cultural Organization shall inform the States referred to in Articles 30 and 32, as well as the United Nations, of the deposit of all the instruments of ratification, accession or acceptance provided for in Articles 31, 32 and 39 and of the notifications and denunciations provided for respectively in Articles 35, 37 and 39.

Article 39. Revision of the Convention and of the Regulations for its execution

1. Any High Contracting Party may propose amendments to the present Convention or the Regulations for its execution. The text of any proposed amendment shall be communicated to the Director-General of the United Nations Educational, Scientific and Cultural Organization who shall transmit it to each High Contracting Party with the request that such Party reply within four months stating whether it:
   (a) desires that a Conference be convened to consider the proposed amendment;
   (b) favours the acceptance of the proposed amendment without a Conference; or
   (c) favours the rejection of the proposed amendment without a Conference.
2. The Director-General shall transmit the replies, received under paragraph 1 of the present Article, to all High Contracting Parties.
3. If all the High Contracting Parties which have, within the prescribed time-limit, stated their views to the Director-General of the United Nations Educational, Scientific and Cultural Organization, pursuant to paragraph 1(b) of this Article, inform him that they favour acceptance of the amendment without a Conference, notification of their decision shall be made by the Director-General in accordance with Article 38. The amendment shall become effective for all the High Contracting Parties on the expiry of ninety days from the date of such notification.
4. The Director-General shall convene a Conference of the High Contracting Parties to consider the proposed amendment if requested to do so by more than one-third of the High Contracting Parties.
5. Amendments to the Convention or to the Regulations for its execution, dealt with under the provisions of the preceding paragraph, shall enter into force only

after they have been unanimously adopted by the High Contracting Parties represented at the Conference and accepted by each of the High Con-tracting Parties.

6. Acceptance by the High Contracting Parties of amendments to, the Convention or to the Regulations for its execution, which have been adopted by the Conference mentioned in paragraphs 4 and 5, shall be effected by the deposit of a formal instrument with the Director-General of the United Nations Educational, Scientific and Cultural Organization.
7. After the entry into force of amendments to the present Convention or to the Regulations for its execution, only the text of the Convention or of the Regulations for its execution thus amended shall remain open for ratification or accession.

Article 40. Registration

In accordance with Article 102 of the Charter of the United Nations, the present Convention shall be registered with the Secretariat of the United Nations at the request of the Director-General of the United Nations Educational, Scientific and Cultural Organization.

IN FAITH WHEREOF the undersigned, duly authorized, have signed the present Convention.

Done at The Hague, this fourteenth day of May, 1954, in a single copy which shall be deposited in the archives of the United Nations Educational, Scientific and Cultural Organization, and certified true copies of which shall be delivered to all the States referred to in Articles 30 and 32 as well as to the United Nations.

Regulations for the Execution of the Convention for the Protection of Cultural Property in the Event of Armed Conflict

Chapter I. Control

Article 1. International list of persons

On the entry into force of the Convention, the Director-General of the United Nations Educational, Scientific and Cultural Organization shall compile an international list consisting of all persons nominated by the High Contracting Parties as qualified to carry out the functions of Commissioner-General for Cultural Property. On the initiative of the Director-General of the United Nations Educational, Scientific and Cultural Organization, this list shall be periodically revised on the basis of requests formulated by the High Contracting Parties.

Article 2. Organization of control

As soon as any High Contracting Party is engaged in an armed conflict to which Article 18 of the Convention applies:

(a) It shall appoint a representative for cultural property situated in its territory; if it is in occupation of another territory, it shall appoint a special representative for cultural property situated in that territory;

(b) The Protecting Power acting for each of the Parties in conflict with such High Contracting Party shall appoint delegates accredited to the latter in conformity with Article 3 below;

(c) A Commissioner-General for Cultural Property shall be appointed to such High Contracting Party in accordance with Article 4.

Article 3. Appointment of delegates of Protecting Powers

The Protecting Power shall appoint its delegates from among the members of its diplomatic or consular staff or, with the approval of the Party to which they will be accredited, from among other persons.

Article 4. Appointment of 'Commissioner-General

1. The Commissioner-General for Cultural Property shall be chosen from the international list of persons by joint agreement between the Party to which he

will be accredited and the Protecting Powers acting on behalf of the opposing Parties.

2. Should the Parties fail to reach agreement within three weeks from the beginning of their discussions on this point, they shall request the President of the International Court of Justice to appoint the Commissioner-General, who shall not take up his duties until the Party to which he is accredited has approved his appointment.

Article 5. Functions of delegates

The delegates of the Protecting Powers shall take note of violations of the Convention, investigate, with the approval of the Party to which they are accredited, the circumstances in which they have occurred, make representations locally to secure their cessation and, if necessary, notify the Commissioner-General of such violations. They shall keep him informed of their activities.

Article 6. Functions of the Commissioner-General

1. The Commissioner-General for Cultural Property shall deal with all matters referred to him in connexion with the application of the Convention, in conjunction with the representative of the Party to which he is accredited and with the delegates concerned.
2. He shall have powers of decision and appointment in the cases specified in the present Regulations.
3. With the agreement of the Party to which he is accredited, he shall have the right to order an investigation or to, conduct it himself.
4. He shall make any representations to the Parties to the conflict or to their Protecting Powers which he deems useful for the application of the Convention.
5. He shall draw up such reports as may be necessary on the application of the Convention and communicate them to the Parties concerned and to their Protecting Powers. He shall send copies to the Director-General of the United Nations Educational, Scientific and Cultural Organization, who may make use only of their technical contents.
6. If there is no Protecting Power, the Commissioner-General shall exercise the functions of the Protecting Power as laid down in Articles 21 and 22 of the Convention.

Article 7. Inspectors and experts

1. Whenever the Commissioner-General for Cultural Property considers it necessary, either at the request of the delegates concerned or after consultation with them, he shall propose, for the approval of the Party to which he is accredited, an inspector of cultural property to be charged with a specific mission. An inspector shall be responsible only to the Commissioner-General.

2. The Commissioner-General, delegates and inspectors may have recourse to the services of experts, who will also be proposed for the approval of the Party mentioned in the preceding paragraph.

Article 8. Discharge of the mission of control

The Commissioners-General for Cultural Property, delegates of the Protecting Powers, inspectors and experts shall in no case exceed their mandates. In particular, they shall take account of the security needs of the High Contracting Party to which they are accredited and shall in all circumstances act in accordance with the requirements of the military situation as communicated to them by that High Contracting Party.

Article 9. Substitutes for Protecting Powers

If a Party to the conflict does not benefit or ceases to benefit from the activities of a Protecting Power, a neutral State may be asked to undertake those functions of a -Protecting Power which concern the appointment of a Commissioner-General for Cultural Property in accordance with the procedure laid down in Article 4 above. The Commissioner-General thus appointed shall, if need be, entrust to inspectors the functions of delegates of Protecting Powers as specified in the present Regulations.

Article 10. Expenses

The remuneration and expenses of the Commissioner-General for Cultural Property, inspectors and experts shall be met by the Party to which they are accredited. Remuneration and expenses of delegates of the Protecting Powers shall be subject to agreement between those Powers and the States whose interests they are safeguarding.

Chapter II. Special protection

Article 11. Improvised refuges

1. If, during an armed conflict, any High Contracting Party is induced by unforeseen circumstances to set up an improvised refuge and desires that it should be placed under special protection, it shall communicate this fact forthwith to the Commissioner-General accredited to that Party.
2. If the Commissioner-General considers that such a measure is justified by the circumstances and by the importance of the cultural property sheltered in' this improvised refuge, he may authorize the High Contracting Party to display on such refuge the distinctive emblem defined in Article 16 of the Convention. He shall communicate his decision without delay to the delegates of the Protecting Powers who are concerned, each of whom may, within a time limit of 30 days, order the immediate withdrawal of the emblem.

3. As soon as such delegates have signified their agreement or if the time limit of 30 days has passed without any of the delegates concerned having made an objection, and if, in the view of the Commissioner-General, the refuge fulfils the conditions laid down in Article 8 of the Convention, the Commissioner-General shall request the Director-General of the United Nations Educational, Scientific and Cultural Organization to enter the refuge in the Register of Cultural Property under Special Protection.

Article 12. International Register of Cultural Property under Special Protection

1. An 'International Register of Cultural Property under Special Protection' shall be prepared.
2. The Director-General of the United Nations Educational, Scientific and Cultural Organization shall maintain this Register. He shall furnish copies to the Secretary-General of the United Nations and to the High Contracting Parties.
3. The Register shall be divided into sections, each in the name of a High Contracting Party. Each section shall be subdivided into three paragraphs, headed: Refuges, Centers containing Monuments, Other Immovable Cultural Property. The Director-General shall determine what details each section shall contain.

Article 13. Requests for registration

1. Any High Contracting Party may submit to the Director-General of the United Nations Educational, Scientific and Cultural Organization an application for the entry in the Register of certain refuges, centers containing monuments or other immovable cultural property situated within its territory. Such application shall contain a description of the location of such property and shall certify that the property complies with the provisions of Article 8 of the Convention.
2. In the event of occupation, the Occupying Power shall be competent to make such application.
3. The Director-General of the United Nations Educational, Scientific and Cultural Organization shall, without delay, send copies of applications for registration to each of the High Contracting Parties.

Article 14. Objections

1. Any High Contracting Party may, by letter addressed to the Director-General of the United Nations Educational, Scientific and Cultural Organization, lodge an objection to the registration of cultural property. This letter must be received by him within four months of the day on which he sent a copy of the application for registration.
2. Such objection shall state the reasons giving rise to it, the only, valid grounds being that:

(a) the property is not cultural property;
(b) the property does not comply with the conditions mentioned in Article 8 of the Convention.

3. The Director-General shall send a copy of the letter of objection to the High Contracting Parties without delay. He shall, if necessary, seek the advice of the International Committee on Monuments, Artistic and Historical Sites and Archaeological Excavations and also, if he thinks fit, of any other competent organization or person.
4. The Director-General, or the High Contracting Party requesting registration, may make whatever representations they deem necessary to the High Contracting Parties which lodged the objection, with a view to causing the objection to 'be withdrawn.
5. If a High Contracting Party which has made an application for registration in time of peace becomes involved in an armed conflict before the entry has been made, the cultural property concerned shall at once be provisionally entered in the Register, by the Director-General, pending the confirmation, withdrawal or cancellation of any objection that may be, or may have been, made.
6. If, within a period of six months from the date of receipt of the letter of objection, the Director-General has not received from the High Contracting Party lodging the objection a communication stating that it has been withdrawn, the High Contracting Party applying for registration may request arbitration in accordance with the procedure in the following paragraph.
7. The request for arbitration shall not be made more than one year after the date of receipt by the Director-General of the letter of objection. Each of the two Parties to the dispute shall appoint an arbitrator. When more than one objection has been lodged against an application for registration, the High Contracting Parties which have lodged the 'objections shall, by common consent, appoint a single arbitrator. These two arbitrators shall select a chief arbitrator from the international list mentioned in Article 1 of the present Regulations. If such arbitrators cannot agree upon their choice, they shall ask the President of the International Court of Justice to appoint a chief arbitrator who need not necessarily be chosen from the international list. The arbitral tribunal thus constituted shall fix its own procedure. There shall be no appeal from its decisions.
8. Each of the High Contracting Parties may declare, whenever a dispute to which it is a Party arises, that it does not wish to apply the arbitration procedure provided for in the preceding paragraph. In such cases, the objection to an application for registration shall be submitted by the Director-General to the High Contracting Parties. The objection will be confirmed only if the High Contracting Parties so decide by a two-third majority of the High Contracting Parties voting. The vote shall be taken by correspondence, unless the Directory-General of the United Nations Educational, Scientific and Cultural Organization deems it essential to convene a meeting under the powers conferred upon him by Article 27 of the Convention. If the Director-General decides to proceed with the vote by correspondence, he shall invite the High Contracting Parties to transmit their votes by sealed letter within six months from the day on which they were invited to do so.

Article 15. Registration

1. The Director-General of the United Nations Educational, Scientific and Cultural Organization shall cause to be entered in the Register, under a serial number, each item of property for which application for registration is made, provided that he has not received an objection within the time-limit prescribed in paragraph 1 of Article 14.
2. If an objection has been lodged, and without prejudice to the provision of paragraph 5 of Article 14, the Director-General shall enter property in the Register only if the objection has been withdrawn or has failed to be confirmed following the procedures laid down in either paragraph 7 or paragraph 8 of Article 14.
3. Whenever paragraph 3 of Article 11 applies, the Director-General shall enter property in the Register if so requested by the Commissioner-General for Cultural Property.
4. The Director-General shall send without delay to the Secretary-General of the United Nations, to the High Contracting Parties, and, at the request of the Party applying for registration, to all other States referred to in Articles 30 and 32 of the Convention, a certified copy of each entry in the Register. Entries shall become effective thirty days after despatch of such copies.

Article 16. Cancellation

1. The Director-General of the United Nations Educational, Scientific and Cultural Organization shall cause the registration of any property to be cancelled:
   (a) at the request of the High Contracting Party within whose territory the cultural property is situated;
   (b) if the High Contracting Party which requested registration has denounced the Convention, and when that denunciation has taken effect;
   (c) in the special case provided for in Article 14, paragraph 5, when an objection has been confirmed following the procedures mentioned either in paragraph 7 or in paragraph 8 or Article 14.
2. The Director-General shall send without delay, to the Secretary-General of the United Nations and to all States which received a copy of the entry in the Register, a certified copy of its cancellation. Cancellation shall take effect thirty days after the despatch of such copies.

Chapter III. Transport of cultural property

Article 17. Procedure to obtain immunity

1. The request mentioned in paragraph I of Article 12 of the Convention shall be addressed to the Commissioner-General for Cultural Property. It shall mention the reasons on which it is based and specify the approximate number and the importance of the objects-to be transferred, their present location, the location

now envisaged, the means of transport to be used, the route to be followed, the date proposed for the transfer, and any other relevant information.

2. If the Commissioner-General, after taking such opinions as he deems fit, considers that such transfer is justified, he shall consult those delegates of the Protecting Powers who are concerned, on the measures proposed for carrying it out. Following such consultation, he shall notify the Parties to the conflict concerned of the transfer, including in such notification all useful information.
3. The Commissioner-General shall appoint one or more inspectors, who shall satisfy themselves that only the property stated in the request is to be transferred and that the transport is to be by the approved methods and bears the distinctive emblem. The inspector or inspectors shall accompany the property to its destination.

Article 18. Transport abroad

Where the transfer under special protection is to the territory of another country, it shall be governed not only by Article 12 of the Convention and by Article 17 of the present Regulations, but by the following further provisions:

(a) while the cultural property remains on the territory of another State, that State shall be its depositary and shall extend to it as great a measure of care as that which it bestows upon its own cultural property of comparable importance;

(b) the depositary State shall return the property only on the cessation of the conflict; such return shall be effected within six months from the date on which it was requested;

(c) during the various transfer operations, and while it remains on the territory of another State, the cultural property shall be exempt from confiscation and may not be disposed of either by the depositor or by the depositary. Nevertheless, when the safety of the property requires it, the depositary may, with the assent of the depositor, have the property transported to the territory of a third country, under the conditions laid down in the present article;

(d) the request for special protection shall indicate that the State to whose territory the property is to be transferred accepts the provisions of the present Article.

Article 19. Occupied territory

Whenever a High Contracting Party occupying territory of another High Contracting Party transfers cultural property to a refuge situated elsewhere in that territory, without being able to follow the procedure provided for in Article 17 of the Regulations, the transfer in question shall not be regarded as misappropriation within the meaning of Article 4 of the Convention, provided that the Commissioner-General for Cultural Property certifies in writing, after having consulted the usual custodians, that such transfer was rendered necessary by circumstances.

Chapter IV. The distinctive emblem

Article 20. Affixing of the emblem

1. The placing of the distinctive emblem and its degree of visibility shall be left to the discretion of the competent authorities of each High Contracting Party. It may be displayed on flags or armlets; it may be painted on an object or represented in any other appropriate form.
2. However, without prejudice to any possible fuller markings, the emblem shall, in the event of armed conflict and in the cases mentioned in Articles 12 and 13 of the Convention, be placed on the vehicles of transport so as to be clearly visible in daylight from the air as well as from the ground. The emblem shall be visible from the ground:
   (a) at regular intervals sufficient to indicate clearly the perimeter of a centre containing monuments under special protection;
   (b) at the entrance to other immovable cultural property under special protection.

Article 21. Identification of persons

1. The persons mentioned in Article 17, paragraph 2(b) and (c) of the Convention may wear an armlet bearing the distinctive emblem, issued and stamped by the competent authorities.
2. Such persons shall carry a special identity card bearing the distinctive emblem. This card shall mention at least the surname and first names, the date of birth, the title or rank, and the function of the holder. The card shall bear the photograph of the holder as well as his signature or his fingerprints, or both. It shall bear the embossed stamp of the competent authorities.
3. Each High Contracting Party shall make out its own type of identity card, guided by the model annexed, by way of example, to the present Regulations. The' High Contracting Parties shall transmit to each other a specimen of the model they are using. Identity cards shall be made out, if possible, at least in duplicate, one copy being kept by the issuing Power.
4. The said persons may not, without legitimate reason, be deprived of their identity card or of the right to wear the armlet.

First Protocol to the Convention for the Protection of Cultural Property in the Event of Armed conflict 1954

The High Contracting Parties are agreed as follows:

I.

1. Each High Contracting Party undertakes to prevent the exportation, from a territory occupied by it during an armed conflict, of cultural property as defined in Article 1 of the Convention for the Protection of Cultural Property in the Event of Armed Conflict, signed at The Hague on 14 May, 1954.
2. Each High Contracting Party undertakes to take into its custody cultural property imported into its territory either directly or indirectly from any occupied territory. This shall either be effected automatically upon the importation of the property or, failing this, at the request of the authorities of that territory.
3. Each High Contracting Party undertakes to return, at the close of hostilities, to the competent authorities of the territory previously occupied, cultural property which is in its territory, if such property has been exported in contravention of the principle laid down in the first paragraph. Such property shall never be retained as war reparations.
4. The High Contracting Party whose obligation it was to prevent the exportation of cultural property from the territory occupied by it, shall pay an indemnity to the holders in good faith of any cultural property which has to be returned in accordance with the preceding paragraph.

II

5. Cultural property coming from the territory of a High Contracting Party and deposited by it in the territory of another High Contracting Party for the purpose of protecting such property against the dangers of an armed conflict, shall be returned by the latter, at the end of hostilities, to the competent authorities of the territory from which it came.

III

6. The present Protocol shall bear the date of 14 May, 1954 and, until the date of 31 December, 1954, shall remain open for signature by all States invited to the Conference which met at The Hague from 21 April, 1954 to 14 May, 1954.

7. (a) The present Protocol shall be subject to ratification by signatory States in accordance with their respective constitutional procedures.
   (b) The instruments of ratification shall be deposited with the Director General of the United Nations Educational, Scientific and Cultural Organization.
8. From the date of its entry into force, the present Protocol shall be open for accession by all States mentioned in paragraph 6 which have not signed it as well as any other State invited to accede by the Executive Board of the United Nations Educational, Scientific and Cultural Organization. Accession shall be effected by the deposit of an instrument of accession with the Director-General of the United Nations Educational, Scientific and Cultural Organization.
9. The States referred to in paragraphs 6 and 8 may declare, at the time of signature, ratification or accession, that they will not be bound by the provisions of Section I or by those of Section II of the present Protocol.
10. (a) The present Protocol shall enter into force three months after five instruments of ratification have been deposited.
   (b) Thereafter, it shall enter into force, for each High Contracting Party, three months after the deposit of its instrument of ratification or accession.
   (c) The situations referred to in Articles 18 and 19 of the Convention for the Protection of Cultural Property in the Event of Armed Conflict, signed at The Hague on 14 May, 1954, shall give immediate effect to ratifications and accessions deposited by the Parties to the conflict either before or after the beginning of hostilities or occupation. In such cases, the Director-General of the United Nations Educational, Scientific and Cultural Organization shall transmit the communications' referred to in paragraph 14 by the speediest method.
11. (a) Each State Party to the Protocol on the date of its entry into force shall take all necessary measures to ensure its effective application within a period of six months after such entry into force.
   (b) This period shall be six months from the date of deposit of the instruments of ratification or accession for any State which deposits its instrument of ratification or accession after the date of the entry into force of the Protocol.
12. Any High Contracting Party may, at the time of ratification or accession, or at any time thereafter, declare by notification addressed to the Director General of the United Nations Educational, Scientific and Cultural Organization, that the present Protocol shall extend to all or any of the territories for whose international relations it is responsible. The said notification shall take effect three months after the date of its receipt.
13. (a) Each High Contracting Party may denounce the present Protocol, on its own behalf, or on behalf of any territory for whose international relations it is responsible.
   (b) The denunciation shall be notified by an instrument in writing, deposited with the Director-General of the United Nations Educational, Scientific and Cultural Organization.
   (c) The denunciation shall take effect one year after receipt of the instrument of denunciation. However, if, on the expiry of this period, the denouncing

Party is involved in an armed conflict, the denunciation shall not take effect until the end of hostilities, or until the operations of repatriating cultural property are completed, whichever is the later.

14. The Director-General of the United Nations Educational, Scientific and Cultural Organization shall inform the States referred to in paragraphs 6 and 8, as well as the United Nations, of the deposit of all the instruments of ratification, accession or acceptance provided for in paragraphs 7, 8 and 15 and the notifications and denunciations provided for respectively in paragraphs 12 and 13.
15. (a) The present Protocol may be revised if revision is requested by more than one-third of the High Contracting Parties.
    (b) The Director-General of the United Nations Educational, Scientific and Cultural Organization shall convene a Conference for this purpose.
    c) Amendments to the present Protocol shall enter into force only after they have been unanimously adopted by the High Contracting Parties represented at the Conference and accepted by each of the High Contracting Parties.
    (d) Acceptance by the High Contracting Parties of amendments to the present Protocol, which have been adopted by the Conference mentioned in subparagraphs (b) and (c), shall be effected by the deposit of a formal instrument with the Director-General of the United Nations Educational, Scientific and Cultural Organization.
    (e) After the entry into force of amendments to the present Protocol, only the text of the said Protocol thus amended shall remain open for ratification or accession.

In accordance with Article 102 of the Charter of the United Nations, the present Protocol shall be registered with the Secretariat of the United Nations at the request of the Director-General of the United Nations Educational, Scientific and Cultural Organization.

IN FAITH WHEREOF the undersigned, duly authorized, have signed the present Protocol.

Done at The Hague, this fourteenth day of May, 1954, in English, French, Russian and Spanish, the four texts being equally authoritative, in a single copy which shall be deposited in the archives of the United Nations Educational, Scientific and Cultural Organization, and certified true copies of which shall be delivered to all the States referred to in paragraphs 6 and 8 as well as to the United Nations.

Second Protocol to the Hague Convention of 1954 for the Protection of Cultural Property in the Event of Armed Conflict

The Parties,

Conscious of the need to improve the protection of cultural property in the event of armed conflict and to establish an enhanced system of protection for specifically designated cultural property;

Reaffirming the importance of the provisions of the Convention for the Protection of Cultural Property in the Event of Armed Conflict, done at the Hague on 14 May 1954, and emphasizing the necessity to supplement these provisions through measures to reinforce their implementation;

Desiring to provide the High Contracting Parties to the Convention with a means of being more closely involved in the protection of cultural property in the event of armed conflict by establishing appropriate procedures therefor;

Considering that the rules governing the protection of cultural property in the event of armed conflict should reflect developments in international law;

Affirming that the rules of customary international law will continue to govern questions not regulated by the provisions of this Protocol;

Have agreed as follows:

Chapter 1 Introduction

Article 1 Definitions

For the purposes of this Protocol:

a. "Party" means a State Party to this Protocol;
b. "cultural property" means cultural property as defined in Article 1 of the Convention;
c. "Convention" means the Convention for the Protection of Cultural Property in the Event of Armed Conflict, done at The Hague on 14 May 1954;
d. "High Contracting Party" means a State Party to the Convention;
e. "enhanced protection" means the system of enhanced protection established by Articles 10 and 11;

f. "military objective" means an object which by its nature, location, purpose, or use makes an effective contribution to military action and whose total or partial destruction, capture or neutralisation, in the circumstances ruling at the time, offers a definite military advantage;
g. "illicit" means under compulsion or otherwise in violation of the applicable rules of the domestic law of the occupied territory or of international law.
h. "List" means the International List of Cultural Property under Enhanced Protection established in accordance with Article 27, sub-paragraph 1(b);
i. "Director-General" means the Director-General of UNESCO;
j. "UNESCO" means the United Nations Educational, Scientific and Cultural Organization;
k. "First Protocol" means the Protocol for the Protection of Cultural Property in the Event of Armed Conflict done at The Hague on 14 May 1954;

Article 2 Relation to the Convention

This Protocol supplements the Convention in relations between the Parties.

Article 3 Scope of application

1. In addition to the provisions which shall apply in time of peace, this Protocol shall apply in situations referred to in Article 18 paragraphs 1 and 2 of the Convention and in Article 22 paragraph 1.
2. When one of the parties to an armed conflict is not bound by this Protocol, the Parties to this Protocol shall remain bound by it in their mutual relations. They shall furthermore be bound by this Protocol in relation to a State party to the conflict which is not bound by it, if the latter accepts the provisions of this Protocol and so long as it applies them.

Article 4 Relationship between Chapter 3 and other provisions of the Convention and this Protocol

The application of the provisions of Chapter 3 of this Protocol is without prejudice to:

a. the application of the provisions of Chapter I of the Convention and of Chapter 2 of this Protocol;
b. the application of the provisions of Chapter II of the Convention save that, as between Parties to this Protocol or as between a Party and a State which accepts and applies this Protocol in accordance with Article 3 paragraph 2, where cultural property has been granted both special protection and enhanced protection, only the provisions of enhanced protection shall apply.

Chapter 2 General provisions regarding protection

Article 5 Safeguarding of cultural property

Preparatory measures taken in time of peace for the safeguarding of cultural property against the foreseeable effects of an armed conflict pursuant to Article 3 of the Convention shall include, as appropriate, the preparation of inventories, the planning of emergency measures for protection against fire or structural collapse, the preparation for the removal of movable cultural property or the provision for adequate in situ protection of such property, and the designation of competent authorities responsible for the safeguarding of cultural property.

Article 6 Respect for cultural property

With the goal of ensuring respect for cultural property in accordance with Article 4 of the Convention:

a. a waiver on the basis of imperative military necessity pursuant to Article 4 paragraph 2 of the Convention may only be invoked to direct an act of hostility against cultural property when and for as long as:

i. that cultural property has, by its function, been made into a military objective; and

ii. there is no feasible alternative available to obtain a similar military advantage to that offered by directing an act of hostility against that objective;

b. a waiver on the basis of imperative military necessity pursuant to Article 4 paragraph 2 of the Convention may only be invoked to use cultural property for purposes which are likely to expose it to destruction or damage when and for as long as no choice is possible between such use of the cultural property and another feasible method for obtaining a similar military advantage;

c. the decision to invoke imperative military necessity shall only be taken by an officer commanding a force the equivalent of a battalion in size or larger, or a force smaller in size where circumstances do not permit otherwise;

d. in case of an attack based on a decision taken in accordance with sub-paragraph (a), an effective advance warning shall be given whenever circumstances permit.

Article 7 Precautions in attack

Without prejudice to other precautions required by international humanitarian law in the conduct of military operations, each Party to the conflict shall:

a. do everything feasible to verify that the objectives to be attacked are not cultural property protected under Article 4 of the Convention;

b. take all feasible precautions in the choice of means and methods of attack with a view to avoiding, and in any event to minimizing, incidental damage to cultural property protected under Article 4 of the Convention;

c. refrain from deciding to launch any attack which may be expected to cause incidental damage to cultural property protected under Article 4 of the Convention which would be excessive in relation to the concrete and direct military advantage anticipated; and

d. cancel or suspend an attack if it becomes apparent:
   i. that the objective is cultural property protected under Article 4 of the Convention;
   ii. that the attack may be expected to cause incidental damage to cultural property protected under Article 4 of the Convention which would be excessive in relation to the concrete and direct military advantage anticipated.

Article 8 Precautions against the effects of hostilities

The Parties to the conflict shall, to the maximum extent feasible:

a. remove movable cultural property from the vicinity of military objectives or provide for adequate in situ protection;
b. avoid locating military objectives near cultural property.

Article 9 Protection of cultural property in occupied territory

1. Without prejudice to the provisions of Articles 4 and 5 of the Convention, a Party in occupation of the whole or part of the territory of another Party shall prohibit and prevent in relation to the occupied territory:
   a. any illicit export, other removal or transfer of ownership of cultural property;
   b. any archaeological excavation, save where this is strictly required to safeguard, record or preserve cultural property;
   c. any alteration to, or change of use of, cultural property which is intended to conceal or destroy cultural, historical or scientific evidence.
2. Any archaeological excavation of, alteration to, or change of use of, cultural property in occupied territory shall, unless circumstances do not permit, be carried out in close co-operation with the competent national authorities of the occupied territory.

Chapter 3 Enhanced Protection

Article 10 Enhanced protection

Cultural property may be placed under enhanced protection provided that it meets the following three conditions:

a. it is cultural heritage of the greatest importance for humanity;
b. it is protected by adequate domestic legal and administrative measures recognising its exceptional cultural and historic value and ensuring the highest level of protection;
c. it is not used for military purposes or to shield military sites and a declaration has been made by the Party which has control over the cultural property, confirming that it will not be so used.

Article 11 The granting of enhanced protection

1. Each Party should submit to the Committee a list of cultural property for which it intends to request the granting of enhanced protection.
2. The Party which has jurisdiction or control over the cultural property may request that it be included in the List to be established in accordance with Article 27 sub-paragraph 1(b). This request shall include all necessary information related to the criteria mentioned in Article 10. The Committee may invite a Party to request that cultural property be included in the List.
3. Other Parties, the International Committee of the Blue Shield and other non-governmental organisations with relevant expertise may recommend specific cultural property to the Committee. In such cases, the Committee may decide to invite a Party to request inclusion of that cultural property in the List.
4. Neither the request for inclusion of cultural property situated in a territory, sovereignty or jurisdiction over which is claimed by more than one State, nor its inclusion, shall in any way prejudice the rights of the parties to the dispute.
5. Upon receipt of a request for inclusion in the List, the Committee shall inform all Parties of the request. Parties may submit representations regarding such a request to the Committee within sixty days. These representations shall be made only on the basis of the criteria mentioned in Article 10. They shall be specific and related to facts. The Committee shall consider the representations, providing the Party requesting inclusion with a reasonable opportunity to respond before taking the decision. When such representations are before the Committee, decisions for inclusion in the List shall be taken, notwithstanding Article 26, by a majority of four-fifths of its members present and voting.
6. In deciding upon a request, the Committee should ask the advice of governmental and non-governmental organisations, as well as of individual experts.
7. A decision to grant or deny enhanced protection may only be made on the basis of the criteria mentioned in Article 10.
8. In exceptional cases, when the Committee has concluded that the Party requesting inclusion of cultural property in the List cannot fulfil the criteria of Article 10 sub-paragraph (b), the Committee may decide to grant enhanced protection, provided that the requesting Party submits a request for international assistance under Article 32.
9. Upon the outbreak of hostilities, a Party to the conflict may request, on an emergency basis, enhanced protection of cultural property under its jurisdiction or control by communicating this request to the Committee. The Committee shall transmit this request immediately to all Parties to the conflict. In such cases the Committee will consider representations from the Parties concerned on an expedited basis. The decision to grant provisional enhanced protection shall be taken as soon as possible and, notwithstanding Article 26, by a majority of four-fifths of its members present and voting. Provisional enhanced protection may be granted by the Committee pending the outcome of the regular procedure for the granting of enhanced protection, provided that the provisions of Article 10 sub-paragraphs (a) and (c) are met.

10. Enhanced protection shall be granted to cultural property by the Committee from the moment of its entry in the List.
11. The Director-General shall, without delay, send to the Secretary-General of the United Nations and to all Parties notification of any decision of the Committee to include cultural property on the List.

Article 12 Immunity of cultural property under enhanced protection

The Parties to a conflict shall ensure the immunity of cultural property under enhanced protection by refraining from making such property the object of attack or from any use of the property or its immediate surroundings in support of military action.

Article 13 Loss of enhanced protection

1. Cultural property under enhanced protection shall only lose such protection:
   a. if such protection is suspended or cancelled in accordance with Article 14; or
   b. if, and for as long as, the property has, by its use, become a military objective.
2. In the circumstances of sub-paragraph 1(b), such property may only be the object of attack if:
   a. the attack is the only feasible means of terminating the use of the property referred to in sub-paragraph 1(b);
   b. all feasible precautions are taken in the choice of means and methods of attack, with a view to terminating such use and avoiding, or in any event minimising, damage to the cultural property;
   c. unless circumstances do not permit, due to requirements of immediate self-defence:
      i. the attack is ordered at the highest operational level of command;
      ii. effective advance warning is issued to the opposing forces requiring the termination of the use referred to in sub-paragraph 1(b); and
      iii. Reasonable time is given to the opposing forces to redress the situation.

Article 14 Suspension and cancellation of enhanced protection

1. Where cultural property no longer meets any one of the criteria in Article 10 of this Protocol, the Committee may suspend its enhanced protection status or cancel that status by removing that cultural property from the List.
2. In the case of a serious violation of Article 12 in relation to cultural property under enhanced protection arising from its use in support of military action, the Committee may suspend its enhanced protection status. Where such violations are continuous, the Committee may exceptionally cancel the enhanced protection status by removing the cultural property from the List.

3. The Director-General shall, without delay, send to the Secretary-General of the United Nations and to all Parties to this Protocol notification of any decision of the Committee to suspend or cancel the enhanced protection of cultural property.
4. Before taking such a decision, the Committee shall afford an opportunity to the Parties to make their views known.

Chapter 4 Criminal responsibility and jurisdiction

Article 15 Serious violations of this Protocol

1. Any person commits an offence within the meaning of this Protocol if that person intentionally and in violation of the Convention or this Protocol commits any of the following acts:
   a. making cultural property under enhanced protection the object of attack;
   b. using cultural property under enhanced protection or its immediate surroundings in support of military action;
   c. extensive destruction or appropriation of cultural property protected under the Convention and this Protocol;
   d. making cultural property protected under the Convention and this Protocol the object of attack;
   e. theft, pillage or misappropriation of, or acts of vandalism directed against cultural property protected under the Convention.
2. Each Party shall adopt such measures as may be necessary to establish as criminal offences under its domestic law the offences set forth in this Article and to make such offences punishable by appropriate penalties. When doing so, Parties shall comply with general principles of law and international law, including the rules extending individual criminal responsibility to persons other than those who directly commit the act.

Article 16 Jurisdiction

1. Without prejudice to paragraph 2, each Party shall take the necessary legislative measures to establish its jurisdiction over offences set forth in Article 15 in the following cases:
   a. when such an offence is committed in the territory of that State;
   b. when the alleged offender is a national of that State;
   c. in the case of offences set forth in Article 15 sub-paragraphs (a) to (c), when the alleged offender is present in its territory.
2. With respect to the exercise of jurisdiction and without prejudice to Article 28 of the Convention:
   a. this Protocol does not preclude the incurring of individual criminal responsibility or the exercise of jurisdiction under national and international law that may be applicable, or affect the exercise of jurisdiction under customary international law;

b. except in so far as a State which is not Party to this Protocol may accept and apply its provisions in accordance with Article 3 paragraph 2, members of the armed forces and nationals of a State which is not Party to this Protocol, except for those nationals serving in the armed forces of a State which is a Party to this Protocol, do not incur individual criminal responsibility by virtue of this Protocol, nor does this Protocol impose an obligation to establish jurisdiction over such persons or to extradite them.

Article 17 Prosecution

1. The Party in whose territory the alleged offender of an offence set forth in Article 15 sub-paragraphs 1 (a) to (c) is found to be present shall, if it does not extradite that person, submit, without exception whatsoever and without undue delay, the case to its competent authorities, for the purpose of prosecution, through proceedings in accordance with its domestic law or with, if applicable, the relevant rules of international law.
2. Without prejudice to, if applicable, the relevant rules of international law, any person regarding whom proceedings are being carried out in connection with the Convention or this Protocol shall be guaranteed fair treatment and a fair trial in accordance with domestic law and international law at all stages of the proceedings, and in no cases shall be provided guarantees less favorable to such person than those provided by international law.

Article 18 Extradition

1. The offences set forth in Article 15 sub-paragraphs 1 (a) to (c) shall be deemed to be included as extraditable offences in any extradition treaty existing between any of the Parties before the entry into force of this Protocol. Parties undertake to include such offences in every extradition treaty to be subsequently concluded between them.
2. When a Party which makes extradition conditional on the existence of a treaty receives a request for extradition from another Party with which it has no extradition treaty, the requested Party may, at its option, consider the present Protocol as the legal basis for extradition in respect of offences as set forth in Article 15 sub-paragraphs 1 (a) to (c).
3. Parties which do not make extradition conditional on the existence of a treaty shall recognise the offences set forth in Article 15 sub-paragraphs 1 (a) to (c) as extraditable offences between them, subject to the conditions provided by the law of the requested Party.
4. If necessary, offences set forth in Article 15 sub-paragraphs 1 (a) to (c) shall be treated, for the purposes of extradition between Parties, as if they had been committed not only in the place in which they occurred but also in the territory of the Parties that have established jurisdiction in accordance with Article 16 paragraph 1.

Article 19 Mutual legal assistance

1. Parties shall afford one another the greatest measure of assistance in connection with investigations or criminal or extradition proceedings brought in respect of the offences set forth in Article 15, including assistance in obtaining evidence at their disposal necessary for the proceedings.
2. Parties shall carry out their obligations under paragraph 1 in conformity with any treaties or other arrangements on mutual legal assistance that may exist between them. In the absence of such treaties or arrangements, Parties shall afford one another assistance in accordance with their domestic law.

Article 20 Grounds for refusal

1. For the purpose of extradition, offences set forth in Article 15 sub-paragraphs 1 (a) to (c), and for the purpose of mutual legal assistance, offences set forth in Article 15 shall not be regarded as political offences nor as offences connected with political offences nor as offences inspired by political motives. Accordingly, a request for extradition or for mutual legal assistance based on such offences may not be refused on the sole ground that it concerns a political offence or an offence connected with a political offence or an offence inspired by political motives.
2. Nothing in this Protocol shall be interpreted as imposing an obligation to extradite or to afford mutual legal assistance if the requested Party has substantial grounds for believing that the request for extradition for offences set forth in Article 15 sub-paragraphs 1 (a) to (c) or for mutual legal assistance with respect to offences set forth in Article 15 has been made for the purpose of prosecuting or punishing a person on account of that person's race, religion, nationality, ethnic origin or political opinion or that compliance with the request would cause prejudice to that person's position for any of these reasons.

Article 21 Measures regarding other violations

Without prejudice to Article 28 of the Convention, each Party shall adopt such legislative, administrative or disciplinary measures as may be necessary to suppress the following acts when committed intentionally:

a. any use of cultural property in violation of the Convention or this Protocol;
b. any illicit export, other removal or transfer of ownership of cultural property from occupied territory in violation of the Convention or this Protocol.

Chapter 5 The protection of cultural property in armed conflicts not of an international character

Article 22 Armed conflicts not of an international character

1. This Protocol shall apply in the event of an armed conflict not of an international character, occurring within the territory of one of the Parties.

2. This Protocol shall not apply to situations of internal disturbances and tensions, such as riots, isolated and sporadic acts of violence and other acts of a similar nature.
3. Nothing in this Protocol shall be invoked for the purpose of affecting the sovereignty of a State or the responsibility of the government, by all legitimate means, to maintain or re-establish law and order in the State or to defend the national unity and territorial integrity of the State.
4. Nothing in this Protocol shall prejudice the primary jurisdiction of a Party in whose territory an armed conflict not of an international character occurs over the violations set forth in Article 15.
5. Nothing in this Protocol shall be invoked as a justification for intervening, directly or indirectly, for any reason whatever, in the armed conflict or in the internal or external affairs of the Party in the territory of which that conflict occurs.
6. The application of this Protocol to the situation referred to in paragraph 1 shall not affect the legal status of the parties to the conflict.
7. UNESCO may offer its services to the parties to the conflict.

Chapter 6 Institutional Issues

Article 23 Meeting of the Parties

1. The Meeting of the Parties shall be convened at the same time as the General Conference of UNESCO, and in co-ordination with the Meeting of the High Contracting Parties, if such a meeting has been called by the Director-General.
2. The Meeting of the Parties shall adopt its Rules of Procedure.
3. The Meeting of the Parties shall have the following functions:
   (a) to elect the Members of the Committee, in accordance with Article 24 paragraph 1;
   (b) to endorse the Guidelines developed by the Committee in accordance with Article 27 sub-paragraph 1(a);
   (c) to provide guidelines for, and to supervise the use of the Fund by the Committee;
   (d) to consider the report submitted by the Committee in accordance with Article 27 sub-paragraph 1(d);
   (e) to discuss any problem related to the application of this Protocol, and to make recommendations, as appropriate.
4. At the request of at least one-fifth of the Parties, the Director-General shall convene an Extraordinary Meeting of the Parties.

Article 24 Committee for the Protection of Cultural Property in the Event of Armed Conflict

1. The Committee for the Protection of Cultural Property in the Event of Armed Conflict is hereby established. It shall be composed of twelve Parties which shall be elected by the Meeting of the Parties.
2. The Committee shall meet once a year in ordinary session and in extra-ordinary sessions whenever it deems necessary.
3. In determining membership of the Committee, Parties shall seek to ensure an equitable representation of the different regions and cultures of the world.
4. Parties members of the Committee shall choose as their representatives persons qualified in the fields of cultural heritage, defence or international law, and they shall endeavour, in consultation with one another, to ensure that the Committee as a whole contains adequate expertise in all these fields.

Article 25 Term of office

1. A Party shall be elected to the Committee for four years and shall be eligible for immediate re-election only once.
2. Notwithstanding the provisions of paragraph 1, the term of office of half of the members chosen at the time of the first election shall cease at the end of the first ordinary session of the Meeting of the Parties following that at which they were elected. These members shall be chosen by lot by the President of this Meeting after the first election.

Article 26 Rules of procedure

1. The Committee shall adopt its Rules of Procedure.
2. A majority of the members shall constitute a quorum. Decisions of the Committee shall be taken by a majority of two-thirds of its members voting.
3. Members shall not participate in the voting on any decisions relating to cultural property affected by an armed conflict to which they are parties.

Article 27 Functions

1. The Committee shall have the following functions:
   a. to develop Guidelines for the implementation of this Protocol;
   b. to grant, suspend or cancel enhanced protection for cultural property and to establish, maintain and promote the List of Cultural Property under Enhanced Protection;
   c. to monitor and supervise the implementation of this Protocol and promote the identification of cultural property under enhanced protection;
   d. to consider and comment on reports of the Parties, to seek clarifications as required, and prepare its own report on the implementation of this Protocol for the Meeting of the Parties;

   e. to receive and consider requests for international assistance under Article 32;
   f. to determine the use of the Fund;
   g. to perform any other function which may be assigned to it by the Meeting of the Parties.
2. The functions of the Committee shall be performed in co-operation with the Director-General.
3. The Committee shall co-operate with international and national governmental and non-governmental organizations having objectives similar to those of the Convention, its First Protocol and this Protocol. To assist in the implementation of its functions, the Committee may invite to its meetings, in an advisory capacity, eminent professional organizations such as those which have formal relations with UNESCO, including the International Committee of the Blue Shield (ICBS) and its constituent bodies. Representatives of the International Centre for the Study of the Preservation and Restoration of Cultural Property (Rome Centre) (ICCROM) and of the International Committee of the Red Cross (ICRC) may also be invited to attend in an advisory capacity.

Article 28 Secretariat

The Committee shall be assisted by the Secretariat of UNESCO which shall prepare the Committee's documentation and the agenda for its meetings and shall have the responsibility for the implementation of its decisions.

Article 29 The Fund for the Protection of Cultural Property in the Event of Armed Conflict

1. A Fund is hereby established for the following purposes:
   (a) to provide financial or other assistance in support of preparatory or other measures to be taken in peacetime in accordance with, inter alia, Article 5, Article 10 sub-paragraph (b) and Article 30; and
   (b) to provide financial or other assistance in relation to emergency, provisional or other measures to be taken in order to protect cultural property during periods of armed conflict or of immediate recovery after the end of hostilities in accordance with, inter alia, Article 8 sub-paragraph (a).
2. The Fund shall constitute a trust fund, in conformity with the provisions of the financial regulations of UNESCO.
3. Disbursements from the Fund shall be used only for such purposes as the Committee shall decide in accordance with the guidelines as defined in Article 23 sub-paragraph 3(c). The Committee may accept contributions to be used only for a certain programme or project, provided that the Committee shall have decided on the implementation of such programme or project.
4. The resources of the Fund shall consist of:
   (a) voluntary contributions made by the Parties;
   (b) contributions, gifts or bequests made by:
      (i) other States;

(ii) UNESCO or other organizations of the United Nations system;
(iii) other intergovernmental or non-governmental organizations; and
(iv) public or private bodies or individuals;

(c) any interest accruing on the Fund;
(d) funds raised by collections and receipts from events organized for the benefit of the Fund; and
(e) all other resources authorized by the guidelines applicable to the Fund.

Chapter 7 Dissemination of Information and International Assistance

Article 30 Dissemination

1. The Parties shall endeavour by appropriate means, and in particular by educational and information programmes, to strengthen appreciation and respect for cultural property by their entire population.
2. The Parties shall disseminate this Protocol as widely as possible, both in time of peace and in time of armed conflict.
3. Any military or civilian authorities who, in time of armed conflict, assume responsibilities with respect to the application of this Protocol, shall be fully acquainted with the text thereof. To this end the Parties shall, as appropriate:
   (a) incorporate guidelines and instructions on the protection of cultural property in their military regulations;
   (b) develop and implement, in cooperation with UNESCO and relevant governmental and non-governmental organizations, peacetime training and educational programmes;
   (c) communicate to one another, through the Director-General, information on the laws, administrative provisions and measures taken under sub-paragraphs (a) and (b);
   (d) communicate to one another, as soon as possible, through the Director-General, the laws and administrative provisions which they may adopt to ensure the application of this Protocol.

Article 31 International cooperation

In situations of serious violations of this Protocol, the Parties undertake to act, jointly through the Committee, or individually, in cooperation with UNESCO and the United Nations and in conformity with the Charter of the United Nations.

Article 32 International assistance

1. A Party may request from the Committee international assistance for cultural property under enhanced protection as well as assistance with respect to the preparation, development or implementation of the laws, administrative provisions and measures referred to in Article 10.

2. A party to the conflict, which is not a Party to this Protocol but which accepts and applies provisions in accordance with Article 3, paragraph 2, may request appropriate international assistance from the Committee.
3. The Committee shall adopt rules for the submission of requests for international assistance and shall define the forms the international assistance may take.
4. Parties are encouraged to give technical assistance of all kinds, through the Committee, to those Parties or parties to the conflict who request it.

Article 33 Assistance of UNESCO

1. A Party may call upon UNESCO for technical assistance in organizing the protection of its cultural property, such as preparatory action to safeguard cultural property, preventive and organizational measures for emergency situations and compilation of national inventories of cultural property, or in connection with any other problem arising out of the application of this Protocol. UNESCO shall accord such assistance within the limits fixed by its programme and by its resources.
2. Parties are encouraged to provide technical assistance at bilateral or multilateral level.
3. UNESCO is authorized to make, on its own initiative, proposals on these matters to the Parties.

Chapter 8 Execution of this Protocol

Article 34 Protecting Powers

This Protocol shall be applied with the co-operation of the Protecting Powers responsible for safeguarding the interests of the Parties to the conflict.

Article 35 Conciliation procedure

1. The Protecting Powers shall lend their good offices in all cases where they may deem it useful in the interests of cultural property, particularly if there is disagreement between the Parties to the conflict as to the application or interpretation of the provisions of this Protocol.
2. For this purpose, each of the Protecting Powers may, either at the invitation of one Party, of the Director-General, or on its own initiative, propose to the Parties to the conflict a meeting of their representatives, and in particular of the authorities responsible for the protection of cultural property, if considered appropriate, on the territory of a State not party to the conflict. The Parties to the conflict shall be bound to give effect to the proposals for meeting made to them. The Protecting Powers shall propose for approval by the Parties to the conflict a person belonging to a State not party to the conflict or a person presented by the Director-General, which person shall be invited to take part in such a meeting in the capacity of Chairman.

Article 36 Conciliation in absence of Protecting Powers

1. In a conflict where no Protecting Powers are appointed the Director-General may lend good offices or act by any other form of conciliation or mediation, with a view to settling the disagreement.
2. At the invitation of one Party or of the Director-General, the Chairman of the Committee may propose to the Parties to the conflict a meeting of their representatives, and in particular of the authorities responsible for the protection of cultural property, if considered appropriate, on the territory of a State not party to the conflict.

Article 37 Translations and reports

1. The Parties shall translate this Protocol into their official languages and shall communicate these official translations to the Director-General.
2. The Parties shall submit to the Committee, every four years, a report on the implementation of this Protocol.

Article 38 State responsibility

No provision in this Protocol relating to individual criminal responsibility shall affect the responsibility of States under international law, including the duty to provide reparation.

Chapter 9 Final Clauses

Article 39 Languages

This Protocol is drawn up in Arabic, Chinese, English, French, Russian and Spanish, the six texts being equally authentic.

Article 40 Signature

This Protocol shall bear the date of 26 March 1999. It shall be opened for signature by all High Contracting Parties at The Hague from 17 May 1999 until 31 December 1999.

Article 41 Ratification, acceptance or approval

1. This Protocol shall be subject to ratification, acceptance or approval by High Contracting Parties which have signed this Protocol, in accordance with their respective constitutional procedures.
2. The instruments of ratification, acceptance or approval shall be deposited with the Director-General.

Article 42 Accession

1. This Protocol shall be open for accession by other High Contracting Parties from 1 January 2000.
2. Accession shall be effected by the deposit of an instrument of accession with the Director-General.

Article 43 Entry into force

1. This Protocol shall enter into force three months after twenty instruments of ratification, acceptance, approval or accession have been deposited.
2. Thereafter, it shall enter into force, for each Party, three months after the deposit of its instrument of ratification, acceptance, approval or accession.

Article 44 Entry into force in situations of armed conflict

The situations referred to in Articles 18 and 19 of the Convention shall give immediate effect to ratifications, acceptances or approvals of or accessions to this Protocol deposited by the parties to the conflict either before or after the beginning of hostilities or occupation. In such cases the Director-General shall transmit the communications referred to in Article 46 by the speediest method.

Article 45 Denunciation

1. Each Party may denounce this Protocol.
2. The denunciation shall be notified by an instrument in writing, deposited with the Director-General.
3. The denunciation shall take effect one year after the receipt of the instrument of denunciation. However, if, on the expiry of this period, the denouncing Party is involved in an armed conflict, the denunciation shall not take effect until the end of hostilities, or until the operations of repatriating cultural property are completed, whichever is the later.

Article 46 Notifications

The Director-General shall inform all High Contracting Parties as well as the United Nations, of the deposit of all the instruments of ratification, acceptance, approval or accession provided for in Articles 41 and 42 and of denunciations provided for Article 45.

Article 47 Registration with the United Nations

In conformity with Article 102 of the Charter of the United Nations, this Protocol shall be registered with the Secretariat of the United Nations at the request of the Director-General.

IN FAITH WHEREOF the undersigned, duly authorized, have signed the present Protocol.

DONE at The Hague, this twenty-sixth day of March 1999, in a single copy which shall be deposited in the archives of the UNESCO, and certified true copies of which shall be delivered to all the High Contracting Parties.

Act of 19 June 2003 Containing Rules Concerning Serious Violations of International Humanitarian Law* (International Crimes Act)

§ 1. General provisions

Section 1

1. For the purposes of this Act:
   (a) 'the Geneva Conventions' mean:
      (i) the Convention (I) concluded in Geneva on 12 August 1949 for the amelioration of the condition of the wounded and sick in armed forces in the field (Netherlands Treaty Series 1951, 72);
      (ii) the Convention (II) concluded in Geneva on 12 August 1949 for the amelioration of the condition of wounded, sick and shipwrecked members of the armed forces at sea (Netherlands Treaty Series 1951, 73);
      (iii) the Convention (III) concluded in Geneva on 12 August 1949 relative to the treatment of prisoners of war (Netherlands Treaty Series 1951, 74); and
      (iv) the Convention (IV) concluded in Geneva on 12 August 1949 relative to the protection of civilian persons in time of war (Netherlands Treaty Series 1951, 75);
   (b) 'superior' means:
      (i) a military commander, or a person effectively acting as such, who has effective command or authority over or exercises effective control over one or more subordinates;
      (ii) a person who exercises effective authority, in a civilian capacity, over or exercises effective control over one or more subordinates.
   (c) 'deportation or forcible transfer of the population' means the forced removal of persons by expulsion or other coercive acts from the area where they are lawfully present without the existence of any grounds that would justify this under international law;

* This is an English translation of the Dutch *Wet Internationale Misdrijven*. Please note that this English translation is not legally binding. The most recent version of the text of the Act can be found, in Dutch, on the website: http://www.wetten.nl.

(d) 'torture' as referred to in section 4, subsection 1 (f), section 5, subsection 1 (b) and section 6, subsection 1 (a) means the intentional infliction of severe physical or mental pain or suffering upon a person who is in the custody or under the control of the accused, subject to the proviso that the pain or suffering does not result solely from, and is not inherent in or incidental to, lawful sanctions;
(e) 'torture' as referred to in section 8 means the torture as defined in (d) – by or on behalf of a government authority – of a person with a view to extracting information or a confession from him or from a third person, punishing him for an act he or a third person has committed or is suspected of committing, or intimidating him or a third person, or coercing him to do or permit something, or for any reason based on discrimination on any ground whatever;
(f) 'forced pregnancy' means the unlawful imprisonment of a woman forcibly made pregnant, with the intent of affecting the ethnic composition of any population or carrying out other serious violations of international law;
(g) 'the crime of apartheid' means inhumane acts of a character similar to the acts referred to in section 4, subsection 1, committed in the context of an institutionalised regime of systematic oppression and domination by one racial group over any other racial group or groups and committed with the intention of maintaining that regime.

2. The term 'public servant' shall have the same meaning in this Act as in the Criminal Code, subject to the proviso that for the purposes of Dutch criminal law the term includes a person who holds a public office in the service of a foreign State.
3. The terms 'conspiracy' and 'serious bodily injury' shall have the same meaning in this Act as in the Criminal Code.

Section 2

1. Without prejudice to the relevant provisions of the Criminal Code and the Code of Military Law, Dutch criminal law shall apply to:
   (a) anyone who commits any of the crimes defined in this Act outside the Netherlands, if the suspect is present in the Netherlands;
   (b) anyone who commits any of the crimes defined in this Act outside the Netherlands, if the crime is committed against a Dutch national;
   (c) a Dutch national who commits any of the crimes defined in this Act outside the Netherlands.
2. The expression 'any of the crimes defined in this Act' as referred to in subsection 1 shall be equated with the crimes defined in Articles 131-134, 140, 189, 416-417bis and 420bis-420quater of the Criminal Code, if the offence or crime referred to in such articles is a crime defined in this Act.
3. Prosecution on the basis of subsection 1 (c) may also take place if the suspect becomes a Dutch national only after committing the crime.

§ 2. Crimes

Section 3

1. Anyone who: with intent to wholly or partly destroy, any national, ethnic or religious group or a group belonging to a particular race, as such:
   (a) kills members of the group;
   (b) causes serious bodily or mental harm to members of the group;
   (c) deliberately inflicts upon the group conditions of life calculated to bring about the physical destruction of the group, in whole or in part;
   (d) imposes measures intended to prevent births within the group; or
   (e) forcibly transfers children of the group to another group,
   shall be guilty of genocide and liable to life imprisonment or a term of imprisonment not exceeding thirty years or a sixth category fine.
2. Conspiracy and incitement to commit genocide which occur in public, either orally or in writing or by means of images, shall carry the same penalties as prescribed for attempted genocide.

Section 4

1. Anyone who commits one of the following acts shall be guilty of a crime against humanity and liable to life imprisonment or a term of imprisonment not exceeding thirty years or a sixth category fine, if such acts are committed as part of a widespread or systematic attack directed against any civilian population, with knowledge of the attack:
   (a) intentional killing;
   (b) extermination;
   (c) enslavement;
   (d) deportation or forcible transfer of population;
   (e) imprisonment or other severe deprivation of physical liberty in violation of fundamental rules of international law;
   (f) torture (as defined in section 1(1) (d));
   (g) rape, sexual slavery, enforced prostitution, forced pregnancy, enforced sterilisation, or any other form of sexual violence of comparable gravity;
   (h) persecution against any identifiable group or collectivity on political, racial, national, ethnic, cultural, religious, gender or other grounds that are universally recognised as impermissible under international law, in connection with any act referred to in this subsection or any other crime as referred to in this Act;
   (i) enforced disappearance of persons;
   (j) the crime of apartheid;
   (k) other inhumane acts of a similar character which intentionally cause great suffering or serious injury to body or to mental or physical health.
2. For the purposes of this section:
   (a) 'attack directed against any civilian population' means a course of conduct involving the multiple commission of acts referred to in subsection 1 against

any civilian population, pursuant to or in furtherance of a State or organisational policy to commit such attack;
(b) 'enslavement' means the exercise of any or all of the powers attaching to the right of ownership over a person, including the exercise of such power in the course of trafficking in persons, in particular women and children;
(c) 'persecution' means the intentional and severe deprivation of fundamental rights contrary to international law by reason of the identity of the group or collectivity;
(d) 'enforced disappearance of persons' means the arrest, detention or abduction of persons by, or with the authorisation, support or acquiescence of a State or a political organisation, followed by a refusal to acknowledge that deprivation of freedom or to give information on the fate or whereabouts of those persons, with the intention of removing them from the protection of the law for a prolonged period of time.

3. For the purpose of this section, 'extermination' includes the intentional infliction of conditions of life, inter alia the deprivation of access to food and medicine, calculated to bring about the destruction of part of a population.

Section 5

1. Anyone who commits, in the case of an international armed conflict, one of the grave breaches of the Geneva Conventions, namely the following acts if committed against persons protected by the said Conventions:
(a) intentional killing;
(b) torture (as defined in section 1 (1)(d)) or inhuman treatment, including biological experiments;
(c) intentionally causing great suffering or serious injury to body or health;
(d) extensive intentional and unlawful destruction and appropriation of goods without military necessity;
(e) compelling a prisoner of war or other protected person to serve in the armed forces of a hostile power;
(f) intentionally depriving a prisoner of war or other protected person of the right to a fair and regular trial;
(g) unlawful deportation or transfer or unlawful confinement; or
(h) the taking of hostages;
shall be liable to life imprisonment or a term of imprisonment not exceeding thirty years or a sixth category fine.

2. Anyone who commits, in the case of an international armed conflict, one of the grave breaches of the Additional Protocol (I), concluded in Bern on 12 December 1977, to the Geneva Conventions of 12 August 1949, relating to the protection of victims of international armed conflicts (Netherlands Treaty Series 1980, 87), namely:
(a) the acts referred to in subsection 1, if committed against a person protected by the Additional Protocol (I);

(b) any intentional act or omission which jeopardises the health of anyone who is in the power of a party other than the party to which he or she belongs, and which:
  (i) entails any medical treatment which is not necessary as a consequence of the state of health of the person concerned and is not consistent with generally accepted medical standards which would be applied under similar medical circumstances to persons who are nationals of the party responsible for the acts and who are in no way deprived of their liberty;
  (ii) entails the carrying out on the person concerned, even with his consent, of physical mutilations;
  (iii) entails the carrying out on the person concerned, even with his consent, of medical or scientific experiments; or
  (iv) entails removing from the person concerned, even with his consent, tissue or organs for transplantation;
(c) the following acts, when they are committed intentionally and in violation of the relevant provisions of Additional Protocol (I) and cause death or serious injury to body or health:
  (i) making the civilian population or individual citizens the object of attack;
  (ii) launching an indiscriminate attack affecting the civilian population or civilian objects, in the knowledge that such attack will cause excessive loss of life, injury to civilians or damage to civilian objects;
  (iii) launching an attack against works or installations containing dangerous forces, in the knowledge that such an attack will cause excessive loss of life, injury to civilians or damage to civilian objects;
  (iv) making non-defended localities or demilitarised zones the object of attack;
  (v) making a person the object of attack in the knowledge that he is hors de combat; or
  (vi) the perfidious use, in violation of article 37 of Additional Protocol (I), of the distinctive emblem of the red cross or red crescent or of other protective emblems recognised by the Geneva Conventions or Additional Protocol (I); or
(d) the following acts if committed intentionally and in violation of the Geneva Conventions and Additional Protocol (I):
  (i) the transfer by the occupying Power of parts of its own civilian population into the territory it occupies or the transfer of all or part of the population of the occupied territory within or outside this territory in violation of article 49 of the Fourth Geneva Convention;
  (ii) unjustifiable delay in the repatriation of prisoners of war or civilians;
  (iii) practices of apartheid and other inhuman and degrading practices involving outrages upon personal dignity, based on racial discrimination;
  (iv) making clearly recognised historic monuments, works of art or places of worship which constitute the cultural or spiritual heritage of peo-

ples and to which special protection has been given by special arrangement, for example within the framework of a competent international organisation, the object of attack, causing as a result extensive destruction thereof, where there is no evidence of the violation by the adverse Party of Article 53, subparagraph (b), of Additional Protocol (I) and when such historic monuments, works of art and places of worship are not located in the immediate proximity of military objectives; or

(v) depriving a person protected by the Geneva Conventions or Article 85, paragraph 2, of Additional Protocol (I) of the right to a fair and regular trial

shall be liable to life imprisonment or a term of imprisonment not exceeding thirty years or a sixth category fine.

3. Anyone who commits, in the case of an international armed conflict, one of the following acts:
   (a) rape, sexual slavery, enforced prostitution, enforced sterilisation or any other form of sexual violence which can be deemed to be of a gravity comparable to a grave breach of the Geneva Conventions;
   (b) forced pregnancy;
   (c) subjecting persons who are in the power of an adverse party to the conflict to physical mutilation or medical or scientific experiments of any kind, which are neither justified by the medical, dental or hospital treatment of the person concerned nor carried out in his or her interest, and which cause death to or seriously endanger the health of such persons or persons;
   (d) treacherously killing or wounding individuals belonging to the hostile nation or army;
   (e) killing or wounding a combatant who is in the power of the adverse party, who has clearly indicated he wishes to surrender, or who is unconscious or otherwise hors de combat as a result of wounds or sickness and is therefore unable to defend himself, provided that he refrains in all these cases from any hostile act and does not attempt to escape; or
   (f) making improper use of a flag of truce, of the flag or of the military insignia and uniform of the enemy or of the United Nations, as well as of the distinctive emblems of the Geneva Conventions, resulting in death or serious personal injury,

   shall be liable to life imprisonment or a term of imprisonment not exceeding thirty years or a sixth category fine.
4. Anyone who, in the case of an international armed conflict, intentionally and unlawfully commits one of the following acts shall be liable to a term of imprisonment not exceeding fifteen years or a fifth category fine:
   (a) making the object of attack cultural property that is under enhanced protection as referred to in articles 10 and 11 of the Second Protocol, concluded in The Hague on 26 March 1999, to the Hague Convention of 1954 for the Protection of Cultural Property in the Event of Armed Conflict (Netherlands Treaty Series 1999, 107);

(b) using cultural property that is under enhanced protection as referred to in (a) or the immediate vicinity of such property in support of military action;
(c) destroying or appropriating on a large scale cultural property that is under the protection of the Convention, concluded in The Hague on 14 May 1954, for the Protection of Cultural Property in the Event of Armed Conflict (Netherlands Treaty Series 1955, 47) or the Second Protocol thereto;
(d) making cultural property that is under protection as referred to in (c) the object of attack; or
(e) theft, pillaging or appropriation of – or acts of vandalism directed against – cultural property under the protection of the Convention referred to in (c).

5. Anyone who, in the case of an international armed conflict, commits one of the following acts:
(a) intentionally directing attacks against civilian objects, that is, objects that are not military objectives;
(b) intentionally launching an attack in the knowledge that such an attack will cause incidental loss of life or injury to civilians or damage to civilian objects or widespread, long-term and severe damage to the natural environment which would be clearly excessive in relation to the concrete and direct overall military advantage anticipated;
(c) attacking or bombarding, by whatever means, towns, villages, dwellings or buildings which are undefended and which are not military objectives;
(d) the transfer, directly or indirectly, by the occupying Power of parts of its own civilian population into the territory it occupies, or the deportation or transfer of all or part of the population of the occupied territory within or outside this territory;
(e) declaring abolished, suspended or inadmissible in a court of law the rights and actions of the nationals of the hostile party;
(f) compelling the nationals of the hostile party to take part in the operations of war directed against their own country, even if they were in the belligerent's service before the commencement of the war;
(g) employing poison or poisoned weapons;
(h) employing asphyxiating, poisonous or other gases and all analogous liquids, materials or devices;
(i) employing bullets which expand or flatten easily in the human body, such as bullets with a hard envelope which does not entirely cover the core or is pierced with incisions;
(j) committing outrages upon personal dignity, in particular humiliating and degrading treatment;
(k) utilising the presence of a civilian or other protected person to render certain points, areas, or military forces immune from military operations;
(l) intentionally using starvation of civilians as a method of warfare by depriving them of objects indispensable to their survival, including wilfully impeding relief supplies as provided for under the Geneva Conventions;

(m) intentionally directing attacks against the civilian population as such or against individual civilians not taking direct part in hostilities;
(n) intentionally directing attacks against buildings, material, medical units and transport, and personnel using the distinctive emblems of the Geneva Conventions in conformity with international law;
(o) intentionally directing attacks against personnel, installations, material, units or vehicles involved in humanitarian assistance or peace missions in accordance with the Charter of the United Nations, as long as they are entitled to the protection given to civilians or civilian objects under the international law of armed conflict;
(p) intentionally directing attacks against buildings dedicated to religion, education, art, science or charitable purposes, historic monuments, hospitals and places where the sick and wounded are collected, provided they are not military objectives;
(q) pillaging a town or place, even when taken by assault;
(r) conscripting or enlisting children under the age of fifteen years into the national armed forces or armed groups or using them to participate actively in hostilities;
(s) declaring that no quarter will be given; or
(t) destroying or seizing property of the adversary unless such destruction or seizure be imperatively demanded by the necessities of the conflict;

shall be liable to a term of imprisonment not exceeding fifteen years or a fifth category fine.

6. If an act as referred to in subsection 4 or 5:
(a) results in the death of or serious bodily injury to another person or involves rape;
(b) involves violence, committed in association, against one or more persons or violence against a dead, sick or wounded person;
(c) involves destroying, damaging, rendering unusable or removing, in association with others, any property which belongs wholly or partly to another;
(d) involves compelling, in association with others, another person to do, refrain from doing or permit something;
(e) involves pillaging, in association with others, a town or place, even when taken by assault;
(f) involves breaking a promise or breaching an agreement concluded with the adverse party as such; or
(g) involves making improper use of a by the laws and customs protected flag or emblem or of the military insignia and uniform of the enemy,

the perpetrator shall be liable to life imprisonment or a term of imprisonment not exceeding thirty years or a sixth category fine.

7. Subsection 2 (b) (iv) shall not apply if the act described therein:
(a) is consistent with the generally accepted medical standards which would be applied under similar medical circumstances to persons who are nationals of the party responsible for the acts and who are in no way deprived of their liberty; or

(b) concerns a case in which blood is donated for transfusion or skin for transplantation, provided that this occurs voluntarily and without compulsion or insistence and only for therapeutic purposes, in circumstances that are in keeping with generally accepted medical standards and supervisory measures intended to protect the interests of both donor and recipient.

Section 6

1. Anyone who, in the case of an armed conflict not of an international character, commits a violation of article 3 common to all of the Geneva Conventions, namely the commission against persons taking no active part in the hostilities, including members of armed forces who have laid down their arms and those who are placed hors de combat by sickness, wounds, detention, or any other cause, of one of the following acts:
   (a) violence to life and person, in particular killing of all kinds, mutilation, cruel treatment and torture (as defined in section 1 (1) (d));
   (b) the taking of hostages;
   (c) outrages upon personal dignity, in particular humiliating and degrading treatment; or
   (d) the passing of sentences and the carrying out of executions without previous judgement pronounced by a regularly constituted court, affording all the judicial guarantees which are generally recognised as indispensable;

   shall be liable to life imprisonment or a term of imprisonment not exceeding thirty years or a sixth category fine.
2. Anyone who, in the case of an armed conflict not of an international character, commits one of the following acts:
   (a) rape, sexual slavery, enforced prostitution, enforced sterilisation or any other form of sexual violence which can be deemed to be of any gravity comparable to a grave breach of the Geneva Conventions;
   (b) forced pregnancy;
   (c) subjecting persons in the power of another party to the conflict to physical mutilation or medical or scientific experiments of any nature whatever, which are neither justified by the medical, dental or hospital treatment of the person concerned nor carried out in his or her interest and which cause death to or can seriously endanger the health of such persons or persons; or
   (d) treacherously killing or wounding individuals belonging to the hostile nation or army;

   shall be liable to life imprisonment or a term of imprisonment not exceeding thirty years or a sixth category fine.
3. Anyone who, in the case of an armed conflict not of an international character, commits one of the following acts:
   (a) intentionally directing attacks against the civilian population as such or against individual civilians not taking direct part in hostilities;

(b) intentionally directing attacks against buildings, material, medical units and transport, and personnel using the distinctive emblems of the Geneva Conventions in conformity with international law;
(c) intentionally directing attacks against personnel, installations, material, units or vehicles involved in humanitarian assistance or peace missions in accordance with the Charter of the United Nations, as long as they are entitled to the protection given to civilians or civilian objects under the international law of armed conflict;
(d) intentionally directing attacks against buildings dedicated to religion, education, art, science or charitable purposes, historic monuments, hospitals and places where the sick and wounded are collected, provided they are not military objectives;
(e) pillaging a town or place, even when taken by assault;
(f) conscripting or enlisting children under the age of fifteen years into the national armed forces or armed groups or using them to participate actively in hostilities;
(g) declaring that no quarter will be given; or
(h) destroying or seizing the property of an adversary unless such destruction or seizure be imperatively demanded by the circumstances of the conflict; or
(i) giving instructions for the transfer of the civilian population for reasons connected with the conflict, other than on account of the safety of the citizens or where imperatively demanded by the circumstances of the conflict;

shall be liable to a term of imprisonment not exceeding fifteen years or a fifth category fine.

4. Section 5, subsection 6, shall apply mutatis mutandis to an act as referred to in subsection 3.

Section 7

1. Anyone who, in the case of an international or non-international armed conflict, commits a violation of the laws and customs of war other than as referred to in sections 5 or 6 shall be liable to a term of imprisonment not exceeding ten years or a fifth category fine.
2. A term of imprisonment not exceeding fifteen years or a fifth category fine shall be imposed:
   (a) if an act as referred to in subsection 1 is likely to result in the death of or serious bodily injury to another person;
   (b) if an act as referred to in subsection 1 involves one or more outrages committed upon personal dignity, in particular humiliating and degrading treatment;
   (c) if an act as referred to in subsection 1 involves compelling another person to do, refrain from doing or permit something, or
   (d) if an act as referred to in subsection 1 involves pillaging a city or place, even when taken by assault.

3. Section 5, subsection 6, shall apply mutatis mutandis to an act as referred to in subsection 1.

Section 8

1. Torture committed by a public servant or other person working in the service of the authorities in the course of his duties shall carry a sentence of life imprisonment or a term of imprisonment not exceeding twenty years or a fifth category fine.
2. The following shall be liable to similar sentences:
   (a) a public servant or other person working in the service of the authorities who, in the course of his duties and by one of the means referred to in Article 47, paragraph 1 (ii), of the Criminal Code, solicits the commission of torture or intentionally permits another person to commit torture;
   (b) a person who commits torture, if this has been solicited or intentionally permitted by a public servant or another person working in the service of the authorities, in the course of his duties and by one of the means referred to in Article 47, paragraph 1 (ii), of the Criminal Code.

§ 3. Extension of criminal responsibility

Section 9

1. A superior shall be liable to the penalties prescribed for the offences referred to in § 2 if he:
   (a) intentionally permits the commission of such an offence by a subordinate;
   (b) intentionally fails to take measures, in so far as these are necessary and can be expected of him, if one of his subordinates has committed or intends to commit such an offence.
2. Anyone who culpably neglects to take measures, in so far as these are necessary and can be expected of him, where he has reasonable grounds for suspecting that a subordinate has committed or intends to commit such an offence, shall be liable to no more than two-thirds of the maximum of the principal sentences prescribed for the offences referred to in § 2.
3. If, in the circumstances referred to in subsection 2, the maximum sentence prescribed for the offence is life imprisonment, the term of imprisonment imposed shall not exceed fifteen years.

§ 4. General provisions of criminal law and criminal procedure

Section 10

The offences referred to in this Act are crimes.

Section 11

1. The fact that a crime as defined in this Act was committed pursuant to a regulation issued by the legal power of a State or pursuant to an order of a superior does not make that act lawful.
2. A subordinate who commits a crime referred to in this Act in pursuance of an order by a superior shall not be criminally responsible if the order was believed by the subordinate in good faith to have been given lawfully and the execution of the order came within the scope of his competence as a subordinate.
3. For the purposes of subsection 2, an order to commit genocide or a crime against humanity is deemed to be manifestly unlawful.

Section 12

The crimes defined in this Act shall be deemed not to be offences of a political nature for the purposes of the Extradition Act (Uitleveringswet) or the Surrender of War Crime Suspects Act (Wet overlevering inzake oorlogsmisdrijven).

Section 13

Articles 70 and 76 of the Criminal Code shall not apply to the crimes defined in this Act, with the exception of the offences referred to in section 7, subsection 1, and, in so far as connected with such offences, the offences referred to in section 9.

Section 14

Where a sentence of imprisonment of at least one year is imposed for one of the crimes defined in this Act, an order may also be made depriving the person concerned of the rights referred to in Article 28 (1) (iii) of the Criminal Code.

Section 15

The Hague District Court shall take cognizance of the crimes defined in this Act, subject to the provisions of the Military Justice Administration Act (Wet militaire strafrechtspraak).

Section 16

Criminal prosecution for one of the crimes referred to in this Act is excluded with respect to:

(a) foreign heads of state, heads of government and ministers of foreign affairs, as long as they are in office, and other persons in so far as their immunity is recognised under customary international law;
(b) persons who have immunity under any Convention applicable within the Kingdom of the Netherlands.

§ 5. Amendment of other Acts

Section 17

The Wartime Offences Act (Wet Oorlogsstrafrecht) is amended as follows:

A.

Section 1 is amended as follows:

1. In subsection 1 parts (iii)-(v) are replaced by a part (iii) which reads:

'sections 4-7 of this Act'.

2. In subsection 1, part (vi) is renumbered as (iv).
3. In subsection 2, the words 'sections 4-9' are replaced by 'sections 4-7'.

B.

Section 3 is amended as follows:

1. Part (i) is deleted and parts (ii)-(iv) are renumbered as parts (i)-(iii).
2. In part (i) (new) the words 'or in sections 1 and 2 of the Genocide Convention Implementation Act' are deleted.
3. In part (ii) (new) the words 'and (ii)' are deleted.

C.

Sections 8-10 are deleted.

D.

In sections 10a and 11, the words 'sections 4-9' are in each case replaced by 'sections 4-7'.

E.

A sentence reading 'It may also be provided that the special courts may also take cognizance of crimes defined in the International Crimes Act' shall be added to section 12, subsection 3.

Section 18

A.

The part of the sentence before the comma in Article 5, paragraph 2, of the Criminal Code shall read: 'Prosecution may also take place in the cases referred to in paragraph 1 (ii)'.

B.

Article 364a, paragraphs 1 and 2 of the Criminal Code shall read:

Article 364a

1. With respect to articles 361, 362 and 363, 'public servants' shall include persons in the public service of a foreign state or an international organisation.
2. With respect to article 362 (20 and 40) and article 363 (20 and 40), 'public servants' shall include former public servants.

Section 18a

In section 1 of the Surrender of War Crime Suspects Act, 'one of the crimes referred to in sections 8 and 9 of the Wartime Offences Act, sections 1 and 2 of the Genocide Convention Implementation Act or sections 1 and 2 of the Torture Convention Implementation Act,' shall be replaced by:
one of the crimes defined in sections 3, 5 to 8 and, in so far as it is connected with the offences referred to in those sections, section 9 of the International Crimes Act.

§ 6. Final provisions

Section 19

The Genocide Convention Implementation Act (Uitvoeringswet genocideverdrag) is repealed.

Section 20

The Torture Convention Implementation Act (Uitvoeringswet folteringverdrag) is repealed.

Section 21

1. If, at the time when this Act enters into force, a prosecution in respect of genocide, torture (as defined in section 1(1)(e)) or a crime that corresponds to a crime referred to in sections 5, 6 or 7 of this Act has already been instituted in accordance with the old law before a court other than as referred to in section 15 of this Act, the case shall be continued before that court.
2. Section 13 shall also apply to offences punishable under the Torture Convention Implementation Act which were committed before the entry into force of this Act.

Section 22

This Act shall enter into force on a date to be determined by Royal Decree.

Section 23

This Act may be cited as the International Crimes Act.

Act of 8 March 2007 Containing Rules on the Taking into Custody of Cultural Property from an Occupied Territory During an Armed Conflict and for the Initiation of Proceedings for the Return of Such Property (Cultural Property Originating from Occupied Territory (Return) Act)*

Chapter 1. General Provisions

Section 1

In this Act the following terms have the following meanings:

a) Our Minister: Our Minister of Education, Culture and Science;
b) Protocol: the Protocol of 14 May 1954 to the Convention for the Protection of Cultural Property in the Event of Armed Conflict, done at The Hague on that date (Dutch Treaty Series 1955, 47);
c) cultural property: cultural property as referred to in article 1 (a) of the Convention referred to under b) above;
d) occupied territory: a territory occupied on or after 14 January 1959 during an armed conflict, to which article 1 of the Protocol applies.

Section 2

It is prohibited to import cultural property from an occupied territory into the Netherlands or to have such property in one's possession in the Netherlands.

Chapter 2. Custody

Section 3

1. Where there is a reasonable suspicion that the prohibition in section 2 has been contravened Our Minister is to take into custody the cultural property concerned:
   a) of his own volition at the time of importation into the Netherlands; or
   b) at the request of the authorities of the relevant occupied territory or previously occupied territory.

* This is the English translation of the Dutch *Wet tot teruggave cultuurgoederen afkomstig uit bezet gebied.* Please note that this English translation is not legally binding. The most recent version of the text of the Act can be found, in Dutch, on the website: http://www.wetten.nl.

2. Our Minister may also take into custody of his own volition cultural property discovered in the Netherlands in respect of which a suspicion as referred to in subsection 1 exists if there is also a reasonable expectation that a request as referred to in subsection 1 b) will be made.

Section 4

1. Our Minister records his decision in writing before taking property into custody. The written decision constitutes an administrative decision.
2. The decision is notified as quickly as possible to:
   a) the authorities of the occupied territory concerned;
   b) the owner of the cultural property taken into custody, if his identity is known;
   c) persons with limited rights to the property, if their identity is known;
   d) the person in possession of the property at the time it is taken into custody.
3. If the situation is so urgent that Our Minister is unable to record the decision to take the property into custody in writing in advance, he must arrange for it to be recorded in writing and published as quickly as possible thereafter.

Section 5

1. All or part of the costs of taking property into custody may, where appropriate, be charged by decision of Our Minister to the person contravening the prohibition in section
2. No costs are in any event payable if:
   a) the claim referred to in section 7 is dismissed or indemnification or fair compensation as referred to in section 7, subsection 3, is awarded by unappealable judgment, or
   b) Our Minister definitively decides against returning the cultural property.
3. If a case as referred to in subsection 2 occurs after Our Minister has made a decision as referred to in subsection 1 he must revoke his decision.
4. The decision states the amount to be charged. The costs may include the costs of making preparations for the property to be taken into custody.
5. Our Minister may collect the costs owed pursuant to the above subsections from the offender, together with the costs incurred in the collection, by warrant of execution.
6. The warrant of execution is served at the expense of the offender by bailiff's notification and constitutes an enforceable order within the meaning of Book 2 of the Code of Civil Procedure. However, no enforcement will take place as long as the situation envisaged in subsection 2 a) can still occur.
7. An action to have the warrant of execution set aside may be brought within six weeks of the day of service by service of a writ of summons on Our Minister.
8. Enforcement of the warrant of execution is suspended pending the action. The court may lift the suspension at the request of Our Minister.

Section 6

1. Custody ends:
   a) upon the return of the cultural property to the authorities of the relevant occupied territory or previously occupied territory following the granting of a claim under legal proceedings as referred to in section 7;
   b) upon the dismissal of the claim for return as referred to in section 7;
   c) by decision of Our Minister if the authorities of the relevant occupied territory or previously occupied territory withdraw a request submitted by them for cultural property to be taken into custody or if they declare, in the event of the property being taken into custody by Our Minister of his own volition, that they will not submit a request for the return of the cultural property, or
   d) by decision of Our Minister for reasons other than those referred to at a), b) or c).
2. If custody ends without the cultural property being returned to the authorities referred to in subsection 1 a), the property is then handed over to the person in possession of it at the start of custody or to the person who can reasonably be designated as legally entitled to it.

Chapter 3. Legal Proceedings For Return

Section 7

1. After taking cultural property into custody Our Minister must lodge a claim in proceedings for the return of the cultural property against the possessor, whom failing against the holder, before the court having jurisdiction in accordance with the rules of the Code of Civil Procedure.
2. Neither articles 86, 88, paragraph 1, and 99, paragraph 1 of Book 3 of the Civil Code nor agreements alienating or encumbering cultural property from occupied territory can be invoked against Our Minister where he is claiming cultural property under subsection 1.
3. A court which grants a claim as referred to in subsection 1 makes an order against the State awarding the possessor or holder:
   a) an indemnification if he shows that he owns or acquired ownership of the cultural property, or in other cases
   b) such compensation as is fair in the circumstances if the possessor or holder exercised due care and attention in acquiring the cultural property.
4. If the possessor or holder from whom the return of cultural property is claimed does not comply with the obligation imposed on him by article 87 of Book 3 of the Civil Code, the provisions of subsection 3 b) do not apply to him.
5. A claim under legal proceedings as referred to in subsection 1 is not subject to a time limit.

Chapter 4. Enforcement

Section 8

The following are responsible for supervising compliance with the provisions of this Act:
a) the inspector referred to section 1 (f) of the Cultural Heritage Preservation Act and the officials referred to in section 15, subsection 1 of that Act, and
b) customs officials of the Tax and Customs Administration.

Section 9

The officials referred to in section 8 (a) are empowered to:
a) enter a dwelling without the consent of the occupant and to take with them the necessary equipment;
b) demand that the occupant show them the cultural property present in the dwelling;
c) seal off areas and objects in so far as this is reasonably necessary for the exercise of the powers referred to in section 5:17 of the General Administrative Law Act;
d) exercise the power referred to in section 5:17 of the General Administrative Law Act, if necessary with the help of the police.

Section 10

Chapters 2 and 3 of the Customs Act, with the exception of section 10 of chapter 2 of that Act, apply *mutatis mutandis* to the officials referred to in section 8 (b).

Chapter 5. Amendments to other Acts

Section 11

Book 3 of the Civil Code is amended as follows:

A.

In article 238, paragraph 4, the words 'article 86a, paragraphs 1 and 2' are replaced by 'article 86a, paragraphs 1 and 2 or in accordance with section 7 of the Cultural Property Originating from Occupied Territory (Return) Act'.

B.

A third paragraph which reads as follows is added to article 291:

> '3. The creditor may not invoke the right of lien against the Minister of Education, Culture and Science where the Minister lodges a claim under legal proceedings for return of cultural property from an occupied territory.'

Chapter 6. Concluding Provisions

Section 12

This Act enters into force with effect from the day after the date of publication of the Bulletin of Acts and Decrees in which it appears.

Section 13

This Act may be cited as the Cultural Property Originating from Occupied Territory (Return) Act.

International Tribunal for the Former Yugoslavia

Excerpts from: *Prosecutor v. Pavle Strugar*

Case No. IT-01-42-T (Trial Judgment), 31 January 2005; at
http://www.icty.org/x/cases/strugar/tjug/en/str-tj050131e.pdf

176. The evidence reviewed to this point shows that on 6 December 1991 the Old Town of Dubrovnik was heavily shelled over some ten and a half hours. As is detailed later in this decision, there was extensive damage to property, even though the Old Town was a World Heritage protected site. There was also injury to, and death of, civilians from the shelling. It should be clearly recorded that at the time of the shelling the Old Town was occupied by a civilian population. The Old Town was their place of living and working. Because of the blockade that had been enforced by the JNA the population of Dubrovnik, including the Old Town, had been without normal running water and electricity supplies for some weeks and essential products to sustain the population, such as food and medical supplies, were in extremely short supply.

183. By way of general observation, to which the Chamber attaches significant weight, the Chamber notes that by 6 December 1991 there were quite compelling circumstances against the proposition that the Croatian defenders had defensive military positions in the Old Town. To do so was a clear violation of the World Heritage protected status of the Old Town. The Chamber accepts there was a prevailing concern by the citizens of the Old Town not to violate the military free status of the Old Town. That is the view of the Chamber, notwithstanding suggestions in the evidence that at times in earlier stages of the conflict there were violations of this by Croatian defending forces. Whether or not that was so, in particular by early December 1991, independent ECMM military monitors had again established themselves at Dubrovnik and were specifically concerned *inter alia* to look out for violations of ceasefire agreements. United Nations Agency officials had also arrived, including the witness Colin Kaiser who was actually staying in the Old Town on 5 and 6 December, for whom the protection, and military free status, of the Old Town were matters of direct responsibility. The events over the preceding weeks had also attracted reporters and cameramen of the world media to Dubrovnik and the Old Town.

Paragraphs 223 – 233

223. The offence of attacking civilian objects is a breach of a rule of international humanitarian law. As already ruled by the Chamber in the present case and upheld by the Appeals Chamber, Article 52, referred to in respect of the count of attacking civilian objects, is a reaffirmation and reformulation of a rule that had previously attained the status of customary international law.

224. The Chamber observes that the prohibition of attacks on civilian objects is set out only in Article 52 of Additional Protocol I, referred to in relation to Count 5. Additional Protocol II does not contain provisions on attacking civilian objects. Nonetheless, as the Appeals Chamber found, the rule prohibiting attacks on civilian objects has evolved to become applicable also to conflicts of an internal nature. The Appeals Chamber noted that already during the Spanish Civil War the tendency to disregard the distinction between international and internal armed conflicts could be observed. Both the republican Government and third States insisted that certain rules applicable to international wars applied also to that war. Among those rules there was the prohibition of attacks on non-military objectives. The Appeals Chamber further referred to the 1970 General Assembly resolution concerning the protection of civilians in "armed conflicts of all types". In that resolution the General Assembly affirmed a number of basic principles, including the prohibition of making dwellings and other installations used only by civilian populations, as well as places and areas designated for the sole protection of civilians, the object of military operations. The Chamber therefore concludes that despite the lack of a provision similar to Article 52 in Additional Protocol II, the general rule prohibiting attacks on civilian objects also applies to internal conflicts. Accordingly, the first and second jurisdictional requirements are met.

225. As regards the third *Tadić* condition, the Chamber notes that the prohibition of attacks on civilian objects is aimed at protecting those objects from the danger of being damaged during an attack. It further reiterates that a prohibition against attacking civilian objects is a necessary complement to the protection of civilian populations. The Chamber observes that in the abovementioned 1970 resolution of the General Assembly the prohibition of making civilian dwellings and installations the object of military operations was listed among the "basic principles for the protection of civilian populations in armed conflicts". Those principles were reaffirmed because of the "need for measures to ensure the better protection of human rights in armed conflicts". The General Assembly also emphasised that civilian populations were in "special need of increased protection in time of armed conflicts". The principle of distinction, which obliges the parties to the conflict to distinguish between civilian objects and military objectives, was considered "basic" by the drafters of Additional Protocol I. The Chamber therefore finds that the prohibition at issue is a rule protecting important values. Similarly to what it has found in respect of the attacks on civilians, the Chamber considers that, in view of the fundamental nature of this prohibition, any attack against civilian objects, even if it did not cause any damage, can be considered a serious violation of international humanitarian law. All the same, the Chamber recalls that the requirement of seriousness contains also the element of gravity of consequences for the victim. The Chamber is of the view that, unlike in the case of attacks on civilians, the offence at hand may not necessarily meet the threshold of "grave consequences" if no damage occurred. Therefore, the assessment of whether those consequences were grave enough to bring the offence into the scope of the Tribunal's jurisdiction under Article 3 of the Statute should be carried out on the basis of the facts of the case. The Chamber observes that in the present case it is alleged that the attacks against civilian objects, with which the Accused is charged, did incur damage to those objects. It will thus pursue the examination of the case on the assumption that the attacks as charged in the Indictment did bring about grave consequences for their victims and the third *Tadić* condition is met. The Chamber would only need to return to the analysis of applicability of Article 3 of the Statute if the evidence on the alleged damage were to fail to demonstrate the validity of the Prosecution allegations to such an extent as to render it questionable whether the consequences of the attack were grave for its victims. As will be seen later in this decision, that is not the case.

226. As recalled above, the fourth *Tadić* condition concerns individual criminal responsibility. The Appeals Chamber has found that under customary international law a violation of the rule prohibiting attacks on civilian objects entails individual criminal responsibility. Furthermore, the Chamber recalls its above findings as to the SFRY regulations establishing criminal responsibility for violations of Additional Protocol I.

[3. Destruction and devastation of property, including cultural property]

227. As to the first and the second *Tadić* conditions, the Chamber observes that Article 3(b) is based on Article 23 of the Hague Convention (IV) of 1907 and the annexed Regulations. Both The Hague Convention (IV) of 1907 and The Hague Regulations are rules of international humanitarian law and they have become part of customary international law.

228. Recognising that the Hague Regulations were made to apply only to international armed conflicts, the Chamber will now examine whether the prohibition contained in Article 3(b) of the Statute covers also non-international armed conflicts. The rule at issue is closely related to the one prohibiting attacks on civilian objects, even though certain elements of those two rules remain distinct. Both rules serve the aim of protecting property from damage caused by military operations. In addition, the offence of devastation charged against the Accused is alleged to have occurred in the context of an attack against civilian objects. Therefore, and having regard to its conclusion that the rule prohibiting attacks on civilian objects applies to non-international armed conflicts, the Chamber finds no reason to hold otherwise than that the prohibition contained in Article 3 (b) of the Statute applies also to non-international armed conflicts.

229. Turning now to the crime charged under Article 3(d), the Chamber notes that this provision is based on Article 27 of the Hague Regulations. Moreover, protection of cultural property had developed already in earlier codes. The relevant provisions of the Hague Convention for the Protection of Cultural Property in the Event of Armed Conflict of 1954 confirm the earlier codes. The Appeals Chamber in the

Tadić case explicitly referred to Article 19 of the Hague Convention of 1954, as a treaty rule which formed part of customary international law binding on parties to non-international armed conflicts. More generally, it found that the customary rules relating to the protection of cultural property had developed to govern internal strife. The Chamber additionally notes that it is prohibited "to commit any act of hostility directed against [cultural property]" both in Article 53 of Additional Protocol I relating to international armed conflicts and Article 16 of Additional Protocol II governing non-international armed conflicts.

230. In view of the foregoing, the Chamber is satisfied that Article 3(d) of the Statute is a rule of international humanitarian law which not only reflects customary international law but is applicable to both international and non-international armed conflicts. Accordingly, the first and second *Tadić* conditions with regard to Article s 3(b) and 3(d) are met.

231. As to the third *Tadić* condition, the Chamber recalls its conclusion that the offence of attacking civilian objects fulfils this condition when it results in damage severe enough to involve "grave consequences" for its victims. It is of the view that, similarly to the attacks on civilian objects, the crime of devastation will fall within the scope of the Tribunal's jurisdiction under Article 3 of the Statute if the damage to property is such as to "gravely" affect the victims of the crime. Noting that one of the requirements of the crime is that the damage be on a large scale, the Chamber has no doubt that the crime at hand is serious.

232. As regards the seriousness of the offence of damage to cultural property (Article 3 (d)), the Chamber observes that such property is, by definition, of "great importance to the cultural heritage of every people". It therefore considers that, even though the victim of the offence at issue is to be understood broadly as a "people", rather than any particular individual, the offence can be said to involve grave consequences for the victim. In the *Jokić* case, for instance, the Trial Chamber noted that the destruction and damage inflicted to the Old Town of Dubrovnik were very serious crimes. It found that "since it is a serious violation of international humanitarian law to attack civilian buildings, it is a crime of even greater seriousness to direct an attack on an especially protected site, such as the Old Town [of Dubrovnik]." In view of the foregoing, the Chamber finds that the offences under Articles 3(b) and 3(d) of the Statute are serious violations of international humanitarian law. Hence, the third *Tadić* condition is satisfied.

233. As to the fourth *Tadić* condition, the Chamber notes that Article 6 of the Charter of the Nuremberg International Military Tribunal already provided for individual criminal responsibility for war crimes, including devastation not justified by military necessity, which is listed in Article 3(b) of the Statute. Concerning Article 3(d) of the Statute, the Chamber recalls that Article 28 of the Hague Convention of 1954 stipulates that "the high contracting parties undertake to take, within the framework of their ordinary criminal jurisdiction, all necessary steps to prosecute and impose penal or disciplinary sanctions upon those persons, of whatever nationality, who commit or order to be committed a breach of the Convention." Furthermore, the case law of this Tribunal provides several examples of individuals convicted under Articles 3(b) or 3(d), or both, of the Statute. Accordingly, the Chamber finds that Articles 3(b) and 3(d) of the Statute entail individual criminal responsibility. Thus, the fourth *Tadić* condition is fulfilled.

279. In the Chamber's view, the facts established in this case make it unnecessary to consider many of the legal and factual issues raised by the submissions of the parties. We would however make the following general observations. The Indictment in this case is confined to an artillery attack on the Old Town which occurred on 6 December 1991. There was also shelling of the wider city of Dubrovnik on that day. The Old Town is a physically distinct part of the wider city. Its geographical location in the wider city, and its clearly visible boundaries as marked by the medieval walls that surround the Old Town, provide an immediate and obvious demarcation of the Old Town from the rest of the city. It is a demarcation which is plain to see at a distance and was obvious to the JNA forces on 6 December 1991. The Old Town is also legally distinct from the rest of the wider city because the Old Town, in its entirety including the medieval walls, enjoys a World Heritage listing and the protections and immunities that are consequent on that listing. In the context of this particular case there is a further basis for distinguishing the Old Town from the remainder of the wider city of Dubrovnik. As found by the Chamber in this decision, on 6 December 1991 there were a few Croatian military positions in the wider city of Dubrovnik that were relevant to the JNA attempt to capture Srd that day, whereas there were none in the Old Town, and it was not believed by the JNA forces responsible for the shelling that there were. For all of these quite compelling reasons it is legally and factually appropriate, in the circumstances of this case, to consider the targeting and shelling of the Old Town in isolation, and in distinction from, the targeting and shelling of the remainder of the wider city of Dubrovnik. That is so for all counts.

285. On 6 December 1991, the evidence is unequivocal that the Old Town was, as it still is, a living town. Though a protected World Heritage site, it had a substantial resident population of between 7,000 and 8,000, many of whom were also employed in the Old Town, as were very many others who came to the Old Town from the wider Dubrovnik to work. The Old Town was also a centre of commercial and local government activity and religious communities lived within its walls. Because of, and under the terms of, the JNA blockade, some women and children had temporarily left the Old Town, but many remained. In addition, families and individuals displaced by the JNA advance on Dubrovnik had found shelter in the Old Town. Some people from the wider Dubrovnik had also been able to take up temporary residence in the Old Town during the blockade in the belief that its World Heritage listing would give them protection from military attack. The existence of the Old Town as a living town was a renowned state of affairs which had existed for centuries. The residential situation in the wider Dubrovnik was, in many respects quite similar and a renowned state of affairs. The wider Dubrovnik was a substantial residential and commercial centre with a large resident population the numbers of whom had been swelled by refugees who had been displaced from other towns and villages by the JNA advance.

Paragraphs 290 – 312

[C. Crimes against property, including cultural property (Counts 4 and 6)]

[1. Law on devastation not justified by military necessity (Count 4)]

290. Count 4 of the Indictment charges the Accused with devastation not justified by military necessity, punishable as a violation of the laws or customs of war under Article 3(b) of the Statute.

291. Article 3(b) codifies two crimes: "wanton destruction of cities, towns or villages, or devastation not justified by military necessity." Only the latter is charged in the present case. From a linguistic point of view, the meaning of the two terms, "devastation" and "destruction," is largely identical. Moreover, the two offences have been treated together by a number of instruments of international humanitarian law. At least in the context of this case, which is concerned with the destruction of buildings in the Old Town of Dubrovnik, the Chamber considers it appropriate to equate the two crimes, while recognising that in other contexts, *e.g.* laying waste to crops or forests, the crime of devastation may have a wider application.

292. While the crime of "devastation not justified by military necessity" has scarcely been dealt with in the Tribunal's jurisprudence, the elements of the crime of "wanton destruction not justified by military necessity" were identified by the Trial Chamber in the *Kordić* case, and recently endorsed by the Appeals Chamber in that same case, as follows:

(i) the destruction of property occurs on a large scale;
(ii) the destruction is not justified by military necessity; and
(iii) the perpetrator acted with the intent to destroy the property in question or in reckless disregard of the likelihood of its destruction.

293. At least in the context of the present trial this definition appears equally applicable to devastation. The Chamber will adopt this definition, with appropriate adaptions to reflect "devastation," for the crime of "devastation not justified by military necessity." Both the Prosecution and the Defence submit that this should be done.

294. Turning to the first element, that is, that the devastation occurred on a "large scale", the Chamber is of the view that while this element requires a showing that a considerable number of objects were damaged or destroyed, it does not require destruction in its entirety of a city, town or village. The Chamber will not pronounce on the question whether there is any identity between the term "large scale" in this context and the term "extensive" in the context of the crime of "extensive destruction of property" pursuant to Article 2(d) of the Statute. The facts of this case do not require it.

295. The second requirement is that the act is "not justified by military necessity". The Chamber is of the view that military necessity may be usefully defined for present purposes with reference to the widely acknowledged definition of military objectives in Article 52 of Additional Protocol I as "those objects which by their nature, location, purpose or use make an effective contribution to military action and whose total or partial destruction, capture or neutralization, in the circumstances ruling at the time, offers a definite military advantage." Whether a military advantage can be achieved must be decided, as the Trial Chamber in the *Galić* case held, from the perspective of the "person contemplating the attack, including the information available to the latter, that the object is being used to make an effective contribution to military action." In other words, each case must be determined on its facts. Recalling its earlier finding that there were no military objectives in the Old Town on 6 December 1991, the Chamber is of the view that the question of proportionality in determining military necessity does not arise on the facts of this case.

296. According to the consistent case-law of the Tribunal the *mens rea* requirement for a crime under Article 3(b) is met when the perpetrator acted with either direct or indirect intent, the latter requiring knowledge that devastation was a probable consequence of his acts.

297. In sum, the elements of the crime of "devastation not justified by military necessity", at least in the present context, may be stated as: (a) destruction or damage of property on a large scale; (b) the destruction or damage was not justified by military necessity; and (c) the perpetrator acted with the intent to destroy or damage the property or in the knowledge that such destruction or damage was a probable consequence of his acts.

[2. Law on destruction or wilful damage of cultural property (Count 6)]

298. Count 6 of the Indictment charges the Accused with destruction or wilful damage done to institutions dedicated to religion, charity and education, the arts and sciences, historic monuments and works of art and science, punishable under Article 3(d) of the Statute.

299. Article 3(d) of the Statute reads:

> The International Tribunal shall have the power to prosecute persons violating the laws or customs of war. Such violations shall include, but not be limited to:
> [...]
> (d) seizure of, destruction or wilful damage done to institutions dedicated to religion, charity and education, the arts and sciences, historic monuments and works of art and science;

300. This provision has been interpreted in several cases before the Tribunal to date. The *Blaskić* Trial Chamber adopted the following definition:

> The damage or destruction must have been committed intentionally to institutions which may clearly be identified as dedicated to religion or education and which were not being used for military purposes at the time of the acts. In addition, the institutions must not have been in the immediate vicinity of military objectives.

301. The *Naletilić* Trial Judgement, while rejecting the *Blaskić* holding that, in order to be protected, the institutions must not have been located in the immediate vicinity of military objectives, held that the elements of this crime with respect to destruction of institutions dedicated to religion would be satisfied if: "(i) the general requirements of Article 3 of the Statute are fulfilled; (ii) the destruction regards an institution dedicated to religion; (iii) the property was not used for military purposes; (iv) the perpetrator acted with the intent to destroy the property."

302. Further, the *Kordić* Trial Judgement held that while this offence overlaps to a certain extent with the offence of unlawful attacks on civilians objects, when the acts in question are directed against cultural heritage, the provision of Article 3(d) is *lex specialis*.

303. In order to define the elements of the offence under Article 3(d) it may be useful to consider its sources in international customary and treaty law. Acts against cultural property are proscribed by Article 27 of the Hague Regulations of 1907, by the Hague Convention of 1954, by Article 53 of Additional Protocol I and by Article 16 of Additional Protocol II.

304. Article 27 of the Hague Regulations of 1907 reads:

> In sieges and bombardments all necessary steps must be taken to spare, as far as possible, buildings dedicated to religion, art, science, or charitable purposes, historic monuments, hospitals, and places where the sick and wounded are collected, provided they are not being used at the time for military purposes.

305. Article 4 of The Hague Convention of 1954 requires the States Parties to the Convention to:

> 1. [...] respect cultural property situated within their own territory as well as within the territory of other High Contracting Parties by refraining from any use of the property and its immediate surroundings or of the appliances in use for its protection for purposes which are likely to expose it to destruction or damage in the event of armed conflict; and by refraining from any act of hostility directed against such property.
> 2. The obligations mentioned in paragraph 1 of the present Article may be waived only when military necessity imperatively requires such a waiver.
>
>   [...]
> 4. They shall refrain from any act directed by way of reprisals against cultural property.

306. Article 53 of Additional Protocol I reads:

> Without prejudice to the Provisions of the Hague Convention for the Protection of Cultural Property in the Event of Armed Conflict of 1954, and of other relevant international instruments, it is prohibited:
> (a) to commit any acts of hostility directed against the historic monuments, works of art or places of worship which constitute the cultural or spiritual heritage of peoples;
> (b) to use such objects in support of the military effort;
> (c) to make such objects the object of reprisals.

This text is almost identical in content to the analogous provision in Additional Protocol II (Article 16) the only differences being the absence in the latter of a reference to "other relevant international instruments" and the prohibition on making cultural property the object of reprisals.

307. The Hague Convention of 1954 protects property "of great importance to the cultural heritage of every people." The Additional Protocols refer to "historic monuments, works of art or places of worship which constitute the cultural or spiritual heritage of peoples." The *Kordić* Appeals Judgement, referring to the ICRC Commentary to Article 53 of Additional Protocol I, stated that despite this difference in terminology, the basic idea [underlying the two provisions] is the same. Whether there may be precise differences is not an issue raised by the facts of this case. The Chamber will limit its discussion to property protected by the above instruments (hereinafter "cultural property").

308. While the aforementioned provisions prohibit acts of hostility "directed" against cultural property, Article 3(d) of the Statute explicitly criminalises only those acts which result in damage to, or destruction of, such property. Therefore, a requisite element of the crime charged in the Indictment is actual damage or destruction occurring as a result of an act directed against this property.

309. The Hague Regulations of 1907 make the protection of cultural property dependent on whether such property was used for military purposes. The Hague Convention of 1954 provides for an obligation to respect cultural property. This obligation has two explicit limbs, *viz.* to refrain "from any use of the property and its immediate surroundings [...] for purposes which are likely to expose it to destruction or damage in the event or armed conflict", and, to refrain "from any act of hostility directed against such property." The Convention provides for a waiver of these obligations, however, but only when "military necessity imperatively requires such a waiver." The Additional Protocols prohibit the use of cultural property in support of military efforts, but make no explicit provision for the consequence of such a use, *i.e.* whether it affords a justification for acts of hostility against such property. Further, the Additional Protocols prohibit acts of hostility against cultural property, without any explicit reference to military necessity. However, the relevant provisions of both Additional Protocols are expressed to be "[w]ithout prejudice to" the provisions of the Hague Convention of 1954. This suggests that in these respects, the Additional Protocols may not have affected the operation of the waiver provision of the Hague Convention of 1954 in cases where military necessity imperatively requires waiver. In this present case, no military necessity arises on the facts in respect of the shelling of the Old Town, so that this question need not be further considered. For the same reason, no consideration is necessary to the question of what distinction is intended (if any) by the word "imperatively" in the context of military necessity in Article 4, paragraph 2 of the Hague Convention of 1954.

310. Nevertheless, the established jurisprudence of the Tribunal confirming the "military purposes" exception which is consistent with the exceptions recognised by the Hague Regulations of 1907 and the Additional Protocols, persuades the Chamber that the protection accorded to cultural property is lost where such property is used for military purposes. Further, with regard to the differences between the *Blaskić* and *Naletilić* Trial Judgements noted above (regarding the use of the immediate surroundings of cultural property for military purposes), and leaving aside any implication of the issue of imperative military necessity, the preferable view appears to be that it is the use of cultural property and not its location that determines whether and when the cultural property would lose its protection. Therefore, contrary to the Defence submission, the Chamber considers that the special protection awarded to cultural property itself may not be lost simply because of military activities or military installations in the immediate vicinity of the cultural property. In such a case, however, the practical result may be that it cannot be established that the acts which caused destruction of or damage to cultural property were "directed against" that cultural property, rather than the military installation or use in its immediate vicinity.

311. As for the *mens rea* element for this crime, the Chamber is guided by the previous jurisprudence of the Tribunal that a perpetrator must act with a direct intent to damage or destroy the property in question. There is reason to question whether indirect intent ought also to be an acceptable form of *mens rea* for this crime, but that is an issue not directly raised by the circumstances of this case.

312. In view of the above, the definition established by the jurisprudence of the Tribunal appears to reflect the position under customary international law. For the purposes of this case, an act will fulfil the elements of the crime of destruction or wilful damage of cultural property, within the meaning of Article 3(d) of the Statute and in so far as that provision relates to cultural property, if: (i) it has caused damage or destruction to property which constitutes the cultural or spiritual heritage of peoples; (ii) the damaged or destroyed property was not used for military purposes at the time when the acts of hostility directed against these objects took place; and (iii) the act was carried out with the intent to damage or destroy the property in question.

Paragraphs 316 – 322

316. In general terms, the Chamber's findings on these Counts are based on the evidence which it has accepted of citizens of Dubrovnik or persons visiting the Old Town during or immediately after the attack, and evidence such as that of a monitor from the ECMM, Per Hvalkof, who walked around in the Old Town on the day after the attack and described the town as "horrible" looking and "very badly damaged"; he thought the Old Town looked like a "missile garbage lot". In reaching its finding the Chamber has also relied on video evidences and various reports compiled after the attack, and has been assisted by its site visit. The Chamber has also relied on this evidence in the determination of how many, and exactly which, buildings and structures were damaged during the 6 December shelling of the Old Town.

317. As discussed above, the Chamber has found that there was an artillery attack by the JNA forces under the command of the Accused on the Old Town of Dubrovnik on 6 December 1991.

318. The Chamber finds that of the 116 buildings and structures it listed in the Annex to its Rule 98*bis* Decision, 52 were destroyed or damaged during the 6 December shelling of the Old Town by the JNA. The Chamber's findings in relation to these 52 buildings and structures are included in an Annex attached to this Judgement, and the evidence upon which the Chamber has relied in making these findings is referenced therein. The Chamber will set out below why it cannot be satisfied to the required standard that the other 64 buildings and structures of the 116, and the additional building (C 1), were destroyed or damaged in that attack. The Chamber emphasises that the list of 52 should not be understood as representing an exhaustive list of the buildings and structures damaged during the 6 December 1991 JNA attack. The Chamber has necessarily had to confine its findings to those buildings listed in the Indictment and which remained listed in the Annex to the Rule 98*bis* Decision. In particular, it was not always possible to relate evidence of damage to the buildings listed therein.

319. The nature and extent of the damage to the 52 buildings and structures from the 6 December 1991 attack varied considerably as is apparent from the evidence identified in the footnotes in the Annex. It is unnecessary to attempt to detail all of the damage in this decision. The most seriously affected were six buildings which were completely destroyed, *i.e.* burned out, on 6 December 1991. Several of the 52 buildings and structures had sustained some degree of damage from earlier shelling in October and November. This earlier damage has been identified by the Chamber so that it is not attributed to the 6 December 1991 attack. In the result, from its analysis of the damage, the Chamber is satisfied that the previously damaged buildings sustained further and significant damage during the 6 December attack.

320. The Chamber also observes that among those buildings which were damaged in the attack, were monasteries, churches, a mosque, a synagogue and palaces. Among the other buildings affected were residential blocks, public places and shops; damage to these would have entailed grave consequences for the residents or the owners, *i.e.* their homes and businesses suffered substantial damage.

321. In reaching its findings that the evidence is insufficient in respect of the other 64 buildings and structures the Chamber is lead by the following considerations. The evidence of damage to hose 64 buildings and structures derives from the extracts from the "Preliminary Report on War Destruction Sustained by the Ancient City Centre of Dubrovnik in October, November and December 1991" compiled by the "Institute for Protection and Conservation of the Historical Monuments" of Dubrovnik (hereinafter "Institute Report"). The Institute Report purports to deal with damage between 1 October and 31 December 1991, which of course includes damage caused on 6 December 1991, and subject of the Indictment, but it is necessary to be able to separate damage of 6 December from all other damage. While the Institute Report itself purports to specify damage occurring on 6 December 1991 by the date of damage given for each object surveyed, this specification has been shown not to be always accurate.

322. Although two witnesses, architects Lucjiana Peko and Slobodan Vuković, who personally carried out inspections of the damage sustained by the buildings and structures in the Old Town, vouched generally for the accuracy and reliability of the extracts from the Institute Report, the Chamber notes that the entries in the Institute Report were recorded on the basis of hearsay evidence. In most of the cases, information was collected from unknown persons who are described merely as neighbours or tenants. Whether those neighbours or tenants spoke from personal knowledge or hearsay knowledge is not known.

Index

L

M

N

U

W

Y

International Humanitarian Law Series

1 Michael J. Kelly, *Restoring and Maintaining Order in Complex Peace Operations: The Search for a Legal Framework*, 1999 ISBN 90 411 1179 4

2 Helen Durham and Timothy L.H. McCormack (eds.), *The Changing Face of Conflict and the Efficacy of International Humanitarian Law*, 1999 ISBN 90 411 1180 8

3 Richard May, David Tolbert, John Hocking, Ken Roberts, Bing Bing Jia, Daryl Mundis and Gabriël Oosthuizen (eds.), *Essays on ICTY Procedure and Evidence in Honour of Gabrielle Kirk McDonald*, 2001 ISBN 90 411 1482 3

4 Elizabeth Chadwick, *Traditional Neutrality Revisited: Law, Theory and Case Studies*, 2002 ISBN 90 411 1787 3

5 Lal Chand Vohrah, Fausto Pocar, Yvonne Featherstone, Olivier Fourmy, Christine Graham, John Hocking and Nicholas Robson (eds.), *Man's Inhumanity to Man: Essays on International Law in Honour of Antonio Cassese*, 2003 ISBN 90 411 1986 8

6 Gideon Boas and William A. Schabas (eds.), *International Criminal Law Developments in the Case Law of the ICTY*, 2003 ISBN 90 411 1987 6

7* Karen Hulme, *War Torn Environment: Interpreting the Legal Threshold*, 2004 ISBN 90 04 13848 x

8 Helen Durham and Tracey Gurd (eds.), *Listening to the Silences: Women and War*, 2005 ISBN 90 04 14365 3

9* ** Marten Zwanenburg, *Accountability of Peace Support Operations*, 2005 ISBN 90 04 14350 5

10 Hirad Abtahi and Gideon Boas (eds.), *The Dynamics of International Criminal Law*, 2006 ISBN 90 04 14587 7

11 Frits Kalshoven, *Belligerent Reprisals*, 2005 ISBN 90 04 14386 6

12 Pablo Antonio Fernández-Sánchez (ed.), *The New Challenges of Humanitarian Law in Armed Conflicts: In Honour of Professor Juan Antonio Carrillo-Salcedo*, 2005 ISBN 90 04 14830 2

13 Ustinia Dolgopol and Judith Gardam (eds.), *The Challenge of Conflict: International Law Responds*, 2006 ISBN 90 04 14599 0

14* Laura Perna, *The Formation of the Treaty Law of Non-International Armed Conflicts*, 2006 ISBN 90 04 14924 4

15 Michael Schmitt and Jelena Pejic (eds.), *International Law and Armed Conflict: Exploring the Faultlines, Essays in Honour of Yoram Dinstein*, 2007 ISBN 978 9004154 28 5

16 Ola Engdahl, *Protection of Personnel in Peace Operations: The Role of the 'Safety Convention' against the Background of General International Law*, 2007 ISBN 978 9004154 66 7

17 Frits Kalshoven, *Reflections on the Law of War: Collected Essays*, 2007 ISBN 978 90 04 15825 2

18 Héctor Olásolo, *Unlawful Attacks in Combat Situations: From the ICTY's Case Law to the Rome Statute*, 2007 ISBN 978 90 04 15466 7

19 José Doria, Hans-Peter Gasser and M. Cherif Bassiouni (eds.), *The Legal Regime of the International Criminal Court: Essays in Honour of Professor Igor Blishchenko*, 2008 ISBN 978 90 04 16308 9

20 David A. Blumenthal and Timothy L.H. McCormack (eds.), *The Legacy of Nuremberg: Civilising Influence or Institutionalised Vengeance?*, 2008 ISBN 978 90 04 15691 3

21 Omar Abdulle Alasow, *Violations of the Rules Applicable in Non-International Armed Conflicts and Their Possible Causes: The Case of Somalia*, 2010 ISBN 978 90 04 16475 8

22 Ola Engdahl and Pål Wrange (eds.), *Law at War: The Law as it Was and the Law as it Should Be – Liber Amicorum Ove Bring*, 2008 ISBN 978 90 04 17016 2

23 Pablo Antonio Fernández-Sánchez (ed.), *International Legal Dimension of Terrorism*, 2009 ISBN 978 90 04 17053 7

---

* Winner of the ASIL Francis Lieber Prize.

** Winner of the 2006 Paul Reuter Prize.

24 Rob McLaughlin, *United Nations Naval Peace Operations in the Territorial Sea*, 2009 ISBN 978 90 04 17479 5

25 Ian Henderson, *The Contemporary Law of Targeting*, 2009 ISBN 978 90 04 17480 1

26 Cecilia M. Bailliet (ed.), *Security: A Multidisciplinary Normative Approach*, 2009 ISBN 978 90 04 17296 8

27 Kristen Eichensehr and W. Michael Reisman (eds.), *Stopping Wars and Making Peace: Studies in International Intervention*, 2009 ISBN 978 90 04 17855 7

28 Noelle Higgins, *Regulating the Use of Force in Wars of National Liberation – The Need for a New Regime: A Study of the South Moluccas and Aceh*, 2009 ISBN 978 90 04 17287 6

29 Nout van Woudenberg and Liesbeth Lijnzaad (eds.), *Protecting Cultural Property in Armed Conflict: An Insight into the 1999 Second Protocol to the Hague Convention of 1954 for the Protection of Cultural Property in the Event of Armed Conflict*, 2010 ISBN 978 9004 18377 3

www.ingramcontent.com/pod-product-compliance
Lightning Source LLC
LaVergne TN
LVHW061943171026
850499LV00005B/105
9789004183773